Bloom's Literary Themes

ENSLAVEMENT AND EMANCIPATION

Bloom's Literary Themes

ENSLAVEMENT AND EMANCIPATION

Edited and with an introduction by
Harold Bloom
Sterling Professor of the Humanities
Yale University

Volume Editor
Blake Hobby

BLOOM'S
LITERARY CRITICISM
An imprint of Infobase Publishing

Bloom's Literary Themes: Enslavement and Emancipation

Copyright © 2010 by Infobase Publishing
Introduction © 2010 by Harold Bloom

Bloom's Literary Criticism
An imprint of Infobase Publishing
132 West 31st Street
New York NY 10001

Library of Congress Cataloging-in-Publication Data
Bloom's literary themes. Enslavement and emancipation / edited and with an introduction
  by Harold Bloom ; volume editor, Blake Hobby.
    p. cm.
  Includes bibliographical references and index.
   ISBN 978-1-60413-441-4 (hc : alk. paper) 1. Slavery in literature. 2. Liberty
in literature. I. Bloom, Harold. II. Hobby, Blake. III. Title: Enslavement and
emancipation.

  PN56.S5765B56 2010
  809'.933552—dc22

Series design by Kerry Casey
Cover design by Takeshi Takahashi
Composition by IBT Global, Inc.
Cover printed by IBT Global, Inc., Troy, NY
Book printed and bound by IBT Global, Inc., Troy, NY
Date printed: January 2010
Printed in the United States of America

10 9 8 7 6 5 4 3 2 1

Contents

Series Introduction by Harold Bloom: Themes and Metaphors

1. Topos and Trope

What we now call a theme or topic or subject initially was named a *topos*, ancient Greek for "place." Literary *topoi* are commonplaces, but also arguments or assertions. A topos can be regarded as literal when opposed to a trope or turning which is figurative and which can be a metaphor or some related departure from the literal: ironies, synecdoches (part for whole), metonymies (representations by contiguity) or hyperboles (overstatements). Themes and metaphors engender one another in all significant literary compositions.

As a theoretician of the relation between the matter and the rhetoric of high literature, I tend to define metaphor as a figure of desire rather than a figure of knowledge. We welcome literary metaphor because it enables fictions to persuade us of beautiful untrue things, as Oscar Wilde phrased it. Literary *topoi* can be regarded as places where we store information, in order to amplify the themes that interest us.

This series of volumes, *Bloom's Literary Themes*, offers students and general readers helpful essays on such perpetually crucial topics as the Hero's Journey, the Labyrinth, the Sublime, Death and Dying, the Taboo, the Trickster and many more. These subjects are chosen for their prevalence yet also for their centrality. They express the whole concern of human existence now in the twenty-first century of the Common Era. Some of the topics would have seemed odd at another time, another land: the American Dream, Enslavement and Emancipation, Civil Disobedience.

I suspect though that our current preoccupations would have existed always and everywhere, under other names. Tropes change across the centuries: the irony of one age is rarely the irony of another. But the themes of great literature, though immensely varied, undergo transmemberment and show up barely disguised in different contexts. The power of imaginative literature relies upon three constants: aesthetic splendor, cognitive power, wisdom. These are not bound by societal constraints or resentments, and ultimately are universals, and so not culture-bound. Shakespeare, except for the world's scriptures, is the one universal author, whether he is read and played in Bulgaria or Indonesia or wherever. His supremacy at creating human beings breaks through even the barrier of language and puts everyone on his stage. This means that the matter of his work has migrated everywhere, reinforcing the common places we all inhabit in his themes.

2. CONTEST AS BOTH THEME AND TROPE

Great writing or the Sublime rarely emanates directly from themes since all authors are mediated by forerunners and by contemporary rivals. Nietzsche enhanced our awareness of the agonistic foundations of ancient Greek literature and culture, from Hesiod's contest with Homer on to the Hellenistic critic Longinus in his treatise *On the Sublime*. Even Shakespeare had to begin by overcoming Christopher Marlowe, only a few months his senior. William Faulkner stemmed from the Polish-English novelist Joseph Conrad and our best living author of prose fiction, Philip Roth, is inconceivable without his descent from the major Jewish literary phenomenon of the twentieth century, Franz Kafka of Prague, who wrote the most lucid German since Goethe.

The contest with past achievement is the hidden theme of all major canonical literature in Western tradition. Literary influence is both an overwhelming metaphor for literature itself, and a common topic for all criticism, whether or not the critic knows her immersion in the incessant flood.

Every theme in this series touches upon a contest with anteriority, whether with the presence of death, the hero's quest, the overcoming of taboos, or all of the other concerns, volume by volume. From Monteverdi through Bach to Stravinsky, or from the Italian Renaissance through the agon of Matisse and Picasso, the history of all the arts demonstrates the same patterns as literature's thematic struggle with itself. Our country's great original art, jazz, is illuminated by what the great creators called "cutting contests," from Louis Armstrong and Duke Ellington on to the emergence of Charlie Parker's Bop or revisionist jazz.

A literary theme, however authentic, would come to nothing without rhetorical eloquence or mastery of metaphor. But to experience the study of the common places of invention is an apt training in the apprehension of aesthetic value in poetry and in prose.

Volume Introduction by Harold Bloom

As more than half this volume is devoted to the tragic history of Africa-American enslavement and its ongoing aftermath, any further commentary on this by me would be redundant. I turn instead to the second book of _Tanakh,_ the Hebrew Bible, now commonly called Exodus.

The pattern of departure for the Promised Land—by Abraham and Moses alike—is the Yahwistic command: _yetziat_ or "get up and go." It will be repeated in another mode as the Hebrew Bible ends, in Chronicles II, where Cyrus the Persian emperor urges the exiles in Babylon to "go up" to Jerusalem. The Old Testament, which is the Christian revision of _Tanakh,_ ends deliberately with the latecomer, nameless prophet Malachi (whose name means "messenger") who warns that parents and children must turn to one another again, lest Yahweh come to smite the earth with a curse.

Exodus essentially is the story of Moses, the reluctant prophet compelled by Yahweh to a great career of triumphant suffering, or should we call it triumph? The heroes of _Tanakh,_ when they bear the Blessing, have an oxymoronic destiny, since whatever their final sorrow, they remain chosen. There are tragic, cast-out figures, like the poignant King Saul, but Moses is a spiritual triumph, though a personal loser, since he is not permitted to enter Canaan.

Exodus, as much as Genesis, is Yahweh's book, and he can be regarded as the most troublesome of all literary characters ever. I devoted most of a book to him, _Jesus and Yahweh,_ and remember crying out in that I did not trust him, did not like him, and wished he would go away—but he won't. Of all literary representations he is the most outrageous and the most sublime. Whether or not you care for him, he is great art, unlike his involuntary parody who is the one blemish of Milton's *Paradise Lost*.

Exodus is the Hebrew epic, fully comparable to Homer, but surpassing all the disciples of Homer, from Virgil to James Joyce. Liberation movements to come will go on finding their model in it.

THE ADVENTURES OF HUCKLEBERRY FINN (MARK TWAIN)

"The Paradox of Liberation in *Huckleberry Finn*" by Neil Schmitz, in *Texas Studies in Literature and Language* (1971)

INTRODUCTION

In his consideration of the ending of *The Adventures of Huckleberry Finn,* Neil Schmitz explores the way Jim is represented, especially during all of the machinations Tom Sawyer dreams up to effect Jim's "escape," a horrific, brutal experience where Jim undergoes great suffering. For Schmitz, "Jim's situation at the end of *Huckleberry Finn* reflects that of the Negro in the Reconstruction, free at last and thoroughly impotent, the object of devious schemes and a hapless victim of constant brutality." Schmitz sees Jim and Huck's "liberation" as bitterly ironic, reflecting both the era in which the text was written and also Twain's sentimentalized vision of black identity. Thus, the central question for Schmitz "is not Jim's freedom per se, but whether he will seize it or be given it, and then, most horrifying of all—what

Schmitz, Neil. "The Paradox of Liberation in *Huckleberry Finn*." *Texas Studies in Literature and Language* Vol. 13, No. 1 (Spring 1971): 125–36.

is to be done with him in either case, this emancipated, alien black man?"

❧

The perennial dispute over the ending of the *Adventures of Huckleberry Finn*, whether Mark Twain's ingenious resolution possesses a "formal aptness," as Lionel Trilling reads it, or is a "failure of nerve," as Leo Marx would have it, regularly invokes that crucial term *freedom*. It is, as Marx so capably argued, what the book is about, but his own judgment that freedom in *Huckleberry Finn* "specifically means freedom from society and its imperatives,"[1] is far from satisfactory, if not simplistic, and the problem remains. Twain was rarely, if ever, a successful philosopher in his fiction. The aphorism was his mode of analysis and Pudd'nhead Wilson, an embittered crank, his notion of a radical theoretician. In *Huckleberry Finn*, where Twain restricts his tortured vision of the world to the consciousness of an urchin, this limitation is something of a dangerous virtue. Those large, potent abstractions—*freedom, civilization, morality*—are not dealt with conceptually, but rather issue their significance through the wrenching of Huck's psyche, through muted cries of pain. There is no Grand Inquisitor passage in the novel. Colonel Sherburn is the closest Twain comes to a *raissoneur*. We are instead made to feel the achievement and loss of freedom in the sensuous context of tight collars and loose rags, floating rafts and cramped sheds. Yet the forces engendering the calamities which pass before Huck's ingenuous gaze drag with them perplexing problems, the darkness of Twain's thought. That is the bewitching thing about *Huckleberry Finn*: it arouses such large and difficult ideas, and then gives us only feelings about those ideas. What Marx demanded some fifteen years ago was an ending to the novel that would elucidate those contorted lines of thought, a conclusion. Unfortunately we do not have it, but we do have, amid all the confusion and dead-ends, strokes of the imagination that cut, however clumsily, very near the bone of our experience.

"Our philosophical tradition," Hannah Arendt writes in *Between Past and Future*, "is almost unanimous in holding that freedom begins where men have left the realm of political life inhabited by the many, and that it is not experienced in association with others but in intercourse with one's self."[2] She then proceeds to argue the contrary: that the only meaningful freedom men can possess must be won in the sociopolitical realm. The notion that men can constitute an impregnable inner freedom within the self simply by taking themselves out of the social world, she argues, is essentially illusory, an escape from the responsibilities of action. Mrs. Arendt's critique of those who would separate freedom from politics, placing it either in the withdrawn self or in a mythicized state of nature, is useful to keep in mind when discussing the nature of freedom in *Huckleberry Finn*, if only because it makes us re-examine the idyllic life established on the river, that "free zone" cutting through the murderous world of politics. What student of the novel does not know that the Shore signifies constraint and the River freedom, or that the "free and easy" life on the raft affirms the sacred practice of brotherhood, specifically Huck's celebrated leap over the color bar? The word keeps bubbling up, often simply serving as a convenient heading for all those apolitical things that Huck and Jim desire. Yet Twain's understanding of what constitutes freedom in his book is largely intuitive, not systematic, and consequently does not fit into the libertarian categories that have been painstakingly constructed to hold it. Indeed, there is a kind of pathos in that criticism which neatly irons out all the contradictions in *Huckleberry Finn*, turning that sprawling, ambivalent narrative into a finely contrived Austenian novel. This approach constrains the most sensitive of Twain's critics. Huck "knows how he feels about Jim, but he also knows what he is expected to do about Jim. This division within his mind corresponds to the division of the novel's moral terrain into the areas represented by the raft on the one hand and society on the other."[3] In short, there is a shared concept of freedom that Huck and Jim struggle to obtain, "their code," and a common understanding of the constrictive rules that society inflicts on its members. The novel's "moral terrain" is accordingly partitioned into precise districts. Only those who do not know the river with its hidden snags and treacherous undercurrents, Twain wrote in *Life on the Mississippi*, can see poetic harmonies in its devious flow.

Clearly Huck and Jim have different ideas of where they want to go and what their flight means, points of view that come increasingly into conflict in the first part of the novel. Faced with a symbolic *point d'appui* as Cairo loomed in his imagination, Twain had to deal with that paradox and found himself staring into the abyss of the Reconstruction. The question is not Jim's freedom per se, but whether he will seize it or be given it, and then, most horrifying of all—what is to be done with him in either case, this emancipated, alien black man? In these proceedings Huck's intentions are finally, though grudgingly, good, but Jim as citizen and dutiful breadwinner is not the Jim who primarily interests him. It is Jim as *magus*, uncomplicated and sensuous, immediate in his feelings, the dark tutor who helps unlock the "sound heart" imprisoned in Huck's breast, who is the cherished soulmate. At the very outset, once Jackson's Island is left behind, the slave and the child are journeying in different directions—Huck within to reassert his instinctual self, Jim outward into the world, toward Cairo and purposeful social activity. It was Twain's recognition of this impending crisis, I feel, that led him to abandon the novel in 1876, leaving Huck and Jim safely neutralized at the bottom of the Mississippi.

The freedom Huck strives to attain is his right to be a child, not an impertinent manikin like Tom Sawyer, but the unregenerate poetic child alive in his body and sensitive to the mystery of being in the world. Miss Watson correctly perceives the subversive nature of this desire, and she moves to suppress it with the conventional weaponry of dutiful elders: grisly textbooks, uncomfortable chairs, "smothery" clothes, and incomprehensible lessons pounded home from a dogmatic religiosity. Twain knew in what small measures and with what anxious solicitude the spirit of a child is curbed. The seductive powers of clean sheets and regular hours keep Tom Sawyer's prankish rebellion in bounds, and for a time in *Huckleberry Finn* almost snare Huck: "So the longer I went to school the easier it got to be. I was getting sort of used to the widow's ways, too, and they warn't so raspy on me" (p. 17).[4] But the "old thing" remains, those rasping arbitrary forms into which the child squeezes his experience. Early in the novel, having been buttoned, buckled, and combed, Huck is driven to the table at the designated time. The dinner plate with its cut and segregated food appalls him. He prefers stew, the meal where "things get mixed up, and the juice kind of swaps around, and the things go better" (p. 7). It is consciousness soaked in the flesh, the self as a fluent whole, that Huck seeks to sustain, and the stakes in that struggle, as Twain represents them, are indeed high. Huck's refusal to become "respectable," to bend his body and then his mind, enables him to keep operative the lucid stare that plumbs hypocrisies and pierces shams. It preserves him from the fate of young Buck Grangerford, who has lost that battle. "Do you like to comb up, Sundays," Huck is asked, "and all that kind of foolishness? You bet I don't, but ma she makes me. Confound these ole britches, I reckon I'd better put 'em on, but I'd ruther not, it's so warm" (p. 81). Buck's acquiescence to that "foolishness" characterizes all the young Grangerfords. Each morning they consecrate themselves to "sir, and Madam," lifting cocktails to their father's rigid, maniacal face and pledging their filial "duty." The continuance of the feud, which ultimately consumes Buck, depends on this ritualistic obeisance, this tacit acceptance of parental madness. "I don't like that shooting from behind a bush," the Colonel reprimands Buck. "Why didn't you step into the road, my boy?" (p. 88). The enemy is sharply focused here. It is the cannibalistic parent or the surrogate Miss Watson "pecking at you all the time" (p. 24). The murderous look Pap Finn casts on Huck is at least undisguised.

Against his powerful elders the child seems to have as his only defense the instinct to be "lazy and jolly," which in *Huckleberry Finn* always figures as a kind of sanctifying grace. Tom Sawyer's antisocial fantasies, acted out in savage games, are "lies," what Huck scornfully calls "just pretending," and have finally all the "marks of a Sunday school" (p. 17). Huck's resistance to oppressive authority always begins at his skin. He chooses "rags and dirt," his tobacco, the good feel of artful "cussing," knowing that they mean an overt repudiation of Miss Watson's meticulous world. There is no posturing or bookish declamation in Huck's rebellion, no desire for the power of revenge. The substance of his challenge is his unwashed face and tattered shirt, that placid concern he manifests for the comfort of his body. Feeling "free and easy" is what he wants, and it is only on the river, cut off from the world of combs and clocks, hard chairs and tight clothes, that he can perfect this liberation. Only there does life become good to possess. When he returns to the raft after the Grangerford catastrophe, Buck's murdered face burning in his memory, his reclamation begins with a feast: "I hadn't had a bite to eat since yesterday; so Jim he got out some corn dodgers and buttermilk, and pork and cabbage, and greens—there ain't nothing in the world so good, when it's cooked right—and whilst I eat my supper we talked and had a good time" (p. 95). The fellowship that follows the feast is also "cooked" in natural juices: the raft is abandoned to the current, Huck and Jim are "always naked, day and night" (p. 97). Huck's description of this idyllic interlude is purely sensuous, redolent with smells and sounds, with the rapture of "listening to the stillness" (p. 96). The mythic imagination flourishes once more: "We used to watch the stars that fell, too, and see them streak down. Jim allowed they'd got spoiled and was hove out of the nest" (p. 97).

What lies coiled in the child is the aboriginal self, an effortless beauty that mocks the repressed, fiercely civilized adult. "This is the grace for which every society longs, irrespective of its beliefs, its political regime, its level of civilization," Claude Lévi-Strauss writes at the end of *Tristes Tropiques*. "It stands, in every case, for leisure, and recreation, and freedom, and peace of body and mind. On this opportunity, this chance of for once detaching oneself from the implacable process, life itself depends."[5] Surely this is the vision Twain glimpsed in Huck's experience, Twain who responded to that "implacable process" with furious anguish all his life. Children were the only savages he knew. Twain rendered Huck "exactly" from his recollection of Tom Blankenship, the only "really independent person" in Hannibal. Ignorant and unwashed, free of parental supervision, Blankenship was "continuously happy" in this wild, unruly state of existence. Both in his fiction and on tour as a performer, Twain constantly impersonated the figure of Blankenship-Huck, the bad boy who fascinates the besieged children around him. There he was in all his colorful extravagance, speaking to staid frock-coated, tightly corseted audiences about the virtue of his vices, those cherished "bad habits" of drinking whisky, smoking cigars, and sleeping late. Then, as now, Twain's audience responded warmly to this pose, remembering their own childish insight into the fraudulence of the great world—in sum, the whole dimly understood drama of their preadolescence. It was the bad boy metamorphosed into the cantankerous uncle drawling blasphemies who reminded them of what they had lost and who brought to life again the villains of childhood, the nay-saying parent and authoritarian teacher. But in *Huckleberry Finn* this was only part of the drama.

What the Brazilian Indian is for Lévi-Strauss, the preceptor of "what our species has been and still is, beyond thought and beneath society,"[6] Jim in his blackness is for Twain, the dark guide who welcomes Huck back to the raft, whose presence relieves him of an aimless loneliness. On Jackson's Island Jim assumes almost immediately the role of interpreter. He understands the natural world, ciphers a certain flight of "little birds," takes Huck literally out of the rain, gives him a short course in reading signs, and in general sharpens Huck's sense of being in the woods, which, given the baneful moons and ominous snakeskins, is not all holiday loveliness. Daniel G.

Hoffman has explored this aspect of Jim at great length in *Form and Fable in American Fiction*, suggesting that these powers enhance Jim's stature in the novel and endow him with "moral energy." Indeed this is the Jim who gains Huck's loving admiration: "Jim knowed all kinds of signs. He said he knowed most everything" (p. 41). It is a relationship that would seem to fit easily into a familiar pattern. Yet Jim is unlike Queequeg and Chingachgook, or any of that legion of dusky mates in nineteenth-century American fiction, not in what he has to give to his white companion, but in what he wants. For Huck the raft is the symbolic center of his flight, the attained end of his quest, but for Jim it is at first a precarious transport and then a prison. He is an escaped slave struggling for his life under nearly impossible conditions, a reality that haunted Twain.

In the *Autobiography* Twain's remembrance of the wild free life, the "unrestricted liberty" of Tom Blankenship, who served as a model for Huck, is clouded by his memory of the slaves. Were they happy, he wonders between lyrical passages on "the taste of maple sap" and "the look of green apples and peaches and pears on the trees," or were they mistreated?[7] He tries to remember whether there was a slave market in the area of Hannibal and recollects seeing Negroes in chains. Similarly Huck senses in Jim that obstinate dark presence, that lurking omnipresent fact. Jim may well serve him as *shaman*, as a brotherly father figure, but there is also that hidden side, the "nigger you can't learn to argue" (p. 67), the imponderable consciousness of the black man. "We were comrades," Twain wrote of his boyhood black friends, "and yet not comrades; color and condition interposed a subtle line which both parties were conscious of and which rendered complete fusion impossible."[8] Twain understood Huck's relish of the simple sensations and saw clearly enough how the freedom to feel comprehended the freedom to think and act, but he had, like any white man, only a glancing sense of Jim's psyche. Negroes *did* choose not to endure. Every Southerner knew that genial Uncle Dan'ls, marvelous storytellers, were capable of running away to die miserably in the swamps. What happened when the slave stood up, as Jim does on Jackson's Island, and declared, "I owns myself, en I's wuth eight hund'd dollars" (p. 42)? That determination to run, to break from the fixed point of being Miss Watson's "big nigger," imposes a psychical baptism on Jim, the taking of his life and his value into his own hands. It also imposed on Twain, the artist, difficult but unavoidable obligations—Jim's waking to consciousness, his emergence from racial type and ultimate assumption of selfhood, a problem complicated by the fact that this complex process could reveal itself only through Huck's limited vision.

One thing is clear. As long as Jim is headed toward Cairo, life on the raft is not particularly "free and easy." If anything, Twain demonstrates repeatedly the barriers between white and black consciousness—Jim's agony, his "level head," and Huck's inane adventurism. Only by painful degree does Huck come to appreciate Jim's dangerous position, and then it takes a figurative slap on the cheek to rouse him to an awareness of Jim's person. The nature of this perplexed relationship is treated in a number of scenes early in the book, each of which deals variously with their estrangement, all leading up to the climactic scene in which Huck decides to betray Jim. That Jim exists somewhere beyond the pale of Huck's perception is clearly insinuated in those passages. "They're after us," Huck declares at the end of Chapter 11, but his understanding of their mutual peril is almost immediately shown to be flawed by his decision to board the *Walter Scott*, a capricious stunt that nearly loses them the raft, Jim's only means of successfully achieving his escape. His rebuke, "he said he didn't want no more adventures," carefully states his dangerous situation:

> He said that when I went in the texas and he crawled back to get on the raft and found her gone, he nearly died; because he judged it was all up with *him* anyway it could be fixed; for if he didn't get saved he would get drownded; and if he did get saved, whoever saved him would send him back home so as to get the reward, and then Miss Watson would sell him South, sure. Well, he was right; he was most always right; he had an uncommon level head, for a nigger. (p. 64)

The "uncommon level head" belongs to a man intent on surviving, as Huck ruefully recognizes. In the much maligned "Sollermun" episode, where Jim is ostensibly reduced to caricature by the comic device of a minstrel show routine, the "level head," I would argue, remains intact. Huck does assume the role of interlocutor, but Jim is neither the drawling bumpkin nor the capering rascal. The Bible story cloaks social and political realities, realities which Huck fails to discern, and it is an assertive Jim who rears up, suddenly touched and wanting to tell. The books found on the *Walter Scott* are examined, and Huck begins an admiring account of "kings and dukes" that draws steadily closer to an unwitting description of the white man's imperium in the South. Jim asks, "How much do a king git?" Huck replies that "they can have just as much as they want; everything belongs to them" (p. 64). Their life is leisurely, interrupted only by wars and politics, and they have their harems, their "million wives." The conversation then focuses on Solomon, the omnipotent ruler who enigmatically decides the fate of his subjects. Jim spiritedly attacks Solomon's proposal to split the child and when Huck intervenes by asserting that he "don't get the point," Jim passionately sweeps the objection aside:

> Blame de pint! I reck'n I knows what I knows. En mine you, de *real* pint is down furder—it's down deeper. It lays in de way Sollermun was raised. You take a man dat's got on'y one er two chillen; is dat man gwyne to be waseful o' chillen? No, he ain't; he can't 'ford it. *He* know how to value 'em. But you take a man dat's got 'bout five million chillen runnin' round de house, en it's diffunt. *He* as soon chop a chile in two as a cat. Dey's plenty mo'. A chile er two, mo' er less, warn't no consekens to Sollermun, dad fetch him! (p. 65)

The real point *is* "down deeper." Jim has instinctively recognized in Solomon the figure of the slaveholder, the white Southerner who regards the Negro as chattel. He speaks from the depths of his own experience about the "chile er two" that "warn't no consekens to Sollermun," his own children—all the black families dismembered on the block. Significantly Jim refuses to accept Huck's patronizing explanation. Indeed he rebukes the boy for what is essentially an impertinence. "Go 'long. Doan' talk to *me* 'bout yo' pints. I reck'n I knows sense when I sees it; en dey ain' no sense in sich doin's as dat" (p. 65). With crushing authority, he adds, "Doan' talk to me 'bout Sollermun, Huck, I knows him by de back." Dumbfounded not so much by Jim's ignorance as by his refusal to give up the "notion" in his head about Solomon, Huck changes the topic. The subsequent discussion of language twists humorously around Jim's refusal to accept the concept of foreign tongues as "natural." Huck is once more superficially academic, concerned with simply ascertaining the fact, and Jim again is somewhere else rooted in his experience of the world and not to be argued from it. Frenchmen, Huck says by way of introducing the topic, "gets on the police, and some of them learns people how to talk French." They go from there. Language becomes an assertion of estrangement; French, the discourse of authority. Isn't it "natural and right for a *Frenchman* to talk different from us?" Huck asks. "Dad blame it," Jim responds, "Why doan he talk like a man?" (pp. 66–67).

But if Jim proves intractable in Chapter 14, revealing an immovable confidence in what he knows "down deeper," he clearly establishes himself in the succeeding chapter. His celebrated reproach—"En all you wuz thinkin 'bout wuz how you could make a fool uv ole Jim wid a lie. Dat truck dah is *trash* en trash is what people is dat puts dirt on de head or dey fren's en makes 'em ashamed" (p. 71)—places Huck in a genus, white trash, the class that Pap Finn in all his viciousness typifies, and strikes unerringly at a vulnerable spot. The hurt is exchanged. Huck is compelled to recognize not only Jim's outraged self, but also to separate himself from the onerous label Jim has affixed to his behavior. It takes fifteen minutes for Huck to ponder the subtle gravity of the charge. His immediate reaction is simply to prostrate himself, to kiss Jim's foot, but upon reflection he formalizes his apology so that it comes not just from Huck, but from the white boy, and goes not just to Jim, but to the black man, the whole race. Huck has emerged from the "solid white fog" to discover Jim, but the implications of his apology, the fright of suddenly seeing the strangeness of his black friend, are not immediately clear to him.

As Cairo nears, Jim discloses for the first time the full extent of his plan, a scheme that involves not just his own freedom but the deliverance of his family. It is couched in such a way as to disregard the legal right of the slaveholder to his property, and it reveals in one stroke Jim's notion of freedom. This information comes late, it is important to note, only after Huck's abasement. Huck's resentful aside that Jim "wouldn't ever dared" to speak in this fashion before is remarkably apt. "Just see," he continues, "what a difference it made in him the minute he judged he was about free" (p. 73). Jim has broken the confining mask of the loyal slave and this new alien personality, as Huck notes with alarm, "was fidgeting up and down past me" (p. 73). Their quick movement about the raft is skillfully choreographed. Jim dances ecstatically and Huck writhes with anxiety. Jim sings out joyously while Huck's conscience whispers feverishly to him. When Huck finally leaves the raft, Jim incants their names, repeating them in such a way as to knit

Huck-Jim tightly together, a chant that poignantly frames Huck's decision as a loyal white to betray Jim, the disloyal black man. "Pooty soon I'll be a-shout'n for joy, en I'll say it's all on accounts o' Huck; I's a free man, en couldn't ever ben free ef it hadn' ben for Huck; Huck done it. Jim won't ever forgit you, Huck; you's de bes' fren' Jim's ever had; en you's de *only* fren' ole Jim's got now" (p. 74). His final exhortation, called out at a distance of fifty yards—"Dah you goes, de ole true Huck; de on'y white genlman dat ever kep' his promise to ole Jim" (p. 74)—not only suggests Jim's despair, his lingering suspicion of Huck, but also involves a cunning piece of seductive praise. Pap Finn's delinquent, ragtag child is now declared a "white genlman."

What has burst in on Huck is the recognition that the flight down river has meant all along a return to civilization. In effect, Jim is going to leave him. Huck has wanted only to play, to ride the raft, sleep late, eat the fish he has caught, and poke around. The distance between the boy and the man, between the black man desperate for a secure and honorable place in society and the white youth in desperate flight from that same society, is here sharply defined. There is no mention of Huck in the plan which Jim excitedly relates. The Jim that Huck has "helped to run away" is the indulgent primitive black man, a storyteller and companion, certainly not an emancipated Jim free in Illinois and working for wages, involved with conspiratorial Abolitionists: "It was according to the old saying, 'give a nigger an inch and he'll take an ell.' Thinks I, this is what comes of my not thinking." The specter of that black man drives Huck back very close to Pap Finn's dread. In this crisis Huck's instincts serve him well, the swinish voice of his father is repudiated, but the victory is, after all, narrowly accomplished. Even as Huck seems to be delivering Jim, the river is nudging them past Cairo and the practical consequences of that decision. What needs to be stressed is that Huck is harassed from all sides, within and without. He not only defies his social conscience in shielding Jim from capture, but also, to a large extent, his own inner needs. There has been, as I have suggested, no formulation in his flight, no determined place to go. Until Chapter 16 Huck seems not to have understood the significance of Cairo. In a very real sense, Jim's freedom means the termination of his own, the abandonment of the raft and the river for concrete realities in Illinois.

It was at this impasse that Twain halted and shelved his manuscript. In a groping, often strangled fashion, he had uncovered a complex philosophical problem concerning the nature of freedom. Huck desires to be liberated from the trammels of society, to win for himself the freedom to feel and move about at will, but this is possible only in solitude. Here the right to do as one pleases is absolutely guaranteed. By feigning his death and ceasing to exist socially, Huck momentarily enters that condition of being on Jackson's Island: "And so for three days and nights. No difference—just the same thing" (p. 36). Huck, who has wrenched himself out of clock-time, discovers the enormity of inner space and immediately begins to struggle with his loneliness. His main task, as he so curiously phrases it, is to "put in time." It is Jim who nudges the bare fact of Huck's liberation toward the more complex matter of freedom in a sociopolitical context, whose presence as a hunted fugitive drives home the brutal truth that no one is free unless all are free. Huck finally perceives this truth, but he doesn't understand, as Twain did, that Jim is headed toward a catastrophe, the equally brutal truth that such a politically organized world (where all men are free) is not yet found, least of all in pre–Civil War Illinois. So it is that the white youth and the black man pass each other in flight, Huck searching for some primitive community and Jim looking for a place in modern society, a phenomenon that Eldridge Cleaver has brilliantly analyzed in *Soul on Ice*. The Supermasculine Menial (the black man) wishes to reclaim his Mind and the Omnipotent Administrator (the white man) seeks to regain his Body, but both are frustrated in their quest for the fused self (man politically and sensuously free) by a class society whose function depends on the fragmentation of the self. Cleaver's prescription in *Soul on Ice* is revolution, a level of discourse that is assuredly remote in *Huckleberry Finn*. The sweeping current of the Mississippi rushes Huck and Jim, who have no theories, southward. Before they can confront one another on the alien ground of Cairo, the steamboat, bearing its passengers and cargo, churns obliviously over the raft and the problems it represents.

Where the first part of the book narrows to an intense concentration of the "subtle line" dividing Huck and Jim, the second part, opening with the Grangerford episode, simply begins a comprehensive revelation of the ugliness of society, and in this new set of adventures Jim is a supernumerary. "Goodness sakes," Huck exclaims to the confidence men who commandeer the raft, "would a runaway nigger run south?" (p. 102). In fact, Jim has ceased to be a renegade black. The "chilling descent" that most critics find in the ending of the novel begins really at this point, with the deformation of Jim's psyche. The black man who had determined not only to seize his freedom, but who, with an audacity that stunned Huck, planned to return and "steal" his family, now becomes the gowned, besmirched "Sick Arab" amiably howling on the moored raft, the comic shambling burrhead who imperils the future of his own children for the sake of his principal tormentor, Tom Sawyer, an arrogant little white boy. The travesty in the final chapter originates in the travesty embedded in that much-praised idyllic sequence where Jim and Huck, far below Cairo, float down the Mississippi in a golden prelapsarian daze. We are asked there to accept a revised, implausible Jim drifting "free and easy" down river, calmly contemplating the heavens as he moves steadily toward the ninth circle of the black man's hell, the Deep South—the terror of which initially compelled him to make his perilous break. Where is the murder in Jim's heart?

In brief, Twain had turned restively from the difficulties Jim posed, but he could no longer evoke the rhapsodic dream of Huck's emancipation without the vexing clutter of Jim's presence. "What is Jim's function in this novel?" Chadwick Hansen asks. "I think it is, quite simply, to be the white man's burden."[9] By forcing Huck to that crisis of conscience at the Phelps farm, Hansen argues, Jim fulfills his purpose: "Jim's chief function in the novel is over at that point . . . and so is the moral conflict. All that remains is to get the characters off stage as gracefully and plausibly as possible."[10] If that is Jim's significance in *Huckleberry Finn*, then Hansen's phrasing is too felicitous. The problem is how to throw the black man away after he has served as a "moral burden." But in fact Jim has struggled for his own life in the novel, and there is no "graceful" way to get him off the stage. Twain's method is to freeze that struggle and abort the development of Jim's self. What he retrieves in this maneuver is the black man as Uncle Dan'l, the old slave he eulogizes in the *Autobiography*, a "patient" friend who gave him his "strong liking" for the black race, his "appreciation of its fine qualities."[11] Having been shackled like an animal on the river, duped and betrayed at the Phelps farm, Jim suffers a final indignity— the affirmation of his "fine qualities." The alternative to that resolutely humane black man, it would seem, is Melville's Babo, duplicitous and deadly, the shadow who becomes flesh in *Benito Cereno*.

NOTES

1. Leo Marx, "Mr. Eliot, Mr. Trilling, and *Huckleberry Finn*," *The American Scholar*, 22 (Autumn, 1953), p. 439.

2. *Between Past and Future* (New York, 1968), p. 157.

3. Marx, p. 439.

4. All references are to the Norton Critical Edition of the *Adventures of Huckleberry Finn*, ed. Sculley Bradley, Richmond Croom Beatty, and E. Hudson Long (New York, 1961).

5. Claude Lévi-Strauss, *Tristes Tropiques* (New York, 1963), p. 398.

6. Ibid.

7. *The Autobiography of Mark Twain*, ed. Charles Neider (New York, 1959), p. 14.

8. Ibid., p. 6.

9. Chadwick Hansen, "The Character of Jim and the Ending of *Huckleberry Finn*," *Massachusetts Review*, 5 (Autumn, 1963), p. 58.

10. Ibid.

11. *Autobiography*, p. 6.

BELOVED
(TONI MORRISON)

"*Beloved* and the Transforming Power of the Word"
by Louise Cowan, in *Classic Texts and the Nature of Authority* (1993)

INTRODUCTION

In her analysis of Toni Morrison's epic novel *Beloved,* which deals with enslavement and the many struggles that continue after emancipation, Louise Cowan focuses on language and the responsibility of the poet to bear witness to the past while pointing "the way to the future in the reader's imagination." Reading the novel for what it tells us about the understanding of psychological and physical trauma, the persistence of guilt, and the ability to heal through the artful use of language, Cowan finds that Beloved herself "is the whole body of unassimilated wrongs of a people, all their wounds and indignities, all their longing for love to heal injustices. She is a sense of injury so strong that she stands ready to intrude into people's lives and stop them from living in her incessant calling out for the love she was denied." For Cowan, to address the horror of what has been and to forge a new way for the future is

Cowan, Louise. "*Beloved* and the Transforming Power of the Word." *Classic Texts and the Nature of Authority.* Eds. Donald and Louise Cowan. Dallas: Dallas Institute, 1993. 291–303.

to accept the responsibility of the poet, who, in refashioning experience, makes the Word incarnate.

~⚬~

"Listen here, girl," he told her, "you can't quit the Word. It's given to you to speak. You can't quit the Word, I don't care what all happen to you."

In an essay entitled "Memory, Creation, and Writing," Toni Morrison maintains that writers have a far greater task than the mere recording of their own culture; they have an obligation to remember and to "bear witness":

> If my work is to be functional to the group (to the village, as it were), then it must bear witness and identify that which is useful from the past and that which ought to be discarded; it must make it possible to prepare for the present and live it out and it must do that not by avoiding problems and contradictions but by examining them; it should not even attempt to solve social problems, but it should certainly try to clarify them.

Morrison is here implying the writer's responsibility to interpret the past; the "witness" borne by the literary work points the way to the future in the reader's imagination. Through a process that Six-O, one of the slaves in Morrison's fifth novel *Beloved*, calls "gathering" and giving the pieces back "in all the right order," the artist is able to give form to experience, to speak the characterizing word, and thus to clarify the significant elements in the life of a people. For, one could argue, *poiesis*—the making of a work of poetic art—makes clear what is valuable in the past by putting it into words and so finding its parallels in the springs of language, wherein are contained the primordial images of the original creative Word. As the contemporary phenomenologist Paul Ricoeur has written: "Only by its incarnation in repeatedly reinterpreted ancient symbolism by which the word is continually reduced to essentials can the word speak to the heart as well as to the intelligence and the will—to the whole person."

The work of art is, to use the term Ricoeur has chosen, an "incarnation," an image, of the creative word. A noted twentieth-century scriptural authority, Sigmund Mowinckel, comments that in the Biblical tradition, the Word "mediated the creation of the world and constantly creates life anew." Its action in time is constant creation. In such a context, the Word is conceived as dramatic and purposeful, finding its resonance in the hearts of men and women. The author of the Book of Proverbs declares: "I will not let the Word of God depart from me before my eyes; it is life to me for I have found it and it is *health* and *healing* to all my flesh."

If, as in the Biblical view, error can be righted, the wrongdoer changed, and the iron chain of cause and effect broken, then judgment and punishment are no longer the necessary outcome of crimes and misdemeanors; indeed the very scenario of human life may be altered. But such a change hinges on discernment and affirmation of the Word. Thus it could be said that the true *logos*, as meaning, can come into being on the human level only through the imagination, which, as Coleridge perceived it, is indeed a *mimesis*, a "repetition in the finite mind" of the inaugural Word. It is this arduous struggle demanded by imagination that constitutes the central action of Toni Morrison's *Beloved*. In a disturbingly powerful way, the novel traces the process of giving form to experience and thus finding the right path for the future, making use of the "ancient symbolism" of the word.

The metaphorical focus of *Beloved* is incarnation, the embodiment of spirit in the things of matter. The opposite of this genuine incarnation, what Dante called *fraud*, is shown to be the counterfeit that falsifies the fundamental pattern of existence. This ancient spirit of deception takes on in the novel the pieced-together body of a fearfully attractive young woman, who, emerging from primordial water, comes to assume the identity of a baby cut off from life eighteen years ago and now returned from the underworld to her mother, greedy for affection. In terms of the major symbolism of the novel, the creature who calls herself Beloved, far from being an incarnation, is made up of heterogeneous pieces yoked together by violence—pieces that, to use Morrison's expression in another connection, do not become true parts. The young woman who walks out of the water on new feet, her head too heavy to support itself, has taken on her inauthentic existence from a word engraved on a tombstone—*Beloved*—purchased at the cost of a woman's honor, a word conceived in bitterness and despair:

those ten minutes [Sethe] … spent pressed up against dawn-colored stone studded with star chips, her knees wide open as the grave, were longer than life, more alive, more pulsating than the baby blood that soaked her fingers like oil.

This act of paying the engraver by "rutting among the tombstones" engenders Beloved, a kind of succubus christened at this moment of Sethe's abandonment to the powers of darkness. The name the creature takes is the single word Sethe could afford from the preacher's address at the unnamed but "crawlin' already?" baby girl's funeral—"Dearly Beloved." From this incident of her begetting and from other aspects of Beloved's behavior when she later enters Sethe's life, one is gradually made aware that this *revenant* is not the child's ghost now grown to full size but a predatory spirit from another realm, desirous of making the *join*, as she puts it. She combines in herself not only the complicated web of psychic horrors woven out of the circumstances surrounding the child's death—Sethe's degradation in slavery, her indignation at violation, her remorse at killing her child, her shame at selling her body—but also the horrors of slave-ship crossings and other atrocities that make up the negative content of what Pierre Teilhard de Chardin has called cosmic "diminishments."

Near the end of the novel, when Paul D asks Denver if Beloved was "sure nuf" her sister, Denver replies, "Sometimes I think she was—more." Further, the entire last section of the novel, after Beloved's exorcism, serves to indicate that this invading spirit was not simply the baby's ghost but a creature that, in the words of the traditional prayer to Michael the Archangel, "prowls about the world, seeking the ruin of souls."

"There is a loneliness that roams," the reader is told in the last pages of the novel, in a section that plays the part of an epilogue. "It is alive, on its own":

Everybody knew what she was called, but nobody anywhere knew her name. Disremembered and unaccounted for, she cannot be lost because no one is looking for her, and even if they were, how can they call her if they don't know her name? Although she has claim, she is not claimed. In the place where long grass opens, the girl who waited to be loved and cry shame erupts into her separate parts, to make it easy for the chewing laughter to swallow her all away.

We have been witnessing, this lyrical passage informs us, the machinations of a wandering spirit with no real identity. She found a place for herself in Sethe's life where she could "be loved and cry shame." Only guilt could make sufficient darkness in the soul for her to gain entry into the world of the living. But eventually her body falls away, "exploded, some say," and the "chewing laughter" swallows her up—an ironic spirit of evil that dominates the dark, hot place from which she has come. After she has gone, people forget her like a bad dream, remembering nothing whatever about her. Occasionally, however, something shifts and they see the lineaments of a familiar face. But if they touch it, we are told, "they know things will never be the same." For a while her footprints are to be seen in back of 124; but these too disappear, for "this is not a story to pass on." Negative entities have no story; theirs is no *epos* or *mythos*. Memory does not preserve their deeds. If the human race is to continue its progress toward its assigned destiny, it learns to "disremember," to discard those things that, as Morrison has said, "are not useful." In the economy of history, their negation is made to serve the purpose of affirmation; the underworld from which they emerge is to be confronted and overcome; but in themselves they are to be forgotten.

Coming from this underworld, a place not simply of the dead but of those spirits who have ranged themselves on the side of negation, Beloved finds an aperture into the world of light through Sethe's shame. This creature from the outer darkness—a *belle dame sans merci*, a fatal lady without grace, a demon, a double, a projection, or, we could even say, a group psychosis—has gained strength and cunning over the years from the unspoken and unspeakable material concealed in the recesses of Sethe's psyche as she spends a great part of each day "beating back the past." Like all that grows in these inner abysses, this alien spirit has become perversely precious, gradually consuming Sethe's substance and appropriating the particular mark of her identity: "She was my best thing," Sethe laments after Beloved's overthrow. Beloved had come demanding inordinate and exclusive love. In fact, her spiritual greed would have been sufficient, finally, to devour the whole world. The injunction at the end of the novel, "This is not a story to pass on," identifies, as Morrison has said in her essay a novel ought to do, what must be discarded from the past. It is the entire work of the novel to "clarify" the social issue involved in the vampirism exerted by a false image—a false word, as I am speaking of it in this mapping—a predatory spirit that preys upon unexamined memories of victimization and self-recrimination. For Beloved to conquer as she has come to do, to make the *join*, would mean for Sethe to capitulate to guilt and falsehood and, finally, give herself over to outer darkness. Beloved is a false creation engendered by a wrong idea upon nothingness, greedy to enter into existence. Her triumph could mean the loss of souls, the fall of cities, the destruction of civilization. Something like Beloved took over the mind of Nazi Germany when a pseudo-ideal was taken as genuine. In the context of this novel, she represents similarly the specter of racial guilt—all the intricate inter-twinings of recrimination and shame darkening the minds of both victim and victimizer—in an America marked by harrowing memories of slavery. What Morrison's novel "clarifies" is that the horrors of this oppression must be brought forward, identified for what they are, given form, and their negative elements discarded as *not* beloved.

The spectral Beloved is alluringly ambiguous, an invasion of Sethe's most noble aspects: her passionate love and courage, her self-punishing sense of justice. Other elements in the novel, however, are clear manifestations of the sordid face of the demonic at work in the affairs of mortals. Throughout the ages, in the Scriptural tradition, the diabolic has made its creative power known by a fragmentation of the Word into mere "words," as in the Tower of Babel. Certainly the modern world has witnessed the decline of belief in the healing power of the word: language is no longer sacred; people turn to it not for their deepest identity but for factual information and the power to manipulate. Surrounded by a jargon that distracts and deceives, the *logos*, with its pattern of meaning that embraces the totality of things, has become fragmented into meaningless words—signs, signifiers, pointers to objects, abstractions. Language is no longer considered a divine gift by which people may interpret their lives. Michel de Corte diagnoses the modern illness as a separation of mind and soul, with the mind able to disincarnate itself and to discourse as ego unencumbered by the soul, which can only suffer inarticulately at its lack.

This motif of speech and silence runs throughout the novel: the bit in Paul D's mouth, which takes away his manhood; Denver's deafness, brought on in childhood by a terrible "word" from a fellow-student. Terrible indeed is the verbal fragmentation to be seen in Schoolteacher's statistics at Sweet Home and to be heard in the pandemonium of garbled language in 124 before the exorcism of Beloved. In contrast are the poetic songs of the chain gang, a group fettered in every other way, which accomplish the freedom their words express, as do Baby Suggs' "calling" in the clearing and the wordless sound the women make—like the moment of creation itself—when they come to deliver Sethe from the interloper who has taken possession of her psyche. Even in the strictures of slavery, the word is vital among the slaves at Sweet Home during the regime of the Garners; the male slaves learn the concept of manhood and are elevated by it, even if their participation in that state is severely limited; they honor Sethe's "word" in choosing from among them her husband, though all are sick with desire for her; Six-O's Thirty-Mile woman embodies her value in the very name bestowed upon her; and, later, Six-O's jubilant shout, "Seven-O," while he is being lynched, his feet burning, is a word filled with unconquerable victory, since it testifies to the continuation of his seed in the world. The word accomplishes its therapy whenever it is affirmative: when it expresses genuine spirit made flesh in love and hope. We see the power of the Word in Baby Suggs, in Stamp Paid, in Paul D, in the Bodwins, in Miss Lady Jones, Janey Wagon, and Ella.

Beloved herself functions as a powerful, evocative word in the novel, almost as a magic charm; "say my name," she says to Paul D. She is hungry for verbal details of the life she seeks to devour; she cannot have enough of Sethe's memories, fragmenting her organic wholeness as a person. But through Beloved's prodding, Sethe begins to remember things she did not know she knew: her mother's mark, like a word, and her strange African tongue, which, as Deborah Horvitz points out, Sethe reads now from this distance.

The emphasis upon the incarnation of the Word is borne out in Baby Suggs' message when she calls to her people in the Clearing. Baby Suggs, holy, is a sibyl, the prophetess of the novel, seeing everything, finally fallible herself, though her "calling" of others serves to keep them alive as a community. Her homilies glorify embodiment: the body is their freedom, she instructs her people: the hand, the head, the eye, the heart. She is comic in a high sense, summoning everyone to a *komos*, a marriage festival. But the vision she serves should perhaps be designated *mythos* rather than *logos*. She calls these former slaves to love their own existence; in everything she does she is a courageous maternal presence—the image of African motherhood that nourishes them all, someone who can love her children and give them up—in contrast to Sethe, whose love, as Paul D says, is "too thick." But myth is inadequate, finally, for the total task of reclaiming the past: myth too must be transformed if the true Word is once more to be incarnated. The feast is a movement in that direction, beginning with Stamp Paid's offerings; but Sethe's excessive motherhood, intensely personal rather than communal, and tormented beyond bearing, violently cuts short any blessing that could have issued from that meal of multiplied loaves and fishes. After this incident Baby Suggs loses her will to live. "They came in my yard," she repeats, an outrage that she had not expected—a violation of the code by which her community lived; and the only upward motion she can make, out of her myth of the earth and of universal motherhood, is toward the contemplation of colors. Blue, as she says to Stamp Paid, "don't hurt nobody." But he replies, "Ain't nothing harmless down here." His remark implies that colors are still only refractions of the undifferentiated light of the *logos*; it is as though the farthest Baby Suggs can see is still into the myth of matter.

These two—the masculine and feminine principles—who have worked in such harmony for the redemption of their people are now to be separated by Baby Suggs' despair: "Listen here, girl," he tells her, "you can't quit the Word. It's given to you to speak. You can't quit the Word, I don't care what all happen to you." But she doubts even her ability to preach:

> "If I call them and they come, what I'm going to say?" "Say the Word!" Then he whispers. "The Word. The Word." The Word had been given her and she had to speak it. Had to.

If Baby Suggs is one pole of the novel, Stamp Paid is the other. She is, as he says at one point, the mountain to his sky. She is a figure of the mother-goddess; he is, as he means to be, a follower of Christ, the *logos*: "the sly steely old black man: agent, fisherman, boatman, tracker, savior, spy.... But sneaking was his job—his life; though always for a clear and holy purpose." As the central moving force in the novel, Stamp Paid ferries blacks across the river to freedom, assists Sethe and Denver just after Denver's birth, grabs the baby from the maddened Sethe's hands just as she draws back for the second time to swing it against the wall. He encourages every black person he touches to go on without fear, reminding them that their price has been paid and they are now free. But toward the end of the novel he blames himself for revealing the truth about Sethe to Paul D and causing trouble between the two; he must in fact question his own motives: "maybe he was not the high-minded Soldier of Christ he thought he was, but an ordinary, plain meddler who had interrupted something going along just fine for the sake of truth and forewarning, things he set such store by."

Baby Suggs' death leaves Stamp Paid alone in his quiet and unheralded work of redemption. After sheltering Paul D, he tries to look after Sethe, but can gain no entrance into 124, hearing only a jumble of incomprehensible sounds. Within, the fragmentation of the word continues in the refrain, a litany of possessive love that each woman sings to herself: "Beloved, she my daughter. She mine," "Beloved is my sister. She's mine, Beloved. She's mine," and "I am Beloved and she is mine." When the thirty women assemble and walk toward 124, summoned by Denver's courageous rejection of passivity and Janey Wagon's dissemination of the word about Sethe's trouble, they bring with them whatever they can carry, along with their Christian faith. Some of them drop to their knees in prayer, but when Ella begins to "holler," they resort to a more primordial power:

> They stopped praying and took a step back to the beginning. In the beginning there were no words. There was the sound, and they all knew what that sound sounded like. . . . Together they [Sethe and Beloved] stand in the doorway. For Sethe it was as though the Clearing had come to her with all its heat and simmering leaves, where the voices of women searched for the right combination, the key, the code, the sound that broke the back of words. Building voice upon voice until they found it, and when they did it was a wave of sound wide enough to sound deep water and knock the pods off chestnut trees. It broke over Sethe and she trembled like the baptized in its wash.

The triumph of the Word is swift and terrible: Sethe rushes to defend her own once more against the invasion of a white man (the benevolent Mr. Bodwin) but is prevented from doing any harm by Ella and the rest of the community; the devil-child "explodes," some say. Afterward, Paul D and Stamp Paid recount the incident in a kind of *stichomythia*, converting the events of Sethe's attack into a verbal exchange with growing awareness of its potential seriousness. Throughout the novel these two men are the clear manifestations of the *logos*, though both, certainly, have had their failures and perplexities. Here at the end the two suddenly find the right order of things, however, beginning to emphasize in their recital the ridiculousness of obsession, excess, mistaken identity, and the automatic repetition of an action that occurs in Sethe's again picking up a lethal weapon as a white man enters her yard. Paul D's exclamation "That woman is crazy. Crazy," puts the event in the right perspective. They dissolve in helpless laughter. The increasingly hilarious *bon mots* they exchange transform the potentially tragic narrative: "Every time a white man come to the door she got to kill somebody?" Sethe's flying off the handle is rendered farcical; one sees that the women's interpretation of her ferocity as excess rather than as *hybris* has enabled the community to intervene and avert disaster, as it did not the first time. However, her act, though something to marvel at when seen in the benignly malign light of comedy, is decidedly not to be imitated.

Afterwards, when Paul D finds Sethe hovering between life and death, lying, apathetic, in the room where Baby Suggs had died, he is suddenly aware of the quilt on her bed, the best that Baby Suggs could do, with its patchwork of "carnival colors." In contrast, an image of *poiesis* comes to his mind: of the kind of wholeness of which he and Sethe are capable: Six-O had said of the Thirty-Mile Woman: "She gather me, man; the pieces I am she gather and give them back to me in all the right order. It's good, you know, when you got a woman who is a friend of your mind." To have the pieces in all the right order is to bring all one's parts into a harmonious form—the hidden and latent as well as the open and obvious—in an act that distinguishes the genuine from that which ought to be cast aside.

What happens, then, to the false word, the fraudulent act that simulates being? Beloved comes from a hot and crowded realm, heavy, as she tells Denver. One crouches there. In this ghastly and unpleasant place, like Dante's inferno, are the negative deeds from slave ship crossings and other acts of suffering and torture. Likewise there are the things out of the barren and unspeakable past that bore no fruit, that came to no fulfillment. If we posit a kind of *nekros*, a realm of the dead into which the negative flows, we might say that into it goes any guilty event, any dark and intolerable human experience, pain, outrage, injury, wrongs, the need for vengeance, remorse, shame—all the things that speak of annihilation and nothingness. An image in the novel is suggestive in indicating the mystery of this realm of negation. Next to the scene in which two "throwaways do something together and they do it well" (that is, bring a child into life in the midst of pain and hopelessness, a child that will live) is juxtaposed an image of bluefern spores, thousands of them, each carrying the genetic pattern of the race. In each "the whole generation sleeps confident of a future":

> And for a moment it is easy to believe each one has one—will become all of what is contained in the spore: will live out its days as planned. This moment of certainty lasts no longer than that; longer, perhaps than the spore itself.

But, like the wheat sown by the sower, most of the spores are doomed to fall on stony ground or to be eaten by fowls or scorched by the sun. Nature's profusion, like that of the Word of creation, is ceaselessly creating in the midst of all the obstacles that the "enemy," if we may refer to another parable, sows among the great fecundity of life. Thus we may see that the transformation effected by the Word requires not only a creative act on the part of the speaker but good, not stony, soil on the part of the hearer.

On one level, Beloved is the whole body of unassimilated wrongs of a people, all their wounds and indignities, all their longing for love to heal injustices. She is a sense of injury so strong that she stands ready to intrude into people's lives and stop them from living in her incessant calling out for the love she was denied. In its ultimate meaning, however, the novel concerns the question of what we do with guilt—the unspeakable sins we have committed—not just those done against us by others, but the wrongs we ourselves have done. How can anyone ever expiate them, how can one endure them? To enter life again, to allow the springs to flow, we must open the gates—and what is likely to come in is something very beloved: our own grief and horror. If we survive this ordeal (and Sethe has to have help), we discard, as Morrison tells us we must, those negative things from the past and by a process of *poiesis* move on into being alive: what we retain, however, is the result: a new incarnation of the Word, which bestows upon fragmentary experience "all the right order"—openness, community, the possibility of joy. *Beloved* is, certainly, a novel of African-American experience—of the horrors of slavery; but it is ultimately a novel about the imagination and the transforming power of the Word.

"The Death of Ivan Ilych"
(Leo Tolstoy)

"The Death and Emancipation of Ivan Ilych"
by Merritt Moseley, University of
North Carolina at Asheville

Ivan Ilych, the protagonist of Count Leo Tolstoy's late short story, is a prosperous man, successful by all the standards of the society in which he lives. He has family, friends, and a good position (which much of his life has been devoted to cultivating), and all of this affords him a certain degree of social, political, and personal freedom. Indeed, "free and easy" is the tone of Ilych's life: He is repeatedly characterized as "agreeable" and narrative emphasis is placed on the fact that his life has a "due and natural character of pleasant lightheartedness and decorum" (137). In his relationship with his wife, who becomes more and more exasperating to him, Ilych likewise seeks—and finds— freedom: "His aim was to free himself more and more from those unpleasantnesses"—both that of their arguments and his occasional periods of amorousness—"and to give them a semblance of harmlessness and propriety. He attained this by spending less and less time with his family . . ." (135).

Even his affair with a young lady is seen as a part of his amenable life arrangement, rather than a vulgar or illicit act: "It was all done with clean hands, in clean linen, with French phrases, and above all among people of the best society and consequently with the approval of people of rank" (131).

Readers will notice that the language Tolstoy uses to describe Ilych's ideal life—words like "pleasant," "agreeable," "free and easy"—has a rather trivial tone to it. Tolstoy makes it clear that Ilych's ultimate goal in life is to avoid unpleasantness, which makes him (by Tolstoy's standards) a rather selfish, short-sighted, and ultimately mediocre individual. But in this contented mediocrity, is he any different from anybody else in his world (or ours)? The story insists that he is not. His life is "most simple and most ordinary"—and therefore, according to Tolstoy, "most terrible" (129).

But why is ordinary life so terrible? How is Ilych enslaved by his agreeably mediocre life, and what are the conditions from which he needs emancipation? There are two sorts of enslavement dramatized in Tolstoy's story: One is imprisonment within the human body, an enslavement to the mortal condition of life; the other, as we shall see presently, is a thoughtless bondage to a set of false values and ideals.

The condition of living is the certainty of death, a point that Ilych ironically embodies. Having spent the entirety of his moderate life span (he dies at 45) trying to avoid unpleasantness, Ilych falls victim to a terrible and mysterious affliction that no doctor is able to diagnose or treat. Although he suffers for months, Ilych clings to the fact that his ailment is undefined and uses it as a reason to deny that he is facing death. Although he lives with pain and illness every day, he is able to convince himself that the inevitability of death somehow does not apply to him. In order to maintain this false belief in the face of such strong evidence to the contrary, he must imprison himself within a false, delusional world in which death does not exist. This is not as crazy as it sounds, and in fact (Tolstoy wishes to show) it is a shared delusion common to most human beings.

When Ilych's best friend, Peter Ivanovich, hears of his death, his response is representative of the common reaction:

> "Three days of frightful suffering and then the death! Why that might suddenly, at any time, happen to me," he thought, and for a moment felt terrified. But—he did not know how—the customary reflection at once occurred to him that this had happened to Ivan Ilych and not to him, and that it should not and could not happen to him, and that to think that it could would be yielding to depression which he ought not to do, as Schwartz's expression plainly showed. After this

> reflection Peter Ivanovich felt reassured, and began to ask
> with interest about the details of Ivan Ilych's death, as though
> death was an accident natural to Ivan Ilych but certainly not
> to himself. (128)

Tolstoy uses this passage to show that the denial of death is natural to every human, that we all enslave ourselves to the false idea that death will not apply to us. Ivanovich stands for all the people in Ilych's world who spend their lives devoted to agreeableness, what Ilych himself regards as the "legality, correctitude, and propriety of his life" (163). In an effort to maintain their life's focus on pleasantness, they must necessarily distance themselves from the ultimate unpleasantness: death. This is further illustrated by Ilych's family and friends, who have a hard time simulating sorrow at his death, and turn almost immediately to thoughts of their own advantage. Tolstoy is providing a picture of a respectable, worldly world—in short, a world where people care about propriety and being *comme il faut*, and vehemently deny the starker realities of life, including that of death.

There are two characters, however, that stand alone in their transcendence of this superficiality. One of them is the servant Gerasim, the butler's assistant, who is seen in Section I strewing fragrant herbs to cover the smell of decomposition. The other is Ilych's son, Vasya. One is of a lesser class, the other of a lesser age, but both are able to confront and express what those of the upper ranks cannot.

Though Gerasim is a menial household worker, he is an important character in Tolstoy's story. As Ivanovich takes his leave with an expression of insincere reflection on the death, Gerasim responds, "It's God's will. We shall all come to it some day," and displays his teeth—"the even, white teeth of a healthy peasant . . ." (129). His peasant class is critical, because Tolstoy's story is in part a critique of what passes for high civilization. Gerasim seems to be the only person who can openly acknowledge what is happening to Ilych and respond with genuine sympathy. He is also the only truly spiritual figure and the character who is able by bear in mind that death is a shared, universal fate. Although he is the least free person in the story, he is the only character not enslaved by a denial of the reality of death.

Gerasim acts as a nurse to the ailing Ilych, but his services are more extensive and more important than just his physical care. As he empties Ilych's commode, Ilych apologizes to him and receives this response: "'O, why, sir,' Gerasim's eyes beamed and he showed his glistening white teeth, 'what's a little trouble? It's a case of illness with you, sir'" (153). Soon Gerasim will sit with Ilych for hours, holding up his legs to lessen his pain; and he does so uncomplainingly and with an understanding of Ivan's suffering and an honesty about its outcome. A contrast here emerges between the straightforwardness and compassion that Gerasim is able to manifest in response to Ilych's condition and the ignorance and detachment of his contemporaries, who refuse to even admit that he is dying.

The clearest account of Gerasim's role is offered in the following narrative passage:

> The awful, terrible act of his dying was, he could see, reduced by those about him to the level of a casual, unpleasant, and almost indecorous incident (as if someone entered a drawing-room diffusing an unpleasant odour) and this was done by that very decorum which he had served his whole life long. He saw that no one felt for him, because no one even wished to grasp his position. Only Gerasim recognized it and pitied him. And so Ivan Ilych felt at ease only with him. He felt comforted when Gerasim supported his legs (sometimes all night long) and refused to go to bed, saying: "Don't you worry, Ivan Ilych. I'll get sleep enough later on," or when he suddenly became familiar and exclaimed: "If you weren't sick it would be another matter, but as it is, why should I grudge a little trouble?" Only Gerasim did not lie; everything showed that he alone understood the facts of the case and did not consider it necessary to disguise them, but simply felt sorry for his emaciated and enfeebled master. Once when Ivan Ilych was sending him away he even said straight out: "We shall all of us die, so why should I grudge a little trouble?"—expressing the fact that he did not consider his work burdensome because he was doing it for a dying man and hoped someone would do the same for him when his time came. (154)

There is one other person who seems to genuinely care for the dying Ilych: his son, Vasya. He is observed by Ivanovich at the funeral: "His tear-stained eyes had in them the look that is seen in the eyes of boys of thirteen or fourteen who are not pure-minded" (129). His youthful tears contrast with the dry-eyed widow, and his age is singled out as contributing to his weakness (both emotional and, it seems, physical). This link between his age, his impurity, and his weakness is further emphasized in the scene where Vasya goes to visit his father in the sickroom:

> ... the schoolboy crept in unnoticed, in a new uniform, poor little fellow, and wearing gloves. Terribly dark shadows showed under his eyes, the meaning of which Ivan Ilych knew well [supposedly evidence of masturbation].
> His son had always seemed pathetic to him, and now it was dreadful to see the boy's frightened look of pity. It seemed to Ivan Ilych that Vasya was the only one besides Gerasim who understood and pitied him. (159)

Only a peasant and a guilt-ridden schoolboy (guilty because he too is enslaved by the body's compulsions) are able to really pity Ivan Ilych; everyone else is too self-centered, too well-bred, *too civilized* to acknowledge his suffering and impending death and to recognize that our shared mortality is what links one person to another.

Admittedly, this is a lesson that even Ilych has a hard time taking to heart, and he is the one dying. In a late internal dialogue he keeps coming back to the question:

> "What is this? Can it be that it is Death?" And the inner voice answered: "Yes, it is Death."
> "Why these sufferings?" And the voice answered, "For no reason—they just are so." Beyond and besides this, there was nothing. (162)

This torment is vivid, perhaps because it echoes Tolstoy's own "deep spiritual fear of death" (which brings him, in the 1860s, to the brink of suicide) (Pachmuss 73). However at the end of his life, Ilych is able to think and feel beyond himself and his selfishness, a change that is stimulated by his son Vasya:

> Then he felt that someone was kissing his hand. He opened his eyes, looked at his son, and felt sorry for him. His wife came up to him and he glanced at her. She was gazing at him

open-mouthed, with undried tears on her nose and cheek and a despairing look on her face. He felt sorry for her too.

"Yes, I am making them wretched," he thought.... He was sorry for them, he must act so as not to hurt them: release them and free himself from these sufferings. (166–67)

Finally, Ilych is able to get beyond his selfish resistance to and resentment of death, and he is able to reach a kind of sympathetic understanding that illustrates the truth of his death. However, Ilych is not enslaved only by his beliefs about mortality; much worse, and the stronger part of Tolstoy's message, is that Ilych is enslaved to a false value system. His life has been all wrong. Recognizing this is the other necessary part of Ilych's reconciliation to his fate: He must find the meaning of his death in the life that preceded it.

Tolstoy admired Henry David Thoreau and quoted him often, as critics such as Clarence Manning have noted. He may have known the lines from *Walden* in which Thoreau writes:

I wished to live deliberately, to front only the essential facts of life, and see if I could not learn what it had to teach, and not, when I came to die, discover that I had not lived. I did not wish to live what was not life, living is so dear; nor did I wish to practice resignation, unless it was quite necessary. I wanted to live deep and suck out all the marrow of life ... (Thoreau 88)

These words might serve as a commentary on the life of Ivan Ilych. Ilych moves through life "successfully" doing just what is expected, living in a way calculated to be the most free and easy and agreeable. This is what is meant by the powerful statement at the beginning of Section II (which details the story leading up to Ilych's death): "Ivan Ilych's life had been most simple and most ordinary and therefore most terrible" (129). In Thoreau's cautionary terms, Ilych comes to the end of life and discovers that he has not lived.

The story not only critiques Ilych's way of life: It also, by implication and with rare exception, critiques the lives of most people living in modern civilization, including Tolstoy's readers and even the author himself. Motivated by powerful, radical Christian beliefs and anarchic political views, Tolstoy held a set of rigid moral standards to which even he himself could not remain faithful. As Anthony

Daniels unsympathetically comments, "After he had written *Anna Karenina* [1873–76], Tolstoy reacted against literature. He wanted henceforth to be a moral philosopher, a prophet, a sage, and a saint, rather than an artist. (How often we mistake the nature of our own gifts!)" (31). Vladimir Nabokov, always mistrustful of didacticism in literature, also comments on Tolstoy's would-be rejection of the novel for "simple tales for the people, for peasants, for school children, pious educational fables, moralistic fairy tales, that kind of thing," but concludes:

> Here and there in "The Death of Ivan Ilych" there is a half-hearted attempt to proceed with this trend, and we shall find samples of a pseudo-fable style here and there in the story. But on the whole it is the artist who takes over. This story is Tolstoy's most artistic, most perfect, and most sophisticated achievement. (237–38)

The artistry of course does not replace or preclude the prophetic denunciation of a life lived falsely; it simply makes it a work of fiction rather than a jeremiad.

What is the matter with the life to which Ivan Ilych has willingly indentured himself? Again, Daniels provides a sardonic summary:

> Tolstoy's relentless indictment of Ivan Ilych's life includes his work as a judge. "Snide" is the best way to describe Tolstoy's treatment of his protagonist.... [Ivan's] main pleasure in life is playing bridge with his friends and colleagues, which Tolstoy tries to get us to condemn as vicious because, like music at the *conservatoire*, it is frivolous, artificial, and inauthentic. By all means let us recognize that playing bridge is not man's highest spiritual or cultural accomplishment, but we should surely also recognize that it hardly registers on the scale of human wickedness. (33)

This is well put, but misses the point somewhat. No, Ivan Ilych is not really wicked. His life is *most ordinary*—he is no more wicked than anybody else. So what has been the matter with Ivan Ilych's life?

Can he really be condemned for wishing to live properly and pleasantly, for liking antiques and enjoying bridge? It seems that this is precisely the message that Tolstoy wishes to impart to the reader, although the reader is of course free to dissent from his stark and uncompromising verdict. Rima Salys writes that "Ivan's existence turns out to have been a living death, while his death is a rebirth into a new spiritual life" (21). "Spiritual" is important here: Ivan's life, though perhaps lived in loose conformity with conventional religion (a priest presides at the funeral) is entirely secular. He takes Communion, on his deathbed, to please his wife, but his mind is on the vermiform appendix. He lives, in other words, in a "spiritual void," which the commentator Victor Brombert identifies as his fatal flaw. Brombert explains:

> Ivan Ilych learns—the lesson may come too late—that emptiness, self-deception, and false values have been at the core of his life, that in the process of living we all deny the truth of our human condition, that we lie to ourselves when we pretend to forget about death, and that this lie is intimately bound up with all the other lies that vitiate our moral being. It is a denunciation of a spiritual void. (155)

In other words, Ilych has been living a literal, physical life, but he has been spiritually dead. James Olney's thoughtful discussion of the story distinguishes between "life as experience" and "life as meaning," and concludes that by his vivid fictional representation Tolstoy helps the reader to *feel* a truth that was in fact ever-present in his own soul. Olney explains:

> Life would be one thing were we not all going to die; then it might be indulging in parties, cards, and pleasure every night, or tastefully decorating an apartment, or lying in bed reading French romances and eating gingerbread and honey (a pleasure Tolstoy once, as a boy, pursued for three days when the certainty of death and the vanity of life were especially vivid and present to him). But life, in fact and meaning, is something very different from this for Tolstoy, and different solely because we all exist under more or less immediate sentence of that death which, according to Tolstoy, worked as a great reordering power over life. (102; and see Rogers 214)

The closer Ilych gets to death, the closer he gets to understanding his author's message, declaring (in a spasm of hatred toward his wife): "All you've lived for and still live for is falsehood and deception, hiding life and death from you" (165). However, as he demonstrates in his rough sort of final epiphany, he is still missing the point:

> "Yes, it was all not the right thing," he said to himself, "but that doesn't matter. The 'right thing' can still be done. But what *is* the right thing?" he asked himself, and suddenly grew quiet.
>
> This occurred at the end of the third day, two hours before his death. (166)

The "reordering power" (also interpretable as a liberating power) of death over the life of Ilych explains why the story is called "The Death of Ivan Ilych" rather than "The *Life* of Ivan Ilych." Ilych's ignorantly blissful lifestyle and total denial of death imprison him within a delusion about his own mortality. He enslaves himself to a set of skewed values and false ideals that hide from him the greatest, most basic truth his life: his inevitable death. Ironically, it is these very values and ideals that prove fatal to Ilych, as his only freedom from them can come through physical death and (one would hope) spiritual rebirth.

WORKS CITED

Brombert, Victor. "The Ambiguity of 'Ivan Ilych,'" *Raritan* 26 (Summer 2006): 152–62.

Daniels, Anthony. "Chekhov & Tolstoy." *The New Criterion* 23 (April 2005): 31–36

Dayananda, Y. J. "*The Death of Ivan Ilych*: A Psychological Study *On Death and Dying.*" From *Literature and Psychology* 22 (1972): 191–98; reprinted in Michael R. Katz, ed. *Tolstoy's Short Fiction*, Norton Critical Edition (New York: W. W. Norton, 1991): 423–34.

Manning, Clarence A. "Thoreau and Tolstoy." *The New England Quarterly* 16 (June 1943): 234–43.

Nabokov, Vladimir. *Lectures on Russian Literature.* Ed. Fredson Bowers. New York: Harcourt Brace Jovanovich, 1981.

Olney, James. "Experience, Metaphor, and Meaning: 'The Death of Ivan Ilych.'" *The Journal of Aesthetics and Art Criticism* 31 (Autumn, 1972): 101–114.

Pachmuss, Temira. "The Theme of Love and Death in Tolstoy's *The Death of Ivan Ilych.*" *American Slavic and East European Review* 20 (February 1961): 72–83.

Rogers, Philip. "Scrooge on the Neva: Dickens and Tolstoj's Death of Ivan Il'ič." *Comparative Literature* 40 (Summer 1988): 193–218.

Salys, Rima. "Signs on the Road of Life: 'The Death of Ivan Il'ič." *The Slavic and East European Journal* 30 (Spring, 1986): 18–28.

Thoreau, Henry D. *Walden*. Edited and annotated by Jeffrey S. Cramer. New Haven: Yale University Press, 2004.

Tolstoy, Leo. "The Death of Ivan of Ivan Ilych." Translated by Aylmer Maude, revised by Michael R. Katz. In *Tolstoy's Short Fiction*, Norton Critical Edition ed. Michael R. Katz (New York: W. W. Norton, 1991): 123–67.

THE DECLARATION OF INDEPENDENCE
(THOMAS JEFFERSON)

"Thomas Jefferson and the Great Declaration"
by Moses Coit Tyler, in *The Literary History of the American Revolution, 1763–1783* (1897)

In his commentary on this founding document that championed the cause of the American Revolution and declared emancipation from the tyranny of the British monarchy, Moses Coit Tyler explores the history of the Declaration of Independence, tracing Jefferson's compositional process and also examining the Declaration's literary qualities. Important political documents, according to Tyler, stand the test of time and can be judged for their political and historical significance as well as their aesthetic qualities.

I.

On the twenty-first of June, 1775, Thomas Jefferson took his seat for the first time as a member of the Continental Congress, bringing with him into that famous assemblage, as we are told by an older member of it, "a reputation for literature, science, and a happy talent

---

Tyler, Moses Coit. "Thomas Jefferson and the Great Declaration." *The Literary History of the American Revolution, 1763–1783*, Vol. 1. New York: G.P. Putnam Sons, 1897. 494–521.

of composition. Writings of his were handed about, remarkable for the peculiar felicity of expression."[1] He had then but recently passed his thirty-second birthday, and was known to be the author of two or three public papers of considerable note.

Of these, the first one, written in 1769, could hardly have been among those compositions of his which were handed about for the admiration of Congress: it consisted of the "Resolutions of the Virginia House of Burgesses" in response to the speech of their new governor, Lord Botetourt, and was remarkable for nothing so much as for its obsequious tone—especially for its meek assurance on behalf of the burgesses that, in all their deliberations, it should be their "ruling principle" to consider the interests of Virginia and those of Great Britain as "inseparably the same."[2]

His second public paper, written in the early summer of 1774, indicates how perfectly, within that interval of five years, this adept at "felicity of expression" had passed from the stage of deference, to something bordering on that of truculence, as regards the official custodians of authority. The extraordinary composition now referred to, was first published at Williamsburg in the year in which it was written, and bears the following title: "A Summary View of the Rights of British America. Set Forth in Some Resolutions intended for the Inspection of the Present Delegates of the People of Virginia now in Convention."[3] Herein his majesty is informed, without the waste of a single word in mere politeness, that "he is no more than the chief officer of the people, appointed by the laws, and circumscribed with definite powers, to assist in working the great machine of government erected for their use, and consequently subject to their superintendence." This, of course, might be a somewhat novel and startling view of himself for the "chief magistrate of the British empire" to take; but after he shall have got accustomed to it, he would see, doubtless, how eminently fitting it was that he should at last receive from the people of America a "joint address, penned in the language of truth, and divested of those expressions of servility which would persuade his majesty that we were asking favors, and not rights."[4]

> Let those flatter who fear: it is not an American art. To give praise which is not due might be well from the venal, but would ill become those who are asserting the rights of human nature. They know, and will therefore say, that kings are the servants, not

the proprietors, of the people. Open your breast, sire, to liberal
and expanded thought. Let not the name of George the Third
be a blot in the page of history. . . . The whole art of government
consists in the art of being honest. Only aim to do your duty,
and mankind will give you credit where you fail. No longer
persevere in sacrificing the rights of one part of the empire to
the inordinate desires of another, but deal out to all equal and
impartial right. . . . This, sire, is the advice of your great American
council, on the observance of which may perhaps depend your
felicity and future fame, and the preservation of that harmony
which alone can continue both in Great Britain and America
the reciprocal advantages of their connection.[5]

Another notable state paper of Jefferson's, was one on which he had
been engaged immediately prior to his departure from the legislature
of Virginia, in order to take his seat in Congress,—an "Address of the
House of Burgesses,"[6] adopted June 12, 1775, and having reference
to Lord North's plan for conciliating the American colonies. In this
paper, the burgesses of Virginia are made to review the long record of
political blunders and crimes perpetrated by the British government
in its relation to America, and then to declare that, for the further
management of the dispute, they looked to the General Congress.

II.

Certainly, it is not strange that the more radical members of Congress
welcomed among them this young man, who, being in opinion even
more radical than themselves, also possessed so striking a talent
for unabashed and sonorous talk to governors of royal provinces
and even to kings. Moreover, he soon won the hearts of the speech
makers in that body by being himself no speech maker; and while he
thus avoided irritating collisions and rivalries with his associates, he
commanded their further admiration by being always "prompt, frank,
explicit, and decisive upon committees and in conversation,"—not
even Samuel Adams himself being more so.[7] Accordingly, only three
days after he had taken his seat, the great honor was paid him of being
joined with the foremost political writer of the day—the author of the
"Farmer's Letters"—as a special committee for preparing the declaration of the Americans on taking up arms.[8] Furthermore, in less than

a month after his arrival, this novice in congressional business was given the second place on a committee, consisting of such veterans as Franklin, John Adams, and Richard Henry Lee, appointed to draft the American reply to Lord North's conciliatory propositions.[9]

Thus it came to pass, that when, early in June, 1776, Congress saw before it the probability of its soon adopting the tremendous resolution,—"that these United Colonies are, and of right ought to be, free and independent States; that they are absolved from all allegiance to the British crown; and that all political connection between them and the state of Great Britain is, and ought to be, totally dissolved,"[10]— then Thomas Jefferson, receiving the largest number of votes, was placed at the head of the committee of illustrious men to whom was assigned the task of preparing a suitable Declaration of Independence, and thereby he became the draftsman of the one American state paper that has reached to supreme distinction in the world, and that seems likely to last as long as American civilization lasts.

III.

It can hardly be doubted that some hindrance to a right estimate of the Declaration of Independence is occasioned by either of two opposite conditions of mind, both of which are often to be met with among us: on the one hand, a condition of hereditary, uncritical awe and worship of the American Revolution and of this state paper as its absolutely perfect and glorious expression; on the other hand, a later condition of cultivated distrust of the Declaration, as a piece of writing lifted up into inordinate renown by the passionate and heroic circumstances of its origin, and ever since then extolled beyond reason by the blind energy of patriotic enthusiasm. Turning from the former state of mind,—which obviously calls for no further comment,—we may note, as a partial illustration of the latter, that American confidence in the supreme intellectual merit of this all-famous document received a serious wound, some forty years ago, from the hand of Rufus Choate, when, with a courage greater than would now be required for such an act, he characterized it as made up of "glittering and sounding generalities of natural right."[11] What the great advocate then so unhesitantly suggested, many a thoughtful American since then has at least suspected,—that this famous proclamation, as a piece of political literature, cannot stand the test of modern analysis; that it belongs to the immense class of over-praised productions; that it is, in fact, a stately patchwork of sweeping propositions of somewhat doubtful validity; that it has long imposed upon mankind by the well-known effectiveness of verbal glitter and sound; that, at the best, it is an example of florid political declamation belonging to the sophomoric period of our national life—a period which, as we flatter ourselves, we have now outgrown.

Nevertheless, it is to be noted that, whatever authority the Declaration of Independence has acquired in the world, has been due to no lack of criticism, either at the time of its first appearance or since then,—a fact which seems to tell in favor of its essential worth and strength. From the date of its original publication down to the present moment, it has been attacked again and again, either in anger or in contempt, by friends as well as by enemies of the American Revolution, by liberals in politics as well as by conservatives. It has been censured for its substance, it has been censured for its form: for its misstatements of fact, for its fallacies in reasoning; for its audacious novelties and paradoxes, for its total lack of all novelty, for its repetition of old and threadbare statements, even for its downright plagiarisms; finally, for its grandiose and vaporing style.

IV.

One of the earliest and ablest of its assailants was Thomas Hutchinson, the last civil governor of the colony of Massachusetts, who, being stranded in London by the political storm which had blown him thither, published there, in the autumn of 1776, his "Strictures upon the Declaration of the Congress at Philadelphia"[12]; wherein, with an unsurpassed knowledge of the origin of the controversy, and with an unsurpassed acumen in the discussion of it, he traverses the entire document, paragraph by paragraph, for the purpose of showing that its allegations in support of American Independence are "false and frivolous."[13]

A better written, and, upon the whole, a more effective arraignment of the great Declaration, was the celebrated pamphlet by an English barrister, John Lind, "An Answer to the Declaration of the American Congress,"—a pamphlet evidently written at the instigation of the ministry, and sent abroad under its approval. Here, again, the manifesto of Congress is subjected to a searching criticism, in order to show that the theory of government put forward in its preamble is "absurd and visionary"[14]; that its political maxims are not only "repugnant to the British constitution" but "subversive of every actual or imaginable kind of government"[15]; and that its specific charges against the king and parliament are "calumnies,"[16]—since they allege as usurpations and as encroachments certain acts of government under George the Third identical in character with those which had been "constantly exercised by his predecessors and their parliaments," and which had been on many occasions recognized as constitutional by the American colonial assemblies.[17] It is doubtful if any disinterested student of history, any competent judge of reasoning, will now deny to this pamphlet the praise of making out a strong case against the historical accuracy and the logical soundness of many parts of the Declaration of Independence.

Undoubtedly, the force of such censures is for us much broken by the fact that those censures proceeded from men who were themselves partisans in the Revolutionary controversy and bitterly hostile to the whole movement which the Declaration was intended to justify. Such is not the case, however, with the leading modern English critics of the same document, who, while blaming in severe terms the policy of the British government toward the Thirteen Colonies, have also found much to abate from the confidence due to this official announcement of the reasons for our secession from the empire. For example, Earl Russell, after frankly saying that the great disruption proclaimed by the Declaration of Independence, was a result which Great Britain had "used every means most fitted to bring about," such as "vacillation in council, harshness in language, feebleness in execution, disregard of American sympathies and affections," also pointed out that "the truth of this memorable Declaration" was "warped" by "one singular defect," namely, its exclusive and excessive arraignment of George the Third "as a single and despotic tyrant," much like Philip the Second to the people of the Netherlands.[18]

This temperate criticism from an able and a liberal English statesman of the present century, may be said to touch the very core of the problem as to the historic justice of our great indictment of the last king of America; and there is deep significance in the fact, that this is the very criticism upon the document, which, as John Adams tells us, he himself had in mind when it was first submitted to him in committee, and even when, shortly afterwards, he advocated its adoption by Congress. After mentioning certain things in it with which he was delighted, he adds: "There were other expressions which I would not have inserted if I had drawn it up,—particularly that which called the king tyrant. I thought this too personal; for I never believed George to be a tyrant in disposition and in nature. I always believed him to be deceived by his courtiers on both sides of the Atlantic, and, in his official capacity only, cruel. I thought the expression too passionate, and too much like scolding, for so grave and solemn a document; but, as Franklin and Sherman were to inspect it afterwards, I thought it would not become me to strike it out. I consented to report it."[19]

A more minute and a more poignant criticism of the Declaration of Independence has been made in recent years by still another English writer of liberal tendencies, who, however, in his capacity as critic, seems here to labor under the disadvantage of having transferred to the document which he undertakes to judge, much of the extreme dislike which he has for the man who wrote it,—whom, indeed, he regards as a sophist, as a demagogue, as quite capable of inveracity in speech, and as bearing some resemblance to Robespierre "in his feline nature, his malignant egotism, and his intense suspiciousness, as well as in his bloody-minded, yet possibly sincere, philanthropy."[20] In the opinion of Professor Goldwin Smith, our great national manifesto is written "in a highly rhetorical strain"[21]; "it opens with sweeping aphorisms about the natural rights of man, at which political science now smiles, and which . . . might seem strange when framed for slave-holding communities by a publicist who himself held slaves"[22]; while, in its specifications of facts, it "is not more scrupulously truthful than are the general utterances"[23] of the statesman who was its scribe. Its charges that the several offensive acts of the king, besides "evincing a design to reduce the colonists under absolute despotism," "all had as their direct object the establishment of an absolute tyranny," are simply "propositions which history cannot accept."[24] Moreover, the Declaration "blinks the fact that many of the acts, styled steps of usurpation, were measures of repression which, however unwise or excessive, had been provoked by popular outrage."[25] "No government could allow its officers to be assaulted and their houses sacked, its loyal lieges to be tarred and feathered, or the property of merchants sailing under its flag to be thrown by lawless hands into the sea."[26] Even "the preposterous violence and the manifest insincerity of the suppressed clause" against slavery and the slave-trade, "are enough to create suspicion as to the spirit in which the whole document was framed."[27]

V.

Finally, as has been already intimated, not even among Americans themselves has the Declaration of Independence been permitted to pass on into the enjoyment of its superb renown, without much critical disparagement at the hands of statesmen and historians. No doubt Calhoun had its preamble in mind, when he declared that "nothing can be more unfounded and false" than "the prevalent opinion that all men are born free and equal"; for "it rests upon the assumption of a fact which is contrary to universal observation."[28] Of course, all Americans who have shared to any extent in Calhoun's doctrines respecting human society, could hardly fail to agree with him in regarding as fallacious and worthless those general propositions in the Declaration which seem to constitute its logical starting point, as well as its ultimate defense.

Perhaps, however, the most frequent form of disparagement to which Jefferson's great state paper has been subjected among us, is that which would minimize his merit in composing it, by denying to it the merit of originality. For example, Richard Henry Lee sneered at it as a thing "copied from Locke's treatise on government."[29] The author of a life of Jefferson, published in the year of Jefferson's retirement from the presidency, suggests that the credit of having composed the Declaration of Independence "has been perhaps more generally, than truly, given by the public" to that great man.[30] Charles Campbell, the historian of Virginia, intimates that some expressions in the document were taken without acknowledgment from Aphra Behn's tragicomedy, "The Widow Ranter, or, The History of Bacon in Virginia."[31] John Stockton Littell describes the Declaration of Independence as "that enduring monument at once of patriotism, and of genius and skill in the art of appropriation,"—asserting that "for the sentiments and much of the language" of it, Jefferson was indebted to Chief Justice Drayton's charge to the grand jury of Charleston delivered in April, 1776, as well as to the declaration of independence said to have been adopted by some citizens of Mecklenburg County, North Carolina, in May, 1775.[32] Even the latest and most critical editor of the writings of Jefferson calls attention to the fact, that a glance at the declaration of rights, as adopted by Virginia on the 12th of June, 1776, "would seem to indicate the source from which Jefferson derived a most important and popular part" of his famous production.[33] By no one, however, has the charge of a lack of originality been pressed with so much decisiveness as by John Adams, who took evident pleasure in speaking of it as a document in which were merely "recapitulated" previous and well-known statements of American rights and wrongs,[34] and who, as late as in the year 1822, deliberately wrote that "there is not an idea in it but what had been hackneyed in Congress for two years before. The substance of it is contained in the declaration of rights and the violation of those rights, in the journals of Congress, in 1774. Indeed, the essence of it is contained in a pamphlet, voted and printed by the town of Boston, before the first Congress met, composed by James Otis, as I suppose, in one of his lucid intervals, and pruned and polished by Samuel Adams."[35]

VI.

Perhaps nowhere in our literature would it be possible to find a criticism brought forward by a really able man against any piece of writing, less applicable to the case, and of less force or value, than is this particular criticism by John Adams and others, as to the lack of originality in the Declaration of Independence. Indeed, for such a paper as Jefferson was commissioned to write, the one quality which it could not properly have had—the one quality which would have been fatal to its acceptance either by the American Congress or by the American people—is originality. They were then at the culmination of a tremendous controversy over alleged grievances of the most serious kind—a controversy that had been fiercely raging for at least twelve years. In the course of that long dispute, every phase of it, whether as to abstract right or constitutional privilege or personal procedure, had been presented in almost every conceivable form of speech. At last, they had resolved, in view of all this experience, no longer to prosecute the controversy as members of the empire: they had resolved to revolt, and casting off forever their ancient fealty to the British crown, to separate from the empire, and to establish themselves as a new nation among the nations of the earth. In this emergency, as it happened, Jefferson was called upon to put into form a suitable statement of the chief considerations which prompted them to this great act of revolution, and which, as they believed, justified it. What, then, was Jefferson to do? Was he to regard himself as a mere literary essayist, set to produce before the world a sort of prize dissertation,—a calm, analytic, judicial treatise on history and politics with a particular application to Anglo-American affairs,—one essential merit of which would be its originality as a contribution to historical and political literature? Was he not, rather, to regard himself as, for the time being, the very mouthpiece and prophet of the people whom he represented, and as such required to bring together and to set in order, in their name, not what was new, but what was old; to gather up into his own soul, as much as possible, whatever was then also in their souls—their very thoughts and passions, their ideas of constitutional law, their interpretations of fact, their opinions as to men and as to events in all that ugly quarrel; their notions of justice, of civic dignity, of human rights; finally, their memories of wrongs which seemed to them intolerable, especially of wrongs inflicted upon them during those twelve years by the hands of insolent and brutal men, in the name of the king, and by his apparent command?

Moreover, as the nature of the task laid upon him made it necessary that he should thus state, as the reasons for their intended act, those very considerations both as to fact and as to opinion which had actually operated upon their minds, so did it require him to do so, to some extent, in the very language which the people themselves, in their more formal and deliberate utterances, had all along been using. In the development of political life in England and America, there had already been created a vast literature of constitutional progress,—a literature common to both portions of the English race, pervaded by its own stately traditions, and reverberating certain great phrases which formed, as one may say, almost the vernacular of English justice, and of English aspiration for a free, manly, and orderly political life. In this vernacular the Declaration of Independence was written. The phraseology thus characteristic of it, is the very phraseology of the champions of constitutional expansion, of civic dignity and of progress, within the English race ever since Magna Charta; of the great state papers of English freedom in the seventeenth century, particularly the Petition of Right in 1629, and the Bill of Rights in 1689; of the great English charters for colonization in America; of the great English exponents of legal and political progress,—Sir Edward Coke, John Milton, Algernon Sidney, John

Locke; finally, of the great American exponents of political liberty and of the chief representative bodies, whether local or general, which had convened in America from the time of the Stamp Act Congress until that of the Congress which resolved upon our Independence. To say, therefore, that the official Declaration of that resolve is a paper made up of the very opinions, beliefs, unbeliefs, the very sentiments, prejudices, passions, even the errors in judgment and the personal misconstructions—if they were such—which then actually impelled the American people to that mighty act, and that all these are expressed in the very phrases which they had been accustomed to use, is to pay to that state paper the highest tribute as to its fitness for the purpose for which it was framed.

Of much of this, also, Jefferson himself seems to have been conscious; and perhaps never does he rise before us with more dignity, with more truth, than when, late in his lifetime, hurt by the captious and jangling words of disparagement then recently put into writing by his old comrade, to the effect that the Declaration of Independence "contained no new ideas, that it is a commonplace compilation, its sentiments hackneyed in Congress for two years before, and its essence contained in Otis's pamphlet," Jefferson quietly replied that perhaps these statements might "all be true: of that I am not to be the judge.... Whether I had gathered my ideas from reading or reflection, I do not know. I know only that I turned to neither book nor pamphlet while writing it. I did not consider it as any part of my charge to invent new ideas altogether, and to offer no sentiment which had ever been expressed before."[36]

Before passing from this phase of the subject, however, it should be added that, while the Declaration of Independence lacks originality in the sense just indicated, in another and perhaps in a higher sense, it possesses originality—it is individualized by the character and the genius of its author. Jefferson gathered up the thoughts and emotions and even the characteristic phrases of the people for whom he wrote, and these he perfectly incorporated with what was already in his own mind, and then to the music of his own keen, rich, passionate, and enkindling style, he mustered them into that stately and triumphant procession wherein, as some of us still think, they will go marching on to the world's end.

There were then in Congress several other men who could have written the Declaration of Independence, and written it well—

notably, Franklin, either of the two Adamses, Richard Henry Lee, William Livingston, and, best of all—but for his own opposition to the measure—John Dickinson; but had any one of these other men written the Declaration of Independence, while it would have contained, doubtless, nearly the same topics and nearly the same great formulas of political statement, it would yet have been a wholly different composition from this of Jefferson's. No one at all familiar with his other writings as well as with the writings of his chief contemporaries, could ever have a moment's doubt, even if the fact were not already notorious, that this document was by Jefferson. He put into it something that was his own, and that no one else could have put there. He put himself into it,—his own genius, his own moral force, his faith in God, his faith in ideas, his love of innovation, his passion for progress, his invincible enthusiasm, his intolerance of prescription, of injustice, of cruelty, his sympathy, his clarity of vision, his affluence of diction, his power to fling out great phrases which will long fire and cheer the souls of men struggling against political unrighteousness. And herein lies its essential originality, perhaps the most precious, and indeed almost the only, originality ever attaching to any great literary product that is representative of its time. He made for himself no improper claim, therefore, when he directed that upon the granite obelisk at his grave should be carved the words,—"Here was buried Thomas Jefferson, author of the Declaration of Independence."[37]

VII.

If the Declaration of Independence is now to be fairly judged by us, it must be judged with reference to what it was intended to be—namely, an impassioned manifesto of one party, and that the weaker party, in a violent race quarrel; of a party resolved, at last, upon the extremity of revolution, and already menaced by the inconceivable disaster of being defeated in the very act of armed rebellion against the mightiest military power on earth. This manifesto, then, is not to be censured because, being avowedly a statement of its own side of the quarrel, it does not also contain a moderate and judicial statement of the opposite side; or because, being necessarily partisan in method, it is likewise both partisan and vehement in tone; or because it bristles with accusations against the enemy so fierce and so unqualified as now to seem in some respects overdrawn; or because it resounds with certain great aphorisms about the natural rights of man, at which, indeed, political science cannot now smile except to its own discomfiture and shame—aphorisms which are likely to abide in this world as the chief source and inspiration of heroic enterprises among men for self-deliverance from oppression.

Taking into account, therefore, as we are bound to do, the circumstances of its origin, and especially its purpose as a solemn and piercing appeal to mankind, on behalf of a small and weak nation against the alleged injustice and cruelty of a great and powerful one, it still remains our duty to enquire whether, as has been asserted in our time, history must set aside either of the two central charges embodied in the Declaration of Independence.

The first of these charges affirms that the several acts complained of by the colonists, evinced "a design to reduce them under absolute despotism," and had as their "direct object the establishment of an absolute tyranny" over the American people. Was this, indeed, a groundless charge, in the sense intended by the words "despotism" and "tyranny,"—that is, in the sense commonly given to those words in the usage of the English-speaking race? According to that usage, it was not an oriental despotism that was meant, nor a Greek tyranny, nor a Roman, nor a Spanish. The sort of despot, the sort of tyrant, whom the English people, ever since the time of King John and especially during the period of the Stuarts, had been accustomed to look for and to guard against, was the sort of tyrant or despot that could be evolved out of the conditions of English political life. Furthermore, he was not by them expected to appear among them at the outset in the fully developed shape of a Philip or an Alva in the Netherlands. They were able to recognize him, they were prepared to resist him, in the earliest and most incipient stage of his being—at the moment, in fact, when he should make his first attempt to gain all power over his people by assuming the single power to take their property without their consent. Hence it was, as Edmund Burke pointed out in the house of commons only a few weeks before the American Revolution entered upon its military phase, that in England

> the great contests for freedom ... were from the earliest times chiefly upon the question of taxing. Most of the contests in the ancient commonwealths turned primarily on the right of

election of magistrates, or on the balance among the several
orders of the state. The question of money was not with them
so immediate. But in England it was otherwise. On this point
of taxes the ablest pens and most eloquent tongues have been
exercised, the greatest spirits have acted and suffered. . . . They
took infinite pains to inculcate, as a fundamental principle, that
in all monarchies the people must in effect themselves, mediately
or immediately, possess the power of granting their own money,
or no shadow of liberty could subsist. The colonies draw from
you, as with their life-blood, these ideas and principles. Their
love of liberty, as with you, fixed and attached on this specific
point of taxing. Liberty might be safe or might be endangered
in twenty other particulars without their being much pleased or
alarmed. Here they felt its pulse; and as they found that beat,
they thought themselves sick or sound.[38]

Accordingly, the meaning which the English race on both sides
of the Atlantic were accustomed to attach to the words "tyranny" and
"despotism," was a meaning to some degree ideal: it was a meaning
drawn from the extraordinary political sagacity with which that race
is endowed, from their extraordinary sensitiveness as to the use of the
taxing-power in government, from their instinctive perception of the
commanding place of the taxing-power among all the other forms
of power in the state, from their perfect assurance that he who holds
the purse with the power to fill it and to empty it, holds the key of
the situation,—can maintain an army of his own, can rule without
consulting parliament, can silence criticism, can crush opposition, can
strip his subjects of every vestige of political life; in other words, he
can make slaves of them, he can make a despot and a tyrant of himself.
Therefore, the system which in the end might develop into results so
palpably tyrannic and despotic, they bluntly called a tyranny and a
despotism in the beginning. To say, therefore, that the Declaration
of Independence did the same, is to say that it spoke good English.
Of course, history will be ready to set aside the charge thus made in
language not at all liable to be misunderstood, just so soon as history
is ready to set aside the common opinion that the several acts of the
British government, from 1763 to 1776, for laying and enforcing
taxation in America, did evince a somewhat particular and systematic

design to take away some portion of the property of the American people without their consent.

The second of the two great charges contained in the Declaration of Independence, while intimating that some share in the blame is due to the British parliament and to the British people, yet fastens upon the king himself as the one person chiefly responsible for the scheme of American tyranny therein set forth, and culminates in the frank description of him as "a prince whose character is thus marked by every act which may define a tyrant." Is this accusation of George the Third now to be set aside as unhistoric? Was that king, or was he not, chiefly responsible for the American policy of the British government between the years 1763 and 1776? If he was so, then the historic soundness of the most important portion of the Declaration of Independence is vindicated.

Fortunately, this question can be answered without hesitation, and in few words; and for these few words, an American writer of to-day, conscious of his own bias of nationality, will rightly prefer to cite such as have been uttered by the ablest English historians of our time, who have dealt with the subject. Upon their statements alone it must be concluded, that George the Third ascended his throne with the fixed purpose of resuming to the crown many of those powers which by the constitution of England did not then belong to it, and that in this purpose, at least during the first twenty-five years of his reign, he substantially succeeded,—himself determining what should be the policy of each administration, what opinions his ministers should advocate in parliament, and what measures parliament itself should adopt. "The king desired," says Sir Erskine May, "to undertake personally the chief administration of public affairs, to direct the policy of his ministers, and himself to distribute the patronage of the crown. He was ambitious not only to reign, but to govern." "Strong as were the ministers, the king was resolved to wrest all power from their hands, and to exercise it himself." "But what was this, in effect, but to assert that the king should be his own minister? ... The king's tactics were fraught with danger, as well to the crown itself, as to the constitutional liberties of the people."[39]

Already, prior to the year 1778, according to Lecky, the king had "laboriously built up" in England a "system of personal government"; and it was because he was unwilling to have this system disturbed, that he then refused, in defiance of the most earnest representations of his own minister and of the most eminent politicians of every party . . . to send for the greatest of living statesmen at the moment when the empire appeared to be in the very agonies of dissolution. . . . Either Chatham or Rockingham would have insisted that the policy of the country should be directed by its responsible ministers, and not dictated by an irresponsible sovereign.

This refusal of the king to adopt the course which was called for by the constitution, and which would have taken the control of the policy of the government out of his hands, was, according to the same great historian, an act "the most criminal in the whole reign of George the Third, . . . as criminal as any of those acts which led Charles the First to the scaffold."[40]

Even so early as the year 1768, according to John Richard Green, "George the Third had at last reached his aim." In the early days of the ministry which began in that year,

his influence was felt to be predominant. In its later and more disastrous days it was supreme; for Lord North, who became the head of the ministry on Grafton's retirement in 1770, was the mere mouthpiece of the king. "Not only did he direct the minister," a careful observer tells us, 'in all important matters of foreign and domestic policy, but he instructed him as to the management of debates in parliament, suggested what motions should be made or opposed, and how measures should be carried. He reserved for himself all the patronage, he arranged the whole cast of the administration, settled the relative place and pretensions of ministers of state, law officers, and members of the household, nominated and promoted the English and Scotch judges, appointed and translated bishops and deans, and dispensed other preferments in the church. He disposed of military governments, regiments, and commissions, and himself ordered the marching of troops. He gave and refused titles, honors, and pensions." All this immense patronage was steadily used for the creation and maintenance of a party in both houses of parliament attached to the king himself. . . . George was, in fact, sole minister during the fifteen years which followed; and the shame of the darkest hour of English history lies wholly at his door.[41]

Surely, until these tremendous verdicts of English history shall be set aside, there need be no anxiety in any quarter as to the historic soundness of the two great accusations which together make up the principal portion of the Declaration of Independence. In the presence of these verdicts, also, even the passion, the intensity of language, in which those accusations are uttered, seem to find a perfect justification. Indeed, in the light of the most recent and most unprejudiced expert testimony, the whole document, both in its substance and in its form, seems to have been the logical response of a nation of brave men to the great words of the greatest of English statesmen, as spoken in the house of commons precisely ten years before: "This kingdom has no right to lay a tax on the colonies.[42] Sir, I rejoice that America has resisted. Three millions of people so dead to all the feelings of liberty as voluntarily to submit to be slaves, would have been fit instruments to have made slaves of the rest."[43]

VIII.

It is proper for us to remember that what we call criticism, is not the only valid test of the genuineness and worth of any piece of writing of great practical interest to mankind: there is, also, the test of actual use and service in the world, in direct contact with the common sense and the moral sense of large masses of men, under various conditions, and for a long period. Probably no writing which is not essentially sound and true has ever survived this test.

Neither from this test has the great Declaration any need to shrink. Probably no public paper ever more perfectly satisfied the immediate purposes for which it was sent forth. From one end of the country to the other, and as fast as it could be spread among the people, it was greeted in public and in private with every demonstration of approval and delight.[44] To a marvelous degree, it quickened the friends of the Revolution for their great task. "This Declaration," wrote one of its signers but a few days after it had been proclaimed, "has had a glorious effect—has made these colonies all alive."[45] "With the Independency of the American States," said another political leader a few weeks later, "a new era in politics has commenced. Every consideration respecting the propriety or impropriety of a separation from Britain is now entirely out of the question. . . . Our future happiness or misery, therefore, as a people, will depend entirely upon ourselves."[46] Six years afterward, in a review of the whole struggle, a great American scholar expressed his sense of the relation of this document to it, by saying, that "into the monumental act of Independence," Jefferson had "poured the soul of the continent."[47]

Moreover, during the century and a quarter since the close of the Revolution, the influence of this state paper on the political character and the political conduct of the American people has been great beyond all calculation. For example, after we had achieved our own national deliverance, and had advanced into that enormous and somewhat corrupting material prosperity which followed the adoption of the constitution, the development of the cotton interest, and the expansion of the republic into a transcontinental power, we fell, as is now most apparent, under an appalling national temptation,—the temptation to forget, or to repudiate, or to refuse to apply to the case of our human brethren in bondage, the very principles which we ourselves had once proclaimed as the basis of every rightful government, and as the ultimate source of our own claim to an untrammeled national life. The prodigious service rendered to us in this awful moral emergency by the Declaration of Independence was, that its public repetition, at least once every year, in the hearing of vast throngs of the American people, in every portion of the republic, kept constantly before our minds, in a form of almost religious sanctity, those few great ideas as to the dignity of human nature, and the sacredness of personality, and the indestructible rights of man as mere man, with which we had so gloriously identified the beginnings of our national existence, and upon which we had proceeded to erect all our political institutions both for the nation and for the States. It did, indeed, at last become very hard for us to listen each year to the preamble of the Declaration of Independence, and still to remain the owners and users and catchers of slaves; still harder, to accept the doctrine that the righteousness and prosperity of slavery was to be taken as the dominant policy of the nation. The logic of Calhoun was as flawless as usual, when he concluded that the chief obstruction in the way of his system, was the preamble of the Declaration of Independence. Had it not been for the inviolable sacredness given by it to those sweeping aphorisms about the natural rights of man, it may be doubted whether, under the vast practical inducements involved, Calhoun might not have succeeded in winning over an immense majority of the American people to the support of his compact and plausible scheme for making slavery the basis of the republic. It was the preamble of the Declaration of Independence which elected Lincoln, which sent forth the Emancipation Proclamation, which gave victory to Grant, which ratified the Thirteenth Amendment.

Moreover, we cannot doubt that the permanent effects of the great Declaration on the political and even the ethical ideals of the American people are wider and deeper than can be measured by our experience in grappling with any single political problem; for they touch all the spiritual springs of American national character, and they create, for us and for all human beings, a new standard of political justice and a new principle in the science of government. "Much ridicule, a little of it not altogether undeserved," says a brilliant English scholar of our time, who is also nobly distinguished in the sphere of English statesmanship,

> has been thrown upon the opening clause of the Declaration of Independence, which asserts the inherent natural right of man to enjoy life and liberty, with the means of acquiring and possessing property, and pursuing and obtaining happiness and safety. Yet there is an implied corollary in this which enjoins the highest morality that in our present state we are able to think of as possible. If happiness is the right of our neighbor, then not to hinder him but to help him in its pursuit, must plainly be our duty. If all men have a claim, then each man is under an obligation. The corollary thus involved is the corner-stone of morality. It was an act of good augury thus to inscribe happiness as entering at once into the right of all, and into the duty of all, in the very head and front of the new charter, as the base of a national existence, and the first principle of a national government. The omen has not been falsified. The Americans have been true to their first doctrine. They have never swerved aside to set up caste and privilege, to lay down the doctrine that one man's happiness ought to be an object of greater solicitude to society than any other man's, or that one order should be encouraged to seek its prosperity through the depression of any other order. Their example proved infectious. The assertion in the New World, that men have a right to happiness and an obligation to promote the happiness of one another, struck a spark in the Old World.

Political construction in America immediately preceded the last violent stage of demolition in Europe.[48]

We shall not here attempt to delineate the influence of this state paper upon mankind in general. Of course, the emergence of the American Republic as an imposing world-power is a phenomenon which has now for many years attracted the attention of the human race. Surely, no slight effect must have resulted from the fact that, among all civilized peoples, the one American document best known, is the Declaration of Independence,[49] does not shrink from calling it "the paper which is probably the best known that ever came from the pen of an individual." and that thus the spectacle of so vast and beneficent a political success has been everywhere associated with the assertion of the natural rights of man. "The doctrines it contained," says Buckle, "were not merely welcomed by a majority of the French nation, but even the government itself was unable to withstand the general feeling."[50] "Its effect in hastening the approach of the French Revolution . . . was indeed most remarkable."[51] Elsewhere, also, in many lands, among many peoples, it has been appealed to again and again as an inspiration for political courage, as a model for political conduct; and if, as the brilliant English historian just cited has affirmed, "that noble Declaration . . . ought to be hung up in the nursery of every king, and blazoned on the porch of every royal palace,"[52] it is because it has become the classic statement of political truths which must at last abolish kings altogether, or else teach them to identify their existence with the dignity and happiness of human nature.

IX.

It would be unfitting, in a work like the present, to treat of the Declaration of Independence without making more than an incidental reference to its purely literary character.

Very likely, most writings—even most writings of genuine and high quality—have had the misfortune of being too little. There is, however, a misfortune—perhaps, a greater misfortune—which has overtaken some literary compositions, and these not necessarily the noblest and the best,—the misfortune of being read too much. At any rate, the writer of a piece of literature which has been neglected, need not be refused the consolation he may get from reflecting that he is, at least, not the writer of a piece of literature which has become hackneyed. Just this is the sort of calamity which seems to have befallen the Declaration of Independence. Is it, indeed, possible for us Americans, near the close of the nineteenth century, to be entirely just to the literary quality of this most monumental document—this much belauded, much bespouted, much beflouted document?—since, in order to be so, we need to rid ourselves, if we can, of the obstreperous memories of a lifetime of Independence Days, and to unlink and disperse the associations which have somehow confounded Jefferson's masterpiece with the rattle of fire-crackers, with the flash and the splutter of burning tar-barrels, and with that unreserved, that gyratory and perspiratory, eloquence now for more than a hundred years consecrated to the return of our fateful Fourth of July.

Had the Declaration of Independence been, what many a revolutionary state paper is, a clumsy, verbose, and vaporing production, not even the robust literary taste and the all-forgiving patriotism of the American people could have endured the weariness, the nausea, of hearing its repetition, in ten thousand different places, at least once every year, for so long a period. Nothing which has not supreme literary merit has ever triumphantly endured such an ordeal, or ever been subjected to it. No man can adequately explain the persistent fascination which this state-paper has had, and which it still has, for the American people, or for its undiminished power over them, without taking into account its extraordinary literary merits—its possession of the witchery of true substance wedded to perfect form:—its massiveness and incisiveness of thought, its art in the marshaling of the topics with which it deals, its symmetry, its energy, the definiteness and limpidity of its statements,[53] its exquisite diction—at once terse, musical, and electrical; and, as an essential part of this literary outfit, many of those spiritual notes which can attract and enthrall our hearts,—veneration for God, veneration for man, veneration for principle, respect for public opinion, moral earnestness, moral courage, optimism, a stately and noble pathos, finally, self-sacrificing devotion to a cause so great as to be herein identified with the happiness, not of one people only, or of one race only, but of human nature itself.

Upon the whole, this is the most commanding and the most pathetic utterance, in any age, in any language, of national grievances and of national purposes; having a Demosthenic momentum of thought, and a fervor of emotional appeal such as Tyrtaeus might have put into his war-songs. Indeed, the Declaration of Independence is a kind of war-song; it is a stately and a passionate chant of human freedom; it is a prose lyric of civil and military heroism. We may be altogether sure that no genuine development of literary taste among the American people in any period of our future history can result in serious misfortune to this particular specimen of American literature.

Notes

1. John Adams, in "The Life of Timothy Pickering," by Charles Wentworth Upham, iv. 466–467; also, in "The Works of John Adams," ii. 513–514 n.
2. "Journal of the House of Burgesses for 1769," p. 4; reprinted in "The Writings of Jefferson," Ford ed., i. 369.
3. Ibid. 421–447.
4. "The Writings of Thomas Jefferson," Ford ed., i. 429.
5. Ibid. 446.
6. Ibid. 455–459.
7. "The Works of John Adams," ii. 514 n.
8. For this declaration, Jefferson prepared two drafts, both of which are given in Ford's edition of his "Writings," i. 462–476. The famous and noble declaration actually proclaimed by Congress, was wholly the work of Dickinson; although, through an error of memory to which, in such matters, Jefferson was peculiarly liable, he himself, in his "Autobiography," laid claim to the authorship of "the last four paragraphs and the half of the preceding one." Ibid. 17.
9. His rough draft for this important paper is given by Ford, in Jefferson's "Writings," i. 476–482.
10. "Journals of the American Congress," i. 368–369.
11. "Letter of Rufus Choate to the Whigs of Maine," 1856.
12. His pamphlet is dated October 15, 1776. The copy of it now before me, the property of Cornell University, is the very copy presented "To Sir Francis Bernard, Bart., From the Author."
13. "Strictures," etc., 3.
14. "An Answer," etc., i. 119.
15. Ibid. 16.
16. Ibid. 5.

17. Ibid. 123–130.
18. Russell Lord John, "Memorials and Correspondence of Charles James Fox," i. 151–152.
19. "The Works of John Adams," ii. 514 n. The distinction here made by John Adams between the personal and the official character of George III., is quite pointless in its application to the Declaration of Independence; since it is of the King's official character only that the Declaration speaks. Moreover, John Adams's testimony in 1822 that he "never believed George to be a tyrant in disposition and in nature," is completely destroyed by John Adams's own testimony on that subject as recorded at an earlier period of his life. For example, in 1780, in a letter to M. Dumas, he thus speaks of George III.—"Europe, in general, is much mistaken in that character; it is a pity that he. should be believed to be so amiable; the truth is far otherwise. *Nerone neronior* is nearer the truth." Ibid. vii. 327.
20. Goldwin Smith, in "The Nineteenth Century," No. 131, January, 1888, p. 109.
21. "The United States. An Outline of Political History," 88.
22. Ibid. 87–88.
23. "The Nineteenth Century," No. 131, p. 111.
24. "The United States," etc., 88.
25. Ibid.
26. "The Nineteenth Century," No. 131, p. 111.
27. Ibid.
28. "A Disquisition on Government," in "The Works of John C. Calhoun," i. 57.
29. "The Writings of Thomas Jefferson," H. A. Washington ed., vii. 305.
30. Stephen Cullen Carpenter, "Memoirs of Thomas Jefferson," i. 11.
31. "History of Virginia,"317.
32. "Graydon's Men and Times of the American Revolution," 323 n.
33. Paul Leicester Ford, "The Writings of Thomas Jefferson," i. Introd. xxvi.
34. "The Works of John Adams," ii. 377.
35. Ibid. 514 n. Thus, the ingenuous reader has the happiness of seeing the eternal fitness of things complied with, and the chief intellectual merit of the Declaration of Independence brought

back to the place where it belongs, and there divided between the town of Boston, James Otis, and the Adams family.

36. "The Writings of Thomas Jefferson," H. A. Washington ed., vii. 305. This was written to Madison, 30 August, 1823, and should be compared with Madison's letter in reply, 6 September, 1823: "Letters and Other Writings of James Madison," iii. 336–337.

37. Randall, "The Life of Thomas Jefferson," iii. 563.

38. Speech on moving his "Resolutions for Conciliation with the Colonies," March 22, 1775. "The Works of Edmund Burke," ii. 120–121.

39. These sentences occur in the chapter on "The Influence of the Crown during the Reign of George III.," in Sir Erskine May's "Constitutional History of England," i. 11, 12, 14–15.

40. "A History of England in the Eighteenth Century," iv. 457–458.

41. "A Short History of the English People," 736–737.

42. "The Celebrated Speech of a Celebrated Commoner," London, 1766, p. 5.

43. Ibid. 12.

44. Frank Moore, in his "Diary of the American Revolution," i. 269–285, has given extracts from the American newspapers for July and August, 1776, describing the official and popular demonstrations in many of the States at the first reading of the Declaration.

45. William Whipple, of New Hampshire, in Force, "American Archives," 6th series, i. 368.

46. Jonathan Elmer, of New Jersey given in Moore, "Diary of the American Revolution." i. 279–280.

47. Ezra Stiles, president of Yale College, in Connecticut election sermon, for 1783, p. 46.

48. John Morley, "Edmund Burke: A Historical Study," 161–162.

49. The editor of the latest edition of "The Writings of Thomas Jefferson," i. Introd. xxv., does not shrink from calling it "the paper which is probably the best that ever came from the pen of an individual."

50. "History of Civilization in England," 846.

51. Ibid. 847.

52. Ibid. 846.

53. Much has been said of the generalities, whether glittering or otherwise, of the Declaration; yet they who have most objected

to its teachings seem to have found them sufficiently specific and distinct. Its famous assertion that "all men are created equal," has been complained of as liable to be misconstrued; "but," as a recent biographer of Jefferson cleverly says, "no intelligent man has ever misconstrued it, except intentionally." John T. Morse Jr., "Thomas Jefferson," 40.

THE BOOK OF EXODUS

"Exodus"
by Allen Dwight Callahan, in *The Talking Book: African Americans and the Bible* (2006)

INTRODUCTION

Focusing on this book of the Bible that tells the story of Israel's enslavement and subsequent emancipation from Egypt, Allen Dwight Callahan articulates the importance of Exodus for African Americans and shows how this book has shaped African-American religion and culture. Cataloging many ways in which the book and its theology of liberation have pervaded African-American spirituals and literature, Callahan explores the figure of Moses in African-American culture and the complex relationship that African Americans have had with this story of bondage and deliverance. Callahan concludes: "The emancipation of the Exodus is imperfectly realized, however, in the collective historical experience of American slaves and their descendants. The laws of the land of their nativity—that is, the laws of the United States—enshrined the country's founding documents, developed out of a collective historical experience

Callahan, Allen Dwight. "Exodus." *The Talking Book: African Americans and the Bible*. New Haven: Yale UP, 2006. 83–137.

that was not only alien to the African-American aspirations to freedom but was hostile to them."

ᴄᴏ̃ₓᴄᴏ

> We poor creatures have need to believe in God, for if God Almighty will not be good to us some day, why were we born? When I heard of his delivering his people from bondage, I know it means poor Africans.
>
> —Polly, a slave, to her mistress

It literally means "the way out." A loanword from the Greek, *exodus* signifies the road of escape. The biblical drama of Exodus recounts the story of the escape of the ancient Israelites from Egypt and their formation as a new people in Canaan. The Lord had commanded that the Egyptians "let my son [Israel] go" (Exod. 4:23), and the imperative phrase "Let my people go" is repeated seven times in the drama that climaxes in the Israelites' flight across the Red Sea.[1]

African Americans heard, read, and retold the story of the Exodus more than any other biblical narrative. In it they saw their own aspirations for liberation from bondage in the story of the ancient Hebrew slaves. The Exodus was the Bible's narrative argument that God was opposed to American slavery and would return a catastrophic judgment against the nation as he had against ancient Egypt. The Exodus signified God's will that African Americans too would no longer be sold as bondspeople, that they too would go free.

"For it is to me that the Israelites are servants [*'abadim*, literally, "slaves"]: they are my servants, whom I freed from the land of Egypt, I the Lord your God" (Lev. 25:55). The Israelites were set free to be the slaves of God. The foregoing is the concluding verse to the chapter in the book of Leviticus that outlines the conditions of the Jubilee, the last year of a forty-nine-year cycle in which all land returns to ancestral ownership and all Israelite slaves go free in the fiftieth year of the cycle.

> And if thy brother that dwelleth by thee be waxen poor, and be sold unto thee; thou shalt not compel him to serve as a bondservant:
>
> But as a hired servant, and as a sojourner, he shall be with thee, and shall serve thee until the year of jubilee:

> And then shall he depart from thee, both he and his
> children with him, and shall return to his own family, and unto
> the possession of his fathers shall he return. (Lev. 25:39–41)

The legislation of Leviticus concludes with a proscription that
American slaves hoped would one day be applied to themselves: "For
they are my servants, which I brought forth out of the land of Egypt:
they shall not be sold as bondsmen. Thou shalt not rule over him
with rigour; but shalt fear thy God" (Lev. 25:42). African Americans
came to associate the year of jubilee with the freedom for which they
yearned with such longing. Negro spirituals that celebrated freedom
came to be known as jubilee songs, and the word *jubilee* later came to
designate the African-American quartets that sang this music in the
late nineteenth century.

If these verses in Leviticus were the dream of the slaves, the verses
that immediately follow them were their nightmarish reality:

> Both thy bondmen, and thy bondmaids, which thou shalt have,
> shall be of the heathen that are round about you; of them shall
> ye buy bondmen and bondmaids. Moreover of the children of
> the strangers that do sojourn among you, of them shall ye buy,
> and of their families that are with you, which they begat in
> your land: and they shall be your possession. And ye shall take
> them as an inheritance for your children after you, to inherit
> them for a possession; they shall be your bondmen forever. (Lev
> 25:44–46)

These verses, and not the jubilee legislation of Leviticus, informed the
view of slaveowners. Baptist preacher and proslavery apologist Iveson
L. Brookes of South Carolina cited the passage above in 1851 when he
wrote, "It was negro slavery, or the bondage of the Canaanitish descendants of Ham, whom God authorized to be held in hereditary bondage,
under the laws of the Jewish polity."[2] For African Americans, strangers
sojourning in the New Israel, this scripture was horrifically fulfilled.

A FURNACE OF IRON

African Americans were slaves when they collectively encountered
the story of the Exodus: it was as slaves that they first learned of

this story about slaves. The Bible told of a miraculous mass flight of slaves orchestrated by God himself. At the shore of the *yam suph*, the sea of reeds, the escaping Israelites are pursued by Egyptian chariots and cavalry led by Pharaoh to reclaim the Hebrew fugitives. Pinned between the desert and the sea, the Israelites panic at the sight of Pharaoh's army in the distance. God directs Moses to wave his staff over the sea, which divides and allows the Israelites safe passage. When Pharaoh's army attempts to pursue them, the waters come crashing down on the Egyptians, drowning Pharaoh's entire host. On freedom's shore, the Israelites sing one of the oldest canticles in all of scripture, the song of God's miraculous victory over Pharaoh's chariots.

> Sing ye to the Lord;
> for he hath triumphed gloriously;
> the horse and his rider hath he thrown into the sea.
> (Exod. 15:21)

It was precisely the miraculous glory of the Israelites' liberation that African-American slaves embraced so enthusiastically: the Negro spirituals would later echo this exultation of divine triumph. The spirituals sing of God's deliverance of the Israelites at the Red Sea and are our oldest testimony to the Exodus in African-American folk tradition.

The spirituals testify that with a mighty hand and an outstretched arm God intervened in the life of his captive children to free them from bondage. He had seen their affliction, heard their cries, knew their sorrows, and had delivered them. The weeping of the children of Israel and God's belated response to it are acts in the drama of Israel's deliverance celebrated in the Negro spiritual "Go Down, Moses."

> "Thus spoke the Lord,"
> Bold Moses said,
> Let my people go,
> If not I'll smite
> Your first born dead,
> Let my people go.
> Go down, Moses,
> Way down in Egypt land,
> Tell old Pharaoh,
> To let my people go.[3]

The question of the Negro spiritual "Didn't Ol' Pharaoh Get Lost?" becomes jubilantly rhetorical:

> Didn't ol' Pharaoh get lost,
> Get lost, get lost,
> In the Red Sea, true believer,
> O, Didn't ol' Pharaoh get lost,
> Get lost, get lost,
> In the Red Sea.[4]

The singers identified with the Hebrews not only in their bondage but also in their abjection: they too were slaves under an impossibly powerful regime. The story of Exodus provided the slaves with a biblical myth that allowed them to acknowledge the enormity of slavery and their own incapacity to do anything about it, while at the same time maintaining an expectation that God would make a way out of no way. This admixture of haplessness and hope was the faith of the slave.

[...]

MY SERVANT MOSES

The book of Exodus begins by making an irony of the fulfillment of the promise that ends the book of Genesis. God tells Abraham that he will make the patriarch "exceedingly fruitful" (Gen. 17:6). Later in Egypt "the children of Israel were fruitful ... and the land was filled with them" (Exod. 1:7). But it is precisely their greatness that marks them for misery. Pharaoh warns his people, "Behold, the people of the children of Israel are more and mightier than we" (Exod. 1:9). Threatened by the Israelites' high birthrate, the Egyptians reduce the Israelites to slavery. The Israelite population continues to grow, and a frustrated Pharaoh commands that all male Israelite children be killed at birth. It is in the shadow of this pogrom that Moses, the future leader of Israel's long march from slavery to freedom, is born.

Armed with magical powers and aided by his eloquent brother Aaron, Moses returns to Egypt after a long hiatus to confront Pharaoh and demand that he release the Hebrew slaves to serve the mysterious God of the desert. A contest of wills and wonders ensues, and after inflicting a series of ten plagues on the Egyptians, Moses receives Pharaoh's grudging permission for the Israelites to leave.

The Bible ascribes to Moses occult powers greater than those of his adversaries. But what is missing from Moses's wizardry is the very thing that makes magic so desirable—the promise of mastery. Moses is not the master of his own magic:

> And the Lord said unto him, what is that in thine hand? And he said, A rod. And he said, Cast it on the ground. And he cast it on the ground, and it became a serpent: and Moses fled from before it. And the Lord said unto Moses, Put forth thy hand, and take it by the tail. And he put forth his hand, and caught it, and it became a rod in his hand. (Exod. 4:2–4)

Moses is a wizard afraid of his wand, and rightly so: it obeys not his commands but God's. African-American folkloric retellings of the biblical story of Moses's contest with Pharaoh's court wizards emphasize that Moses merely lays his stick down and it does its work of itself.

> One day he was out minding his father-in-law's sheep, and the Lord spoke to Moses and said, "Pull off your shoes, for you is on holy ground. I want you to go back and deliver my children from Egypt." He said, "Moses, what is that you got in your hand?" Moses said, "It's a staff." He said, "Cast it on the ground." And it turned to a snake. And Moses fled from it. The Lord said, "Go back and pick it up." And Moses picked it up, and it turned back into a staff. The Lord said, "Go back and wrought all these miracles in Egypt and deliver my children from bondage."
>
> So Moses goes on back. He goes into to Pharaoh and told him what the Lord had told him to do. Pharaoh said, "Who is he?" "I can show you what He got power to do." And he cast his rod on the floor, and it turned into a serpent. Pharaoh said, "That ain't nothing. I got a magic can do that." So he brought his magicians and soothsayers in, and they cast their rods on the floor. So theirs turned to snakes. And they crawled up to Moses' snake, and Moses' snake swallowed up their snakes. And that's where hoodoo lost its hand, because theirs was evil

power and his was good. They lost their rods and he had his
and theirs too.[5]

"Hoodoo," also known as "voodoo," "rootwork," and "conjure," is
the residue of West African faith and practice flavored with Native
American and European elements that survives in African-American
folk healing and medicine. Hoodoo works cures and prodigies through
occult ritual and herbal remedies. Practitioners, called "conjurors" or
"rootworkers," manipulate words and objects to wield power over
disease and misfortune. The "hand" is conjure terminology for amulets
and other cultic objects fashioned by conjurors to ward off evil. Some
Christian slaves associated "rootwork" with demonic activity: as one
Negro spiritual puts it, "Satan is a liar and a conjurer, too, / If you don't
mind, / He'll conjure you."[6] Resistance to magic inheres in biblical
religion generally, which is hostile to any attempt to manipulate
divine power.[7] In the figure of Moses African Americans could say yes
to the miraculous while also saying no to the magical.

And yet, in the figure of Moses some African Americans said yes
to both. They saw Moses as the conjuror par excellence. A contemporary hoodoo practitioner in New Orleans, calling himself Hoodoo
Book Man, explained to an anthropologist, "Hoodooism started
way back in the time that Moses days, back in old ancient times,
nine thousand years ago. Now you see, Moses, he was a prophet just
like Peter and Paul and James. And then he quit being a prophet
and started the hoodooism."[8] Thomas Smith, a former slave from
Yamacraw, South Carolina, was an octogenarian in the 1930s when
he talked about his knowledge of hoodoo with an oral historian in
the Savannah Unit of the Georgia Writer's Project under the Works
Projects Administration. Smith said that Moses's magical powers
still existed among African Americans. "That happen in Africa the
Bible say. Ain't it show that Africa was a land of magic power since
the beginning of history? Well then, the descendents of Africans
have the same gift to do unnatural thing[s]."[9] Smith had experienced
slavery in the South Carolina low country, where vestiges of West
African culture among the slaves, many of whom had been brought
directly from Africa, were strong: slaves on low country plantations
even continued to observe African ethnic distinctions into the nineteenth century.[10] Elements of West African magic—hoodoo—figured
prominently in the culture of these slaves.

A distinctive element, common to the West African worldview of the Fon, Ewe, Bantu, Dahomey, Whydah, and Yoruba peoples, was the cosmic power symbolized by the snake. The snake was the subject of veneration, fear, and folklore; its skin was used in the manufacture of charms and talismans, and its presence was considered an omen.[11] Some slaves who were hoodoo practitioners were reputed to be snake charmers. The Bible associates Moses with snakes precisely in the exercise of his miraculous powers. Moses's rod transmutes into a snake, and later the rod of his brother Aaron turns into a snake to overpower the transmogrified snakes of Pharaoh's court sorcerers (Exod. 7:10–12). The episode comports with the logic of hoodoo that the only match for strong magic is stronger magic.

African Americans were not the first to associate Moses with magic. In the first century BCE the Roman author Pliny writes in his *Natural History* that Moses was a great magician, as does the Greek author Apuleius in his *Apology*, and Moses figures prominently in esoteric European traditions of magic and secret wisdom. But the folklore of African Americans and other people of African descent elaborated further on this association of Moses with occult powers. On the basis of her ethnographic exploration of hoodoo in New Orleans, Zora Neale Hurston noted that all hoodoo practitioners "hold that the Bible is the great conjure book in the world," as well as that "Moses is honored as the greatest conjuror."[12] Hurston found the same to be so among people of African descent throughout the New World: "Wherever the Negro is found, there are traditional tales of Moses and his supernatural powers that are not in the Bible, nor can they be found in any written life of Moses.... All over the Southern United States, the British West Indies and Haiti there are reverent tales of Moses and his magic."[13]

Hurston's ethnographic studies of African-American culture in the South inform her novel *Moses, Man of the Mountain* (1939), a retelling of the Exodus story in a flavorful African-American Southern idiom. Though faithful to the biblical account, Hurston embellishes Moses's biblical biography with a masterful blend of ethnography, folklore, and flourishes of hoodoo. As a young man Moses has Pharaoh's court magicians teach him their tricks. After reading the book of Thoth, Egyptian god of wisdom and magic, Moses copies the text of the book on a piece of papyrus and washes the writing off with beer, which he then drinks so that he will not forget what he read and wrote.

In Midian, Moses's father-in-law, Jethro, himself a practitioner of hoodoo, instructs Moses in magical arts: Moses's magical powers ultimately surpass even Jethro's, who declares Moses "the finest hoodoo man in the world."[14]

For African Americans, Moses was more than an expert magician or antimagician. He was, first and foremost, a leader of his people. Moses personifies leadership as divine vocation. Moses as an archetype of the faithful community leader is an image with strong antebellum roots. Slaves in the South Carolina low country sang of him as a divinely appointed leader of the people.

> God call Moses! (Ay Lord!)
> God call Moses! (Ay Lord!)
> God call Moses! (Ay Lord!)
> Time is a-rollin' on!
> Moses free the people! (Ay Lord!)
> Moses free the people! (Ay Lord!)
> Moses free the people! (Ay Lord!)
> Time is a-rollin' on![15]

In an essay entitled "Our Greatest Want" (1859), writer and activist Frances E. W. Harper commended to her readers the figure of Moses as an ideal political leader. Harper surveys the violent political leadership of Europe and laments its "carnage and blood." She condemns American politicians as mercenary "worshippers at the shrine of success," an idolatry practiced even by "some of us, upon whose faculties the rust of centuries has lain." Among these Harper indicts the leaders of her own community. "When we have a race of men whom this bloodstained government cannot tempt or flatter, who would sternly refuse every office in the nation's gift, from a president down to a tide-waiter, until she shook her hands from complicity in the guilt of cradle plundering and man stealing, then for us the foundations of an historic character will have been laid." African Americans need more than "gold or silver, talent or genius." The virtues of "unselfishness, earnestness, and integrity" must temper and tether these other possessions to "subserve the case of crushed humanity and carry out the greatest idea of the present age, the glorious idea of human brotherhood." Harper finds these virtues in Moses, who had turned from the privilege and prestige of "the slave power of Egypt" and chose rather "to suffer with the enslaved than rejoice with the free."[16] Later in her literary career Harper would revisit the figure of Moses as exemplar of virtuous leadership in the free-verse epic poem, *Moses: A Story of the Nile* (1869).

Speaking of his black soldiers, white Union Army commander Thomas Wentworth Higginson remarked in 1864, "There is no part of the Bible with which they are so familiar as the story of the deliverance of Israel. Moses is their *ideal* of all that is high, and noble, and perfect, in man. I think they have been accustomed to regard Christ not so much in the light of a *spiritual* Deliverer, as that of a second Moses who would eventually lead them out of their prison-house of bondage."[17] Preachers from antebellum times on have spoken of leadership in the language and image of the call narrative of Moses. A Virginia preacher's description of his calling at the beginning of the twentieth century is illustrative: "One day when I was working in the field all by myself, God told me he wanted me to [be] a leader for my people like Moses. I complained that I was not prepared. And God said, 'you go and I'll go with you and speak for you.' From that day I became some sort of leader of my people."[18]

Harriet Tubman, celebrated escaped slave and Union Army scout, was Moses to her admirers and the many fugitive slaves that she guided to freedom. Tubman crossed the Mason-Dixon Line repeatedly to conduct slaves along the Underground Railroad. For Tubman the image of Exodus and Promised Land had signified her own forays against the American regime of Pharaoh. She reworked the themes of Egypt and Canaan in her self-composed musical repertoire that spoke the secret language of escape. She coined a song to warn slaves in hiding "there's danger in the way" and that they should not come out in the open to meet her.

> Moses go down in Egypt,
> Tell old Pharaoh to let my people go;
> Hadn't been for Adam's fall,
> Shouldn't have to died at all.[19]

Moses continued to be an evocative ideal in African-American representations of authentic leadership in the twentieth century. James Weldon Johnson's sermonic poem "Let My People Go," paraphrases the call narrative of Exodus 3 mediated through a conscious elaboration of the Negro spiritual "Go Down, Moses": "Go down, Moses / Way down in Egypt land / Tell old Pharaoh / To let my people go."[20] Johnson supplements his poetic language with other divine summonses in the Bible. There is the still, small voice reminiscent of Elijah's conversation with God at Kidron: "And after the earthquake a fire; but the Lord was not in the fire: and after the fire a still small voice" (1 Kings 18:12). The reply, "here am I," is the response of Abraham, Samuel, and Isaiah as well: the poet echoes the Bible echoing itself. The invisible voice that speaks to Moses from the burning bush also suggests the story of the Apostle Paul's divine encounter on the Damascus road in Acts 9. The burning bush signifies God's voice, wherever and to whomever it speaks, as a call to leadership in a moment of crisis. It is the imagery of divine vocation.

In Beauford Delaney's painting *Burning Bush* (1932), the conical, fiery mass dominating the foreground implies simultaneously all the encounters on holy ground that mark the career of Moses and the milestones of the Exodus.[21] As the title of the work suggests, the pyramidal flame is the numinous bush from which God speaks to Moses in Exodus 3. But the blazing mound is also the lightning at Sinai where God dictates his law in Exodus 20 and, at the end of the book of Deuteronomy, the summit of Pisgah that Moses mounts in the final moments of his life. The entire career of the divinely appointed leader is signified in the single, flaming image. The painting contains no human figures: the luminous form in the foreground signifies simultaneously the burning bush, Sinai, and Pisgah. But there is no Moses. For Delaney the burning bush is a sign of divine presence that transcends human effort. The Exodus is initiated and consummated in the encounter with God. It is God and God alone who appoints the appointed and anoints the anointed. It is God and God alone who makes Moses the leader of the people. The painting affords the principals of the encounter—Moses, God, the children of Israel—neither foreground nor background. Delaney's image is divine vocation as pure event, a vivid color portrait of Providence.

In *Moses, Man of the Mountain*, Zora Neale Hurston treats the challenges of leading a fearful, recalcitrant people up from slavery. Among other themes, Hurston explores how bondage becomes the psychic norm of the slave born, bred, and expecting to die in slavery. When Moses announces to the Israelites that they are to leave the house of bondage, Hurston writes, "the people cried.... They just sat with centuries in their eyes and cried."[22] Tears and fears show that liberation is a frightening alternative future for the children of Israel. In the play of the figures of Moses and the people that Moses led, Hurston signifies the terror as well as the promise of freedom for African Americans.

The figure of Moses attended African-American restive efforts to participate with greater equity in national life after World War II. Progressive Party politician Charlotta A. Bass appealed to the rhetoric of Exodus when in April 1952 she accepted the nomination as candidate for vice president of the United States on the Progressive ticket with presidential candidate Vincent Halliman. In her acceptance speech before the Progressive Party National Convention she defiantly promised her socialist comrades that "I will not retreat, not one inch, so long as God gives me the vision to see what is happening and strength to fight for the things I know are right." She concluded, "I accept this great honor. I give you as my slogan in this campaign— 'Let my people go.'"[23] And when the Civil Rights Movement of the late 1950s and 1960s brought the cadences of black preaching into the public square, Martin Luther King, Jr., became the Moses of his people, marching toward the promise of a postapartheid society. King called Southern segregationists "pharaohs" who had used every means to hold African Americans in "the Egypt of segregation" and to bar them from the "Promised Land" of full citizenship.[24]

With poignancy King himself takes on the mantle of Moses in his last speech, delivered the night before his assassination in Memphis, Tennessee, on April 4, 1968. King structures his remarks with the same form that we find in Deuteronomy's report of the end of Moses's career on Mount Pisgah. Both testaments, that of King and that of Moses, open with the Exodus of the children of Israel from Egypt. Before ascending Mount Nebo, Moses concludes his address to the Israelites with a retrospective of the Exodus.

> And Moses called unto all Israel, and said unto them, Ye have seen all that the Lord did before your eyes in the land of Egypt unto Pharaoh, and unto all his servants, and unto all his land;
> The great temptations which thine eyes have seen, the signs, and those great miracles:
> Yet the Lord hath not given you a heart to perceive, and eyes to see, and ears to hear, from this day.

And I have led you forty years in the wilderness: your clothes are not waxen old upon you, and thy shoe has not waxen old upon your foot.

Ye have not eaten bread, neither have ye drunk wine or strong drink: that ye might know that I am the Lord your God. (Deut. 29:2–8)

King goes on to say, however, that he would neither stop at the triumph of the Exodus nor choose to live in the moment of entry into the Promised Land of the Israelites.[25] The highlights that King reviews in his historical summary are not those of the biblical Exodus but those of the Civil Rights movement and the movements of emancipation that punctuated the early 1960s.

Strangely enough, I would turn to the Almighty, and say, "if you allow me to live just a few years in the second half of the twentieth century, I will be happy." Now that's a strange statement to make, because the world is all messed up. The nation is sick. Trouble is in the land. Confusion all around. That's a strange statement. But I know, somehow, that only when it is dark enough, can you see the stars. And I see God working in this period of the twentieth century in a way that men, in some strange way, are responding—something is happening in the world. The masses of people are rising up. And wherever they are assembled today, whether they are in Johannesburg, South Africa; Nairobi, Kenya; Accra, Ghana; New York City; Atlanta, Georgia; Jackson, Mississippi; or Memphis, Tennessee—the cry is always the same—"We want to be free."[26]

At the end of the sermon, King turns to the testamentary language of Deuteronomy 34 to refer neither to the people nor to the movement but to himself. King himself has looked over; King himself bequeaths to the children that Moses led the legacy and challenge of the Promised Land he has seen but shall not live to enter.

We've got some difficult days ahead. But it doesn't matter with me now. Because I've seen the mountaintop. And I don't mind. Like anybody, I would like to live a long life. Longevity has its place. But I'm not concerned about that now. I just want to do God's will. And He's allowed me to go up to the mountain. And I've looked over. And I've seen the Promised Land.[27]

Though King's many admirers hailed him as one like unto Moses, only here, in the shadow of death, did King identify himself with the figure of Moses. Like Moses, he looks over into the Promised Land that he knows he will not enter, and like Moses he charges his followers to take the land with a confidence. The mantle of Moses, that venerable ideal of African-American leadership, weighed on Martin Luther King, Jr., throughout his public life. He claimed that mantle only on the eve of his death.

[...]

THE WORDS OF THE COVENANT

In spite of obstacles, and in spite of the Israelites themselves, Moses leads the wandering multitude to Mount Sinai. There, through the mediation of Moses, God draws the fugitive horde into a covenant, a contractual agreement of exclusive fealty to him. The stipulations of the agreement are spelled out in the laws that God dictates to Moses on Sinai. Taken together, the compendium of these laws—henceforth the Law of Moses—becomes Israel's constitution. Israel's collective existence, initiated in the dramatic deliverance by the Lord of Hosts, is consolidated in the commandments of the God of law.

But the earliest summaries of the Exodus in the Bible do not mention Sinai: several ancient variations on Israel's recollection of the Exodus pass over the revelation of God's law in silence.

A wandering Aramean was my ancestor; he went down into Egypt and lived there as an alien, few in number, and there he became a great nation, mighty and populous. When the Egyptians treated us harshly and afflicted us, by imposing hard labor on us, we cried to the Lord, the God of our ancestors; the Lord heard our voice and saw our affliction, our toil, and our oppression. The Lord brought us out of Egypt with a mighty hand and an outstretched arm, with a terrifying display of power, and with signs and wonders; and he brought us into this place and gave us this land, a land flowing with milk and honey. (Deut. 26:5–9)

We find similar summaries in Joshua 24:2–13 and in Psalms 78:12–55, and fulsome poetic rehearsals in Psalms 105, 106, and 136. None of these mention Sinai. We must await Nehemiah 9:7–31, an elaborate penitential prayer composed late in the history of ancient Israel, to find Sinai amid memories of the patriarchs, the Exodus, and the wilderness.

As in the earliest biblical summaries of the Exodus story, the connection between the deliverance at the Red Sea and the law at Sinai is seldom acknowledged in the African-American renderings of the Exodus. The figure of Moses is celebrated in a way that Sinai is not. In one of the additional verses of "Didn't Old Pharaoh Get Lost," we encounter a rare reference to Sinai in the Negro spirituals.

> And the Lord spoke to Moses,
> From Sinai's smoking top,
> Saying, "Moses, lead the people,
> Till I shall bid you stop."[28]

Sound and fury precedes the announcement of the Ten Command-ments: "And it came to pass ... that there were thunders and light-nings, and a thick cloud upon the mount, and the voice of the trumpet exceeding loud; so that all the people that was in the camp trembled" (Exod. 19:16). Likewise "the thunderings, the lightnings, and the noise of the trumpet, and the mountain smoking" punctuate the end of the Commandments (20:18). But in the Negro spiritual there is no mention of the law, not even the Ten Commandments. The revelation is not to Israel but to Moses. Not Ten Commandments but one: keep moving. Sinai is important in the minds of the unknown bards because Moses stood upon it. African-American reading of the revelation of the commandments tends to echo the ancient biblical traditions that remember Exodus without reference to Sinai.

The circumscribed African-American reading of Exodus was also at variance with that of the Puritan founders of what would become the United States. The Puritans imagined their migration from the Old World as an exodus to a New Canaan and an errand in the wilderness of the New World.[29] It is the biblical idea of covenant that informs John Winthrop's sermon "A Modell of Christian Charity," composed on his ship the *Arbella* en route to North America in 1630. Having left Egypt, the sanctified community must now take on the yoke of the covenant that God enjoins upon them on the other side of the Red Sea.

> Beloved there is now set before us life, and good, deathe and evill in that wee are Commanded this day to love the Lord our God, and to love one another, to walke in his wayes and to keepe his Commaundements and his Ordinance, and his lawes, and the Articles of our Covenant with him that wee may live and be multiplied, and that the Lord our God may blesse us in the land whither we goe to posess it: But if our heartes shall turne away soe that wee will not obey, but shall be seduced and worship ... other Gods, our pleasures, and profitts, and serve them; it is propounded unto this day, wee shall surely perishe out of the good Land whither wee passe over this vast Sea to possesse it.[30]

Winthrop delivers this speech en route to the Promised Land, with Egypt far behind at a safe, cisatlantic distance. He refers to the Exodus from England as a fait accompli. In the New World the settlers have the opportunity to realize covenantal life as a new nation, the New Jerusalem, the City upon a Hill.

Puritan theology, which interpreted the experience of the English settlers in North America in terms of biblical typology, had been reading the Exodus as an American story for a century before the Revolution. The Exodus story continued to influence the colonial imagination throughout the revolutionary period. In the discussion of the official seal of the new nation in 1776, Benjamin Franklin proposed the image of Moses, staff in hand, parting the Red Sea as Pharaoh's army is drowned in its waters, with the caption "Rebellion to tyrants is obedience to God." Thomas Jefferson suggested a design with a scene of the Israelites in the wilderness led by cloud and pillar of fire. In the mid-nineteenth century, Herman Melville summarized the national self-understanding in 1850 in his early novel *White Jacket: or, The World in a Man-of-War*. "We Americans are driven to a rejection of the maxims of the Past, seeing that, ere long, the van of nations must, of right, belong to ourselves. ... Escaped from the house of bondage, Israel of old did not follow after the ways of the Egyptians. To her was given an express dispensation; to her were given new things under the sun. And we as Americans are the peculiar, chosen people—the Israel of our time; we bear the ark of the liberties of the world." As late as 1865, James Russell Lowell could still extol America as "the Promised Land / That flows with Freedom's honey and milk."[31]

Puritan preachers took to pulpit and public square to remind the New Israel of duties that attended the blessings of the divine covenant. These calls to covenantal responsibility were warnings to return to a compact with God and with one's fellow citizens that had been effected at the founding of the nation. Jeremiah is the namesake for this form of public rhetoric, the jeremiad, because the prophet had called the kingdom of Judah to remember its covenant with God.

> The word that came to Jeremiah from the Lord, saying, Hear ye the words of this covenant and speak unto the men of Judah and to the inhabitants of Jerusalem; And say thou unto them, Thus saith the Lord God of Israel; Cursed be the man that obeyeth not the words of this covenant, which I commanded your fathers in the day that I brought them forth of, out of the land of Egypt, from the iron furnace, saying, Obey my voice, and do them, according to all which I command you: so shall ye be my people, and I will be your God: That I may perform the oath which I have sworn unto your fathers, to give them a land flowing with milk and honey, as it is this day." (Jer. 11:1–5)

The jeremiad assumes the notion of a shared national covenant, ratified in history and presently in force. Jeremiah called for a renewal of fidelity to a failed covenant that the Israelites would henceforth interiorize: "But this shall be the covenant that I will make with the house of Israel; After those days, saith the Lord, I will put my law in their inward parts, and write it in their hearts; and will be their God, and they shall be my people" (31:33).

African-American prophets demanded in biblical idiom that America live up to a law of liberty whites had never known in its observance and that blacks knew only in its breech. But the characterization of early African-American protests as jeremiads is not quite apt. The commandments to honor the rights of life, liberty, and the pursuit of happiness had been violated even as they were being promulgated by the Founding Fathers. For Americans to live out their founding ideals would be an unprecedented act of covenantal fidelity.

The spirit of African-American frustration with the national covenant—broken in its making—is that of Moses on the mountain, not Jeremiah in the Temple. In Exodus 32 the Bible recounts how, as soon as Moses returned from the mountain with the tablets inscribed with God's law, he found the Israelites in a spree of wanton apostasy. Moses had been on the numinous, terrifying mountain for some time, and the Israelites had become restless and anxious. In his absence, Aaron, Moses's brother, mouthpiece, and the father of what would become the Israelite priesthood, was persuaded by the people to found a cult more accessible than the mysterious God of the mountain. They all melt down their gold to fashion a calf that would serve as the idolatrous focus of the Israelites' adoration. Moses descends from Sinai to encounter the people engaged in orgiastic worship of the calf, violating the very commandments he holds in his hands. The former slaves were even crediting their new idol with their deliverance from Pharaoh. In a fit of fury, Moses dashes the tablets to the ground, shattering them. Moses literally breaks the divine laws, angered that even as they were being coined on Sinai they were being broken in the Israelite camp.

The story suggests why Moses, not Jeremiah, is the proper point of figural reference for African-American protests against slavery. The protests arise very early in the history of American self-identification as the New Israel, too early to be a real analogue to the prophetic complaint of Jeremiah. Jeremiah laments Israelite apostasy at a later, more mature moment in the history of Israel's evolving consciousness of covenant. The African-American oracles decry a breach of national covenant at a time much closer to its ratification. African Americans would condemn the corrupt cult of the self-proclaimed New Israel. Their protests, coeval with the foundation of the nation itself, targeted the golden calf of white supremacy. As furiously as Moses, African-American prophets saw the divine law of freedom violated even as it was being enshrined in the founding documents and championed by the Founding Fathers.

Some even sought to break laws that had already been broken. In the face of slavery's egregious violations, African Americans willfully read scripture contrary to the law's plain sense. The story of the Exodus became an apologia for disregarding the commandment against stealing.[32] In Martin Delany's antebellum novel *Blake*, the protagonist Henry Blake advises two enslaved co-conspirators to pilfer money from their masters. "God told the Egyptian slaves to 'borrow from their neighbors'—meaning their oppressors—'all their jewels,' meaning to take their money and wealth whenever they could get their hands on it, and depart from Egypt."[33] Ex-slave autobiographers Henry Bibb and William Wells Brown both speak of this sanctified stealing and its biblical justification.[34] Breaking the commandments under the slave regime was not merely a personal prerogative of the slave: because the master class had stolen so much from the slave—indeed, the slave's very life—depriving the master of ill-gotten gains became a moral imperative.

The traditions that now make up the biblical account of Exodus highlight the importance of law and covenant. Their canonical sequence shows, however, that the Israelites shared a common obligation to obey the Mosaic Law because they had collectively enjoyed the emancipation that God had secured for them at the Red Sea. The emancipation of the Exodus is imperfectly realized, however, in the collective historical experience of American slaves and their descendants. The laws of the land of their nativity—that is, the laws of the United States—enshrined the country's founding documents, developed out of a collective historical experience that was not only alien to the African-American aspirations to freedom but was hostile to them.

NOTES

Epigraph: Diary entry, Dec. 12, 1857, by her mistress: Barbara Leigh Smith Bodichon, *An American Diary, 1857–8*, ed. Joseph W. Reed, Jr. (London: Routledge and K. Paul, 1972), 65, cited in Albert J. Raboteau, "African-Americans, Exodus, and the American Israel," in Paul E. Johnson, ed., *African-American Christianity: Essays in History* (Berkeley: University of California Press, 1994), 13.

1. Exod. 5:1, 7:16, 8:1, 8:20, 9:1, 9:13, 10:3.

2. Iveson L. Brookes, *A Defense of Southern Slavery, against the Attacks of Henry Clay and Alex'r Campbell* . . . (Hamburg, SC, 1851), 5, quoted in Forrest G. Wood, *The Arrogance of Faith: Christianity and Race in America from the Colonial Era to the Twentieth Century* (New York: Alfred A. Knopf, 1990), 86.

3. "Go Down, Moses," in James Weldon and J. Rosamond Johnson, *The Books of American Negro Spirituals: Including the*

Book of American Negro Spirituals and the Second Book of Negro Spirituals, 2 vols. (New York: Viking Press, 1925–26; reprint ed., New York: Da Capo Press, 1989), 1:51–53.

4. "Didn't Ol' Pharaoh Get Lost?" in ibid., 60–61.

5. In Richard M. Dorson, *American Negro Folktales* (Greenwich, CT: Fawcett, 1967), 256–257.

6. Cited in John W. Roberts, *From Trickster to Badman: The Black Folk Hero in Slavery and Freedom* (Philadelphia: University of Pennsylvania Press, 1989), 155.

7. Gerhard Von Rad, *Old Testament Theology*, trans. D. M. G. Stalker, 2 vols. (New York: Harper, 1962), 1:35.

8. Harry Middleton Hyatt, *Hoodoo—Conjuration—Witchcraft—Rootwork: Beliefs Accepted by Many Negroes and White Persons, These Being Orally Recorded among Blacks and Whites*, 5 vols. (Hannibal, MO: Western, 1970–1978), 2:1758, quoted in Kevin J. Hayes, *Folklore and Book Culture* (Knoxville: University of Tennessee Press, 1997), 14–27.

9. Works Project Administration, *Drums and Shadows: Survival Studies among the Georgia Coastal Negroes* (Garden City, NY: Anchor Books, 1972), 25.

10. Charles Joyner, *Down by the Riverside: A South Carolina Slave Community* (Urbana: University of Illinois Press, 1984), 143.

11. Ibid., 145.

12. Zora Neale Hurston, "Hoodoo in America," *Journal of American Folklore* 44 (October–December 1931): 414.

13. Zora Neale Hurston, *Tell My Horse*, in Cheryl A. Wall, ed., *Zora Neale Hurston: Novels and Stories* (New York: Library of America, 1995), 378.

14. Zora Neale Hurston, *Moses, Man of the Mountain*, in Wall, ed., *Hurston: Novels and Stories*, 443.

15. Quoted in Joyner, *Down by the Riverside*, 164.

16. Frances Harper, "Our Greatest Want," in Gates and McKay, eds., *Norton Anthology*, 431–432.

17. Quoted in Raboteau, "Exodus," 13.

18. In Charles L. Perdue, Jr., Thomas E. Barden, and Robert K. Phillips, *Weevils in the Wheat: Interviews with Virginia Ex-Slaves* (Charlottesville: University of Virginia Press, 1976), 10, quoted in Roberts, *Trickster*, 161.

19. Quoted in Jaqueline L. Tobin and Raymond G. Dobard, *Hidden in Plain View. The Secret Story of Quilts and the Underground Railroad* (New York: Doubleday, 1999), 147.

20. James Weldon Johnson, "Let My People Go," in Johnson, *God's Trombones: Seven Negro Songs in Verse* (New York: Viking Press, 1927), 45–52.

21. Beauford Delaney, *The Burning Bush*, 1941, reproduced in Gary A. Reynolds and Beryl J. Wright, *Against the Odds: African-American Artists and the Harmon Foundation* (Newark, NJ: Newark Museum, 1989), 127, pl. 7.

22. Hurston, *Moses, Man of the Mountain*, 501.

23. Charlotta Bass, "I Accept This Call," *National Guardian* Apr. 2, 1952, reprinted in Gerda Lerner, ed., *Black Women in White America: A Documentary History* (New York: Vintage Books, 1973), 345.

24. Martin Luther King, Jr., *Where Do We Go from Here: Chaos or Community?* (New York: Harper and Row, 1967), 124; King, "Out of the Long Night of Segregation," *Presbyterian Outlook*, Feb. 10, 1958, 6.

25. Martin Luther King, Jr., "I See the Promised Land," in James Melvin Washington, ed., *A Testament of Hope: The Essential Writings and Speeches of Martin Luther King, Jr.* (San Francisco: Harper and Row, 1986), 279.

26. Ibid., 280.

27. Ibid., 286.

28. "Didn't Ol' Pharaoh Get Lost?" in Weldon and Johnson, *Books of American Negro Spirituals*, 1:61.

29. Eddie S. Glaude, Jr., *Exodus! Religion, Race, and Nation in Early Nineteenth-Century Black America* (Chicago: University of Chicago Press, 2002), 46. See David Lyle Jeffrey, "The Bible and the American Myth," in Jeffrey, *People of the Book: Christian Identity and Literary Culture* (Grand Rapids, MI: William B. Eerdmans, 1996), 317–352.

30. *Winthrop Papers*, vol. 2 (Boston: Massachusetts Historical Society, 1931), 282–284, 292–295, reprinted in Conrad Cherry, ed., *God's New Israel: Religious Interpretations of American Destiny* (Englewood Cliffs, NJ: Prentice-Hall, 1971), 43, cited in Raboteau, "Exodus," 10.

31. Werner Sollors, *Beyond Ethnicity: Consent and Descent in American Culture* (New York: Oxford University Press, 1986), 42–44; Herman Melville, *White Jacket: or, The World in a Man-of-War* (New York: Oxford University Press, 1967), 152–153; James Russell Lowell, "Oration Ode," in William Michael Rossetti, ed., *The Poetical Works of James Russell Lowell* (New York, 1889), 298.

32. Martin R. Delany, *Blake, or The Huts of America, a Novel* (Boston: Beacon Press, 1970), 315, n. 3.

33. Ibid., 43.

34. See Gilbert Osofsky, ed., *Puttin' on Ole Massa: The Slave Narratives of Henry Bibb, William Wells Brown, and Solomon Northup* (New York: Harper and Row, 1969), 147, 166, 215.

THE POETRY OF LANGSTON HUGHES

"'Racial Individuality': Enslavement and Emancipation in the Poetry of Langston Hughes"
by Robert C. Evans, Auburn University at Montgomery

As a black man writing (and attempting to publish) poetry in the United States only 60 or so years after the end of the Civil War, a period when manifestations of racism—including blatant discrimination, violence, and even lynchings—were still rampant, Langston Hughes almost inevitably explored such topics as enslavement and emancipation in his work. These themes are often the obvious topics of his poems, for Hughes could never forget that he was not simply an author but was (and would inevitably be read as) a "Negro" author. A desire for freedom, as well as an awareness of the limits to freedom, were thus not only themes in much of his earliest poetry, but they were also issues that helped shape the composition and reception of *The Weary Blues*, his initial book of poems. Reading the early reviews helps one appreciate the complex and often conflicting expectations Hughes faced not simply as a poet but as a *black* poet writing and publishing in the mid-1920s.

Most of the earliest commentary on *The Weary Blues* was complimentary, but reviewers often strongly disagreed about what, precisely, they expected from Hughes and his work, or how they should respond to his writings. Thus John T. Hackett, one early commentator, spoke for several others when he suggested that Hughes might be benefiting from the support of "faddists who have recently hurrahed indiscriminately for every Negro able to hum a tune, mimic a canary or write his name" (Dace 49). "Mr. Hughes," Hackett continued, "is not the awaited Negro Milton, for his are unassuming canticles" (Dace 49). For reviewers such as Hackett, then, Hughes was merely a modestly talented writer whose race, ironically, made him more likely to be over-praised than underappreciated. Likewise, Howard Mumford Jones opined that "the present vogue for Negro art is falsifying a good many values, which, upon cooler inspection after the craze has died, will be found to be fools' gold" (Dace 49). Jones, then, agreed with Hackett that Hughes profited (both literally and figuratively) from being a black writer in the mid-1920s. When anticipating the reactions of critics such as Hackett and Jones, then, one of the constraints Hughes faced was derived from the assumption that he benefited from a kind of literary "affirmative action," and that his work might not really deserve any genuinely intense enthusiasm. Any interest it did excite might derive (according to Hackett, Jones, and others) from a merely temporary fad or "craze" for black writers—a craze fed and stoked by such white admirers of Hughes as Carl Van Vechten, who wrote the introduction to *The Weary Blues* and who is mentioned explicitly both by Hackett and Jones. Paradoxically, then, for critics such as these, Hughes was less a victim of discrimination against blacks than a beneficiary of praise possibly rooted in pity, guilt, shifting fashions, or patronizing condescension.

According to Jones, Hughes was often trapped between his identity as a black man and his desire to be a respectable man of letters. Hughes wrote well (Jones suggested) when he evoked the blues or when he wrote "bitterly and sincerely about the south," but he was much less successful when he merely tried to imitate the works of previous white poets, such as Paul Verlaine or Owen Meredith (the pen name of Robert Bulwer-Lytton). "When Mr. Hughes keeps his eye on the ball," Jones asserted, "he writes keenly and directly and movingly, . . . but half the time he swings around, looks uneasily at his audience and seems to say, 'After all, I am a poet, you know, and not a bright colored boy,'" and his work suffers (Jones thought) as a result (Dace 49–50). Jones seems not to have noticed the very narrow space he had marked out for a black writer such as Hughes. If Hughes wrote too obviously or insistently as a black person, any enthusiasm for his work might seem merely the product of a temporary "craze," but if he wrote too obviously in imitation of canonical white poets, he might seem to be afraid to appear unliterary. Poor Langston Hughes! If he kept in mind the expectations of critics such as Jones when he wrote, and if he took such expectations at all seriously, he must have sensed some real and serious attempts to restrict his imaginative freedom. If a poet such as Hughes were to take seriously the expectations drawn by critics like Jones, that poet would feel enormously the impact of what Harold Bloom has memorably called "the anxiety of influence." If, on the one hand, Hughes was perceived to be too much influenced by his race and by previous black writers and their literature, he might be considered simply a token author, benefiting from a passing fad. If, on the other hand, he was perceived to be too much influenced by accepted white writers, he might be considered merely (and slavishly) imitative.

A further sense of the potential constraints (and censure) Hughes faced in composing and publishing his first volume of poems can be glimpsed in a review by Countee Cullen, himself a talented black poet. Whereas a white reviewer such as Jones felt that Hughes was at his best when dealing with obviously racial themes and obviously "black" settings (such as jazz and Harlem), Cullen reacted in just the opposite way. Cullen wondered "if jazz poems really belong to that dignified company, that select and austere circle of high literary expression which we call poetry" (Dace 56). For Cullen, Hughes's first volume revealed "too much emphasis . . . on strictly Negro themes," and this alleged overemphasis left Cullen feeling a particular "coldness toward the jazz poems" since "they seem to set a too definite limit upon an already limited field" (Dace 57). Ironically, if Jones felt that Hughes was striving to be *too* "literary," Cullen felt that Hughes was not "literary" enough, and if Jones felt that Hughes was at his best (although perhaps also at his most faddish) when he was most obviously writing as a black man, Cullen felt that Hughes was at his best when his race was least an issue. "*De gustibus non est disputandum*": There's no disputing taste, according to the old Latin saying. Every writer knows that every reviewer brings his or her own set of unique expectations and prejudices to the job of reviewing. Hughes, however, could never afford to forget that he would almost inevitably be seen and reviewed not simply as a poet but as a *black* poet, and that he would be viewed as such by reviewers who were themselves either black or white. Indeed, very few of the early commentaries on

The Weary Blues among the many collected by Dace fail to mention Hughes's race. Hughes knew, when writing and preparing to publish his poems, that his works would inevitably be read through a variety of racial lenses. His freedom as a poet was as potentially constrained by racial expectations as his freedom as a person was actually constrained by the same kinds of assumptions.

Hughes's awareness of the dilemmas he faced—and his creative response to those dilemmas—can be seen in his famous essay "The Negro Artist and the Racial Mountain," which was published in the very same year as *The Weary Blues*. The essay opens by rejecting the idea that a black poet should want to write simply as a generic "poet," which, to Hughes, meant actually wanting to write as a *white* poet. Instead, Hughes asserts that "no great poet has ever been afraid of being himself," which, in Hughes's case, meant honestly acknowledging the significance of his undeniable racial identity (1311). Throughout the essay, in fact, Hughes repeatedly links an acknowledgement of his blackness with the achievement of true freedom. He rejects, for instance, any "desire to pour *racial individuality* into the mould of American standardization, and to be as little Negro and as much American as possible" (1311; emphasis added). He argues for the freedom of the black poet to write about "beauty of *his own* people" and he repudiates any mere "aping of things white" (1311; emphasis added). Hughes particularly admires black commoners—whom he calls "the low-down folks"—because "they still hold *their own individuality* in the face of American standardization" (1312; emphasis added). The "truly great Negro artist" will follow the example of these people because he will be "one who is not afraid to *be himself*" (1312; emphasis added).

Rather than seeing any conflict between the impulse to write as a black person and the impulse to write freely, Hughes sought to erase that distinction altogether. For him, freedom did not conflict with his blackness, but was instead rooted in it. For Hughes, being an emancipated black man in America in the early twentieth century meant acknowledging (rather than trying to ignore or deny) the painful history of black enslavement and racial discrimination; being a liberated and creative poet meant accepting (rather than trying to erase or forget) his racial identity. Twice, in fact, Hughes uses the phrase "racial individuality" to express his ideal. To some minds, such a phrase might seem an oxymoron: How can a person think of himself both as an autonomous individual and as a member of a race? For Hughes, however, there is no fundamental paradox in such a phrase. To be truly himself—really free and emancipated—meant also acknowledging, and taking pride in, his heritage as an African American. "Why should I want to be white?" he asks rhetorically near the end of his essay; and then he answers: "'I am a Negro—and beautiful'" (1314). Here, as in the essay as a whole, there is as much emphasis on Hughes's individuality as on his race. Ultimately, in the final paragraph of the essay, Hughes both embraces his racial identity and declares his individual freedom, including his freedom not only from any disapproving whites but also (significantly enough) from any disapproving blacks. "If white people are pleased" with the kind of art that Hughes and his contemporaries create, "we are glad. If they are not, it doesn't matter. . . . If colored people are pleased we are glad. If they are not, their displeasure doesn't matter either" (1314). Hughes's essay amounts, in short, to a declaration of personal and literary independence—but it is a declaration of autonomy that also freely acknowledges the importance of race to Hughes's individual identity. The essay is, in other words, and as Hughes himself plainly puts it, a declaration of "racial individuality."

How is this ideal of "racial individuality" reflected (if at all) in *The Weary Blues*? To begin answering that question, it may be helpful to look at a discrete section of the volume so that it is possible to examine not only individual poems but also the ways in which individual works interact with one another through their near or adjacent positions in the book. For these purposes, the opening portion of the final section of *The Weary Blues* (a section titled "Our Land") is particularly useful. The opening poem, for instance—also titled "Our Land" (and subtitled "Poem for a Decorative Panel")—is not explicitly racial in its language or topics, although the poem cannot help but be "colored" by all the openly racial poems that precede it in the book. "We should have a land," the poem begins, "of sun, / Of gorgeous sun" (ll. 1–2), and in the plainness and simplicity of the phrasing, in the absence of any distinctive dialect, and in the deliberate generality of the word "We," one senses Hughes's desire in this poem to speak to as broad an audience as possible. In this poem he speaks less as a black man than as a generic human being, although of course the desire to live in a land of joy would have been felt especially keenly by people who had, for most of their history in America, been oppressed and denied opportunity. Hughes writes here, as he writes so often in *The Weary Blues*, in a way that could easily have been understood by the "low-down folks" he so admired, but the yearning for freedom and pleasure that the poem expresses is one to which practically any reader, of any race, can relate.

"Our Land" is a poem that deliberately appeals to all five senses— touch, taste, hearing, smell, and vision. It imaginatively evokes a kind of earthly paradise, only to remind us, in lines 7, 12, and 15, that this paradise does not exist in the speaker's (or the reader's) actual here and now. This is not to say, however, that a land of the sort that the speaker describes does not or cannot exist; and in fact the final two lines ("Oh, sweet, away! / Ah, my beloved one, away!"; ll. 16–17) suggest the real possibility of escape to precisely the kind of land the poem so power- fully imagines. Such an escape, however, would implicitly involve a departure from modern, urban, oppressive, and uninspiring America; it might involve relocating to a tropical landscape, or even to Africa. The point of the poem, however, seems less to endorse a literal emigra- tion from the United States than to suggest how "our land" might, ideally, be imaginatively transformed. Hughes splendidly evokes the beauties we could enjoy, and then in the final lines of each of the first three stanzas he snatches those beauties away by reminding us that they do not presently exist. The effect is to suggest what *might* be, what *could* be, if "our land" were not a land where life is figuratively cold and gray and where "joy is wrong" (ll. 7, 12, 15). It is the absence and condemnation of joy, rather than any literal coldness or literal gray- ness, that most troubles the speaker, and although the poem begins by imagining the possibility of a joyous community that might include everyone, it ends by seeking refuge and solace in the company of one person—one "beloved"—in particular.

"Our Land" is the sort of poem that might appeal to any reader, of any racial background or economic status, although it might have a special appeal to poor blacks. In the next poem, however—titled "Lament for Dark Peoples"—Hughes obviously speaks not only to and for African Americans, but also to and for other people of color, especially American Indians. The language of this poem, with its emphasis on the theme of paradise lost, echoes that of "Our Land," but here the political message is much more explicit, and the note of protest is far more obvious and angry. Hughes writes here as a black man, but he assumes the right to speak for other oppressed peoples as well; he thus makes it clear that the desire for freedom is not anything peculiar to African Americans, but is in fact the common heritage of all American minorities. Hughes contends that blacks and native Americans have been treated like animals and have been reduced to the status of trapped beasts in "the circus of civilization" (ll. 10, 12). The word *circus* suggests something trivial, superficial, and demeaning and thus contrasts here with the positive qualities usually associated with the word civilization. By the end of "Lament for Dark Peoples," we are even further distant from the kind of paradise imagined in "Our Land." At least, at the end of that first poem, there seemed some possibility of escape; at the end of the "Lament," however, the sense of being inescapably "caged" (l. 12) is emphasized through the reiterative, circular phrasing that dominates the whole poem, but especially the final stanza.

"Lament for Dark Peoples" makes even more explicit the themes of enslavement and desired emancipation that had already been sounded in "Our Land." By the time one reaches the third poem, "Afraid," however, one finds an interesting and unpredictable shift, which is so brief that it can be quoted in its entirety:

> We cry among the skyscrapers
> As our ancestors
> Cried among the palms in Africa
> Because we are alone,
> It is night,
> And we're afraid.

Here the opening "We" might at first seem to include anyone of any color or background, but by the third line it seems clear that the "We" mainly pertains to blacks. Ironically, however, the pain the poem emphasizes is not caused, in this case, primarily by racial discrimination or prejudice, but by far more elemental human emotions: loneliness, fear of the dark, and fear in general. It would have been easy enough for Hughes, in this poem, to blame whites for transporting blacks from an African pastoral paradise to a land in which alienating urban skyscrapers had become the dominant form of architecture, but in this poem he manages to write openly as a black man while still evoking common human feelings. In the space of the first three poems of this one section of *The Weary Blues*, then, Hughes has managed to write first in a way that seems relatively unconcerned with any open or explicit concern with race (in "Our Land"), then in a way in which racial issues are front and center (in "Lament for Dark Peoples"), and then, finally, in a way in which race is mentioned but in which common human impulses and responses are given the most obvious emphasis ("Afraid"). In these three poems, therefore, Hughes illustrates in miniature the kind of imaginative freedom—the refusal to be stereotyped or pigeonholed—that he extols in his essay "The Negro Artist and the Racial Mountain." He writes unashamedly as a black man, but he refuses to write merely or simply as an African American, as if nothing else about him mattered. He speaks with pride about (and out of) his African-American heritage, but he preserves his individual freedom as a writer to adopt a variety of tones and personae. He acknowledges the history of black enslavement, but through his own creativity and imaginative liberties he also opens the prospect of mental (and perhaps, eventually, political and social) emancipation not only for his own people but (as "Our Land" suggests) for everyone else, as well.

WORKS CITED AND CONSULTED

Bloom, Harold. *The Anxiety of Influence: A Theory of Poetry*. London: Oxford University Press, 1975.

Dace, Tish, ed. *Langston Hughes: The Contemporary Reviews*. Cambridge: Cambridge University Press, 1997.

Hughes, Langston. *The Collected Works of Langston Hughes, Volume 1: The Poems: 1921–1940*. Ed. Arnold Rampersad. Columbia: University of Missouri Press, 2001.

————. "The Negro Artist and the Racial Mountain." *The Norton Anthology of African American Literature*. Ed. Henry Louis Gates, Jr. and Nellie Y. McKay. 2nd ed. New York: Norton, 2004. 1311–14.

Mullen, Edward J., ed. *Critical Essays on Langston Hughes*. Boston, MA: G.K. Hall, 1986.

INCIDENTS IN THE LIFE OF A SLAVE GIRL
(HARRIET JACOBS)

Moral Experience in Harriet Jacobs's
Incidents in the Life of a Slave Girl
by Sarah Way Sherman, in *NWSA Journal* (1990)

INTRODUCTION

In her analysis of this great story of enslavement and emancipation, Sarah Way Sherman focuses on the complex
moral vision of Harriet Jacobs (Linda Brent). Contrasting the
narratives of Jacobs and Frederick Douglass and reading
Jacobs's work in light of the way it undermines conventional
notions of freedom, Sherman concludes, "The power of this
text . . . is its demonstration that moral action is not the work
of pure, ego-less angels but of loving, self-determined women
and men. The community of care cannot be sustained in
a fallen, corrupted world merely through the innocence of
the dove but requires the wisdom of the serpent to survive
and prevail. Principled yet pragmatic, defiant and compassionate, Linda Brent's bittersweet voice is the voice of moral
experience."

Sherman, Sarah Way. "Moral Experience in Harriet Jacobs's *Incidents in the Life
of a Slave Girl*." *NWSA Journal*, Vol. 2, No. 2 (Spring 1990): 167–85.

"Slavery is terrible for men," Harriet Jacobs wrote in 1861, "but it is far more terrible for women." Citing this passage from *Incidents in the Life of a Slave Girl*, Jean Fagan Yellin argues that Jacobs's book was the first to address the sexual exploitation of women under slavery. But Yellin also notes the rhetorical strain of such outspokenness. Compared to the classic *Narrative of the Life of Frederick Douglass* (1845), Jacobs's narrative can appear weakened by conflict. As I hope to show, however, this important book's ambivalence and troubled voice point toward its strength.[1] While the thrust of *Incidents in the Life* comes from its unequivocal denunciation of an evil system, its tension comes from a painful confrontation with moral conflict and moral ambiguity. The pseudonymous narrator, Linda Brent, is caught between the brutal, exploitative bonds of slavery and the idealized, altruistic bonds of true womanhood.[2] The first she resists with great spirit and no ambivalence; the other she resists only with great pain and guilt, after deep disillusionment. Both systems denied her a selfhood; neither had words to authorize her choices.

Jacobs's story, now widely available, has found new readers, particularly in college courses where it is often read alongside Douglass's *Narrative*. The differences between the two are illuminating. I should say, however, that Douglass's text may not itself be a typical slave narrative. One reason he was assimilated into the American literary canon with relative ease may have been his brilliant deployment of white conventions, particularly the developmental drama of the self-made man. There are significant parallels between the trajectory of Benjamin Franklin's rise from obscurity to political office and Douglass's own emergence from slavery into the public forum.[3] One of the most important differences then between Jacobs and Douglass is gender. Gender directly shapes Jacobs's experience both as slave and free woman; moreover, gender shapes the conventions available for her interpretation of these experiences. The exemplary rise of a self-made woman was not a common literary plot. Before addressing gender differences, however, there is another key difference between Jacobs and Douglass: her early literacy and relatively privileged status as a slave.

The text opens with the lines, "I was born a slave, but I never knew it till six years of happy childhood had passed away." Linda and her brother, William, are raised by indulgent owners. Linda's mistress teaches her to read and treats her almost like a daughter. This woman had been herself nursed at the breast of Linda's grandmother; hence she is seen as the "foster sister" of Linda's own mother. Not only are the children taught to read, but they are raised within an intact black family which "fondly shields" them from the realities of slavery. Linda's father is a skilled carpenter. Her grandmother, Martha, has obtained her freedom, owns her own home, and supports herself through a lively business as a baker. This proud family holds Linda and William to the standards of middle-class behavior—the moral codes of free people—even though the two children cannot always fulfill them. The conflicts created by this situation appear early and are central to the text.

Linda, for example, describes how William is called by both his white mistress and his father. Whom should he obey? From an abstract, ideal perspective the moral claim of the father is obviously superior to that of the mistress. But in the fallen world of the slave-holding South, the father's claim is silenced. William assesses the context and goes to his mistress. For the time being, the greater good, greater even than goodness, is survival. But if William thereby escapes a whipping, or worse, he does not escape his father's wrath. He is held morally accountable and reprimanded for making the wrong choice.

The lesson that Linda and William must learn is excruciating. Although the dove of moral idealism may be beautiful, to act in a corrupt world it must learn a lesson from the serpent. Only a "fortunate fall" from innocence can develop a morality adequate to the complexity of human experience.[4] Thus while Douglass's narrative begins with a slave who does not know he is human, this one begins with a child who does not know she is a slave. If she is to survive, she must learn not to express her humanity but to hide it, not to find her tongue but to bite it. Powerless to fulfill the moral codes, one of white society, she develops a powerful critique of those codes that assesses moral action within its human context.

This lesson is complicated by Jacobs's other difference from Douglass—her gender. If "slavery was terrible" for men like William, it was, again in Linda Brent's words, "far more terrible for women." Slavery was acted out on male bodies but also within female ones. As "brood mare" or concubine, wet nurse or mammy, part of a slave woman's productive work was reproduction.[5] Slavery's threat was therefore even the more intimate and brutal. If slavery denied the female slave's selfhood, it tempted her master to monstrous selfishness, unfettered by recognition of their common humanity.

Not only was slavery's threat more sexual for women, but genteel codes for their behavior were more stringent. The standards of free people differed for men and women. With the example of her own mother's chaste courtship and marriage ever before her, Linda is carefully indoctrinated by her mistress and family into the cult of true womanhood. The ideology of woman's innate "piety, purity, submissiveness and domesticity" could be a significant weapon against male aggression, but it also opened new areas of vulnerability. As a model for human behavior, it had, as Linda discovers, serious flaws. "Angels in the house" might win self-respect and private influence but only by renouncing self-assertion and public power.[6]

While Linda's awareness of slavery begins at age six, with her mother's death, her moral education begins at twelve, with the death of her mistress, "almost a mother to her." She is not freed as she had come to expect but is "bequeathed" to her mistress's little niece, Emily Flint. This shock destroys whatever illusions Linda might have had about her actual condition. Not long after this first "fall," Emily's father, Dr. Flint, begins to make sexual advances. The story now takes on some qualities of a conventional seduction novel, a sentimental story of innocence pursued. Linda is not physically coerced, but she is, from puberty onward, relentlessly harassed by Flint, her master until Emily's majority. The language and plot of these sections led some critics, such as John Blassingame, to suspect that Jacobs's white editor, Lydia Maria Child influenced the text. Yellin's research, however, has shown that Jacobs herself was responsible for the text.[7] Its words and story are essentially her own. While the hesitations and expressions of shame associated with Linda's sexual history may be explained by her need to appease white middle-class readers, I believe they also result from Linda's own education in genteel codes of female behavior. Again, the source was from within her own family, particularly her freed grandmother, Martha.

Martha in many ways is a model of womanly strength and integrity. A capable, devout Christian, she has earned the respect of her community, black and white. After serving as wet nurse, cook, and mammy to Mrs. Flint's mother's household for many years, she gained her freedom to become mistress of her own home. This domestic space is not only a "haven in a heartless world" but literally a means to Linda's freedom when she later hides in its shed for seven years. (Confined to a tiny alcove, concealed even from her own children, she waits for a chance to escape to the North.) If her master Dr. Flint is the text's serpent, Linda's strong and kindly grandmother is its dove. Her memory remains with Linda like "light, fleecy clouds floating over a dark and troubled sea."[8] Yet that dark and troubled sea is the one which Linda has to cross.

As a young girl, Linda "had resolved that I would be virtuous, though I was but a slave. I had said, 'Let the storm beat! I will brave it till I die.'"[9] But the storm is ruthless. Not only does Dr. Flint batter her purity of mind with constant insinuations and harassment, but he destroys any hopes for legitimate fulfillment by refusing to allow her to marry the free black man who loves her. Even if he had permitted it, the marriage would have had no legal existence because of her status as a slave. In Samuel Richardson's classic seduction novel *Pamela*, the chaste heroine triumphs when her employer and would-be seducer finally proposes marriage. But, as critic Valerie Smith points out, the happy endings of sentimental novels do not apply to a young slave girl's story. If legitimizing Flint's sexual advances were the only issue, racist laws alone would prevent him from marrying her.[10]

Of course, there is one conventional ending that could apply: martyrdom. Like Clarissa of Richardson's other seduction novel, Linda could choose to die rather than to live an "impure" life: a sullied blossom in a sullied world. As in the opening story of her brother William's choice, the constant question behind Linda's life and text is, when is your humanity worth dying for? At what moment, precisely, is survival as a compromised individual too painful? Her motto, Linda Brent says, is give me liberty or give me death, but the difficulty is knowing when that final choice has come. In this case she does not die in the storm but decides instead to take a free white man as a lover. The decision brings her into direct conflict not only with her master's will but also her grandmother's values. In the genteel code, virginity before marriage was equated with female self-worth and moral integrity. For the free, middle-class woman the choice of husband was *the* choice. Through this choice she exercised the majority of what control she had over her adult life. While agonizingly limited, the choice was, nevertheless, real. Denied this choice, Brent is forced to recognize that it is through the moral exercise of her right to choose that a woman gains moral integrity, not through the physical virginity with which the choice is associated.

Thus, struggling to explain her history to white genteel readers, Brent says, "It seems less degrading to give one's self, than to submit to compulsion. There is something akin to freedom in having a lover who has no control over you, except that which he gains by kindness and attachment."[11] It is the quality of the relationship that marks it as moral or immoral, not its legal status: "A master may treat you as rudely as he pleases, and you dare not speak; moreover, the wrong does not seem so great with an unmarried man, as with one who has a wife to be made unhappy." At this point Brent seems aware of the radical turn her remarks are taking: "There may be sophistry in all this; but the condition of slavery confuses all principles of morality, and, in fact, renders the practice of them impossible."[12] What Brent seems reluctant to say, perhaps for fear of alienating her audience, is that if slavery renders the practice of morality impossible, far from confusing all principles of morality, it may actually clarify them. Under pressure, the genuinely ethical stands out from the merely conventional.

Linda, however, is not ready to dispense with womanly purity as an ideal. She never completely abandons her grandmother's values but argues that only those who are free to uphold them should be judged by them. Thus her voice moves between passionate idealism and calm realism: "I know I did wrong. No one can feel it more sensibly than I do. The painful and humiliating memory will haunt me to my dying day. Still, in looking back, calmly, on the events of my life, I feel that the slave woman ought not to be judged by the same standard as others."[13] In the same passage she bravely takes full responsibility for her choice: "I knew what I did, and I did it with deliberate calculation." But again, she asks her reader to read that confession within its context: "But, O, ye happy women, whose purity has been sheltered from childhood, who have been free to choose the objects of your affection, whose homes are protected by law, do not judge the poor desolate slave girl too severely."

In sum her grandmother's vision of the cult of true womanhood is "beautiful" but unattainable. If Linda had that choice in this world, she would take it. But she does not. Denied the innocence of the dove, she uses the wisdom of the serpent. She chooses survival: selfhood and self-determination. Through her liaison with Mr. Sands she gains some control over her body. If she cannot marry, she can at least choose with whom she will reproduce. Citing her birthright as a mother, she argues that, "Of a man who was not my master I could ask to have my children well supported, and in this case, I felt confident I should obtain the boon. I also felt quite sure that they would be made free."[14] Later she discovers that Sands is only apparently softer than Flint; both are made of the same slaveholding stuff although Sands is shiftier. Nevertheless, the central point remains; she says there is something akin to freedom in this choice, and she takes it.

But this is an understanding her grandmother does not share. She cannot contextualize her moral judgements. When Linda confesses her pregnancy, Martha's judgement is severe: "'I had rather see you dead than to see you as you now are. You are a disgrace to your dead mother.' She tore from my fingers my mother's wedding ring and her silver thimble. 'Go away!' she exclaimed, 'and never come to my house again.'"[15] When Martha finally softens and goes to the terrified, despairing girl, she still does not give up her code:

> She listened in silence. I told her I would bear any thing and do any thing, if in time I had hopes of obtaining her forgiveness. I begged of her to pity me, for my dead mother's sake. And she did pity me. She did not say, 'I forgive you', but she looked at me lovingly, with her eyes full of tears. She laid her old hand gently on my head, and murmured, 'Poor child! Poor child!'[16]

As the text clearly demonstrates, Linda has no ideology or language to justify her choice. After her escape she tells the people sheltering her that she is a mother but not a wife. Although they are understanding, they caution her against such honesty in the future; it could expose her to contempt. The "delicate silence of womanly sympathy" is the best that she can expect, but that is a lot. This silence does not demand the struggle to forge explanations. It acknowledges her history's context and forgives. Hence Jean Fagan Yellin and Hazel Carby read understanding in the silence of Linda's daughter, Ellen, who tells her mother there is nothing in her past she need explain. The daughter's understanding and acceptance heal the pain of the grandmother's first rejection, yet this silence means, again, that there is finally no language of justification.[17] Sexual purity remains an operative fiction: a value for that ideal world whose future possibility Linda is unwilling to give up—at the same time she must live with the reality of slavery in this one.

These issues of voice and virginity have been at the center of much critical discussion of this text. I believe, however, that Linda Brent's sexual initiation is only that, an initiation. The central experience of her mature morality is neither virginity nor its loss, but motherhood. The "moral mother" was a powerful image in Victorian ideology; one has only to think of how skillfully Harriet Beecher Stowe used it.[18] Thus, as Carby suggests, while Linda's fall from sexual innocence presented problems for her white readership, as well as for herself, her resultant motherhood conferred not only new knowledge but new power.[19] It is as a slave mother that Linda Brent addresses her reader; it is through this role that she claims authority to write.

The gift of motherhood, however, is also mixed, and Brent's description offers us another sobering critique. She shows how utterly inadequate the sentimental vision of selfless motherhood was to slave realities. Of her first child, Benjamin, Linda says: "The little vine was taking deep root in my existence, though its clinging fondness excited a mixture of love and pain. . . . I could never forget that he was a slave."[20] "Why," she asks, "does the slave ever love? Why allow the tendrils of the heart to twine around objects which may at any moment be wrenched away by the hand of violence?"[21] The imagery of twining vines and tendrils is a staple of Victorian sentimentalist fiction, but in this narrative the imagery of attachment lies close to the imagery of bondage. The chapter describing Benjamin's birth is "The New Tie to Life," and the one describing Ellen's, "Another Link to Life." These children give her reason to live, but the ties that bind her to motherhood can tighten her to slavery. When Flint suspects that Linda may escape, he threatens to bring Benny and Ellen to the plantation, thinking, she writes, "that my children's being there would fetter me to the spot." He knew "that my life was bound up in my children."[22]

As a slave mother, as in so many of her other roles, Linda must bear moral responsibility virtually without control, with only the slimmest margin of choice. Even before she hides in that tiny, cramped alcove, contingency hems her in at every side. At the Flint's plantation she lies down beside Ellen and "felt how much easier it would be to see her die than to see her master beat her." And earlier, looking on her newborn son, she states: "Sometimes I wished that he might die in infancy. . . . Death is better than slavery."[23] Death is the one choice she always has. While this subtext of infanticide becomes surface in Toni Morrison's

Beloved, as well as *Uncle Tom's Cabin* (where Cassie gives her infant laudanum), in *Incidents in the Life of a Slave Girl* it is the constant, somber background, the desperate horizon.[24] The other direction from freedom is nevertheless an escape. Moreover, it is the final assertion of authority: in death her children would be hers to keep.

The complexities of Linda's situation appear in a passage describing Ellen's christening. Recognizing that Linda cannot give her child the baby's father's name, Linda's father's former mistress comes forward and offers the child her Christian name, to which Linda adds her own father's surname. But, she adds, her father "had himself no legal right to it, for my grandfather on the paternal side was a white gentleman. What tangled skeins are the genealogies of slavery!" Then, the white mistress, by way of a gift, "clasped a gold chain around my baby's neck. I thanked her for this kindness; but I did not like the emblem."[25]

At the close of a chapter entitled "Another Link to Life," this imagery is heavily loaded. William's initial dilemma has become more complex. He finds himself in a double-bind because he was doubly-bound: first by the legal chain of slavery, second by the reproductive chain of kinship. But now we see the two chains entwined, a tangled skein of black and white extending down through the generations. Because the chains themselves are deeply entwined, so are their moral claims. What if one's "owner" is also one's father?

The moral test, throughout the narrative, is love. When Sands takes his daughter Ellen with him to Washington, he does not bother to write her mother. Linda quietly comments: "The links of such relations as he had formed with me, are easily broken and cast away as rubbish." Later, when Linda attempts to tell Ellen about her father, Ellen stops her: "'I am nothing to my father, and he is nothing to me.... I was with him five months in Washington, and he never cared for me.... I thought if he was my own father, he ought to love me. I was a little girl then, and didn't know any better.'"[26]

Brent repeatedly refers to Sands's fatherhood as "a parental relation," a relation which "takes slight hold of the hearts or consciences of slaveholders." Simple biological bonds are easily corrupted by power, greed, and sexuality; but most of all she laments, "how slavery perverted all the natural feelings of the human heart."[27] Sands treats his child as his slave, and therefore is not worthy of being her father, is not her father, and has no rightful authority over her. An umbilical cord is a "tie," but the only tie with moral authority is love.

Thus a third chain is a transcendent chain of affection, of motherly and fatherly, ultimately neighborly love. This chain transcends both slavery and biology; although it might have its roots in biological parenthood and kinship, it is not determined by them. This sacred chain, associated with the ethos of true womanhood and evangelical Christianity, presents Linda with her most painful moral dilemma: whether to run away or stay.

As Mary Helen Washington and Judith Fetterley, among others, point out, there are significant differences between the description of Linda Brent's escape and Frederick Douglass's.[28] Douglass opens by telling us how he was systematically denied the comforts of a mother and family life, then passes over his courtship of his wife-to-be in a few sentences. As in Benjamin Franklin's autobiography, the self which he presents is individual, strikingly outlined against the public sphere. His ultimate liberation is represented by a solitary self speaking in a voice unashamed and unconflicted before a public audience. The story of Douglass's escape from the bonds of slavery is central; the story of his loyalty to the bonds of love and friendship is peripheral.

The two stories, however, are deeply entwined in Linda Brent's narrative, and in many other male and female slave narratives. Indeed Eugene Genovese remarks that "almost every study of runaway slaves uncovers the importance of the family motive: thousands of slaves ran away to find children, parents, wives, or husbands from whom they had been separated by sale."[29] Other slaves, such as Henry Bibb, suffered agonies over the conflict between their desire for freedom and their responsibility to families.[30] Thus while resisting slavery presents no more ethical challenge to Linda Brent than it does to Frederick Douglass (she feels no moral responsibility to the Flints), leaving her children and grandmother presents a severe challenge. Honesty will not allow Linda to minimize the human consequences of this choice: her grandmother's suffering, her children's loneliness. She has defined a self, but she has defined it within the context of other selves. Bound by mutual love and responsibility, their identities are interdependent. If her obligation to her master is void, her obligation to this community is not.

When Martha first suspects Linda is planning to escape, "She looked earnestly at me, and said, 'Linda, do you want to kill your old grandmother? I am old now, and cannot do for your babies as I once did for you.'" Linda argues that only by fleeing can she keep Dr.

Flint from using Benny and Ellen as a weapon to break her. In her absence he would have no reason to threaten them. Her desperate gamble is that she can work for her children's liberation from the North. Perhaps their father could buy them and set them free. But her grandmother is not so hopeful: "'Stand by your own children,'" she says, "'and suffer with them till death. Nobody respects a mother who forsakes her children; and if you leave them, you will never have a happy moment.'"[31]

Linda's conflicts, painful in themselves, are exacerbated by the ideology of true womanhood, represented once again by her grandmother. Both agree on the priority of Linda's duty to her children; how to fulfill that duty is the question. Linda accepts her responsibility to care for this community, but to do so she must care for herself. Her children's freedom depends upon her strength, her will, which must not be broken, despite her grandmother's fear and the genteel images of womanhood to which Linda might once have aspired. Ladylike martyrdom may be an option, but it is not the one Linda chooses. When Linda thinks of her daughter, and what she herself "had suffered in slavery at her age," her "heart was like a tiger's when a hunter tries to seize her young."[32] Moral action, and moral resistance, demand selfhood.

The choice, however, is still painful: "I remembered the grief this step would bring upon my dear old grandmother, and nothing less than the freedom of my children would have induced me to disregard her advice."[33] And her grandmother does not let her off easily: "Whenever the children climbed on my knee, or laid their heads on my lap, she would say, 'Poor little souls! what would you do without a mother? She don't love you as I do.'"[34] Even though she knows the accusation is false and prompted by a human fear, Brent's narrative is haunted by guilt. In the midst of her first escape she imagines her grandmother saying, "'Linda, you are killing me.'"

But if Linda does not obey her grandmother, neither does she judge her, for these feelings are ones she has shared. Early in the story, when her uncle Benjamin tells her about his plan to leave, Linda's first response is "'Go ... and break your mother's heart.'"[35] Though she immediately regrets the words, they are out. When her brother William makes his break, we see again that the heart's spontaneous reaction is not joy but grief: "If you had seen the tears, and heard the sobs, you would have thought the messenger had brought tidings of death instead of freedom."[36] These are people whose lives are bound up with those they love. Even when separation brings freedom, it brings pain. As her ship finally approaches Philadelphia and freedom, Linda sees what she calls not the City of Brotherly Love but "the city of strangers." She looks at her companion, also an escaping slave, "and the eyes of both were moistened with tears. We had escaped from slavery, and we supposed ourselves to be safe from the hunters. But we were alone in the world, and we had left dear ties behind us, ties cruelly sundered by the demon Slavery."[37]

Given the text's focus on mothering, the fact and imagery of nursing—both as physical breastfeeding and as emotional nurturing—are key throughout. If the perversion of human relations appears in the white father who sells his child into oppression, the ennobling of human relations appears in the black mother who nurtures the child of her oppressor. And this, of course, is Martha herself, who takes her own child off her breast in order to suckle the child of her beloved mistress. This white baby becomes in her eyes the "foster-sister" of her own child, Linda's mother. There is indeed a curious doubling in the text. Linda Brent's mother dies but is survived by a twin, Aunt Nancy.[38] The white foster daughter dies but leaves a sister. This sister becomes the revengeful Mrs. Flint, a frightening image of the slave-mistress.

Aunt Nancy's story is one of the most painful stories Brent tells. Nancy sleeps at the foot of Mrs. Flint's bed, undergoing a harrowing series of premature births and miscarriages while waiting on her foster sister, her white mistress. Mrs. Flint in turn gives birth to her own children, whom Nancy must raise. Nancy's fertility is literally sacrificed to her "sister's." When she finally dies, the letter describing her death—a letter probably written by Dr. Flint—blasphemously imitates the language of community: "Could you have seen us round her death bed, mingling our tears in one common stream, you would have thought the same heartfelt tie existed between a master and his servant, as between a mother and her child."[39] But of course the same heartfelt tie does not exist between a master and his servant. Not only is the servant forced to care for the master, but this care is not reciprocated. Mrs. Flint wants Nancy buried in their own plot as a sign of Nancy's devotion to her "family"; Linda's grandmother adamantly refuses. The true family is the one in which Nancy's care was returned. Aunt Martha claims ownership of her daughter's body at last.

But Martha's relationship to Mrs. Flint remains one of the most troubling in the book. This revengeful woman *is* her foster daughter, not just in name but in emotional reality. In extending her care to her owner's child, Martha blurred the boundaries between self and other, and with them, slave and master, white and black. According to racist ideology, a mother's milk cannot miscegenate. The merging of nurse and child was considered free from the taint of racial definition, and in this text its love is innocent: the milk of human kindness. The memory of this bond lays a claim on the old grandmother's loyalty. When Mrs. Flint won't speak to her former nurse, Linda writes, "This wounded my grandmother's feelings, for she could not retain ill will against the woman whom she had nourished with her milk as a babe." When Dr. Flint questions her, Martha simply says, "'Your wife was my foster-child, Dr. Flint, the foster-sister of my poor Nancy, and you little know me if you think I can feel any thing but good will for her children.'" Martha's love for Mrs. Flint was, and remains, unconditional; she is indeed a dove. In a better world such goodness would confer moral authority. Linda admits that Dr. Flint was held at bay many times by her grandmother's reputation, but when Martha goes to Flint to plead for her granddaughter—reminding "him how long and how faithfully she had served in the family, and how she had taken her own baby from her breast to nourish his wife"—the doctor simply ignores her claims.[40] Here the ideology of true womanhood fails. Moral example alone is no match for positive evil.

One could argue, however, as Hazel Carby does, that Martha's behavior in this and other key instances is not submissive, but assertive. She is, Carby writes, "representative of a strong moral code in the midst of an immoral system."[41] She acts on behalf of the entire community of her care, black and white. The problem is that she has no power to enforce that code. By extending her love to a corrupt foster daughter, Martha endangers the other members of the community for whom she cares. By rejecting Mrs. Flint she would lose her Christ-like purity. The dove must learn a lesson from the serpent if it is to survive, and its peaceable kingdom come into this world, not just the next. Finally, even Martha is forced to agree that the greater good of Linda's escape justifies active resistance, including lies and deceit. She hides Linda in that womb-like, coffin-like space for seven years, caring for little Benjamin and Ellen all that time: a brave defiance of her own fear and honesty.[42]

Of course, Aunt Martha's love for her white foster children is not always the case in black literature. In Toni Morrison's *The Bluest Eye*, attachment to the oppressor's child appears as moral failure, a capitulation to white fantasies. In one excruciating scene Pauline rejects her own daughter in favor of the pretty white child who calls her Polly in the fancy house by the lake.[43] The implications and dangers of such nonreciprocal, powerless mothering are heightened in the horrifying violation of Sethe in *Beloved*. Forcibly taking milk meant for her child, the two white boys "with mossy teeth" pervert the sign of Sethe's womanly power and love freely given.[44] In Alice Walker's *The Color Purple* Sofia refuses to lie about loving *her* white "foster daughter's" child: "Some colored people so scared of whitefolks," she says, "they claim to love the cotton gin." Sofia does not deny she "feels something" for Eleanor Jane herself, "because out of all the people in your daddy's house you showed me some human kindness. But on the other hand, out of all the people in your daddy's house, I showed you some." Unlike Aunt Martha's, Sofia's love *is* conditional: "Kind feelings is what I offer you. I don't have nothing to offer your relatives but just what they offer me."[45]

In *Incidents in the Life of a Slave Girl* we see a black nursemaid who slaps the face of her dead mistress while the child she cares for, the child of the dead woman, looks on (the child tells and the nurse is sold). Here, however, as in *The Color Purple*, the white child before the corruption of consciousness *may* be worthy of love because that child may be capable of giving love. At the end of her long flight north, Linda Brent says she was so disillusioned that she was in danger of losing her compassion and hope. In the chapter called "A Home Found" she describes how Mary, her white employer's daughter, "thawed my heart, when it was freezing into cheerless distrust of all my fellow-beings." "I loved Mrs. Bruce's babe. When it laughed and crowed in my face, and twined its little tender arms confidingly about my neck . . . my wounded heart was soothed."[46]

The infant is not the source of the slave woman's exploitation. Although a black baby may be denied nourishment given to its white "sister," the demand is the slaveholder's, not the inarticulate child's. Brent reiterates her faith that "surely little children are true." In one parable-like story we see that truth uncorrupted: "I once saw two beautiful sisters playing together. One was a fair white child; the other was a slave, but also her sister. When I saw them embracing each other, and heard their joyous laughter, I turned sadly away from the lovely sight."[47] This Edenic moment is inevitably doomed. The serpent of slavery and white male sexuality insinuate themselves into the slave girl's innocence. She becomes aware of her difference, her enslavement, and her sexual vulnerability. Finally, she must drain "the cup of sin, and shame, and misery, whereof her persecuted race are compelled to drink."[48]

And what of her white sister? "From childhood to womanhood her pathway was blooming with flowers, and overarched by a sunny sky. Scarcely one day of her life had been clouded when the sun rose on her happy bridal morning."[49] But Brent stops at the bridal morning for good reason. If the serpent enters the slave girl's life at puberty, he enters her white sister's at marriage. Unchecked power and sexual exploitation make betrayal by her husband almost inevitable. Moral corruption blights her happiness and "ravages" her home, with its twining vines, "of all its loveliness."

This is the source, Brent implies, of Mrs. Flint's venom, the motivation behind her attack on the daughter of her foster sister and grandchild of her foster mother. Sexual jealousy, the "green-eyed monster," is personified in this woman's vindictiveness.[50] Brent is unsparing in her portrayal of that vindictiveness, but in an act of remarkable compassion, she writes, "Yet I, whom she detested so bitterly, had far more pity for her than he had, whose duty it was to make her life happy. I never wronged her, or wished to wrong her, and one word of kindness from her would have brought me to her feet."[51] Although deeply corrupted by slaveholding's unchecked power, Mrs. Flint persecutes Linda primarily out of helplessness and misery. The true source of her anger is her husband, but in a patriarchal world she too can be rendered powerless against him.

Linda Brent's story opens with the death of her white mistress. Her grief is real, "for she had been almost like a mother to me."[52] But this death brings another. When the will is read, Linda learns she has not been freed but "bequeathed" as a piece of property. "My mistress taught me the precepts of God's Word: 'thou shalt love thy neighbor as thyself.' 'Whatsoever ye would that men should do unto you, do ye even so unto them.' But I was her slave, and I suppose she did not recognize me as her neighbor."[53] This "one great wrong," emblem of slavery's moral blindness, cannot be forgotten or forgiven, but it is countered at the book's close by an act of neighborly love and courage.

After Linda's escape to the North she is employed by a Mr. and Mrs. Bruce as nursemaid for their daughter. Although the husband appears both obtuse and sympathetic to slaveholding, Mrs. Bruce is remarkable for her understanding and support. When Mrs. Bruce dies, the second wife proves even more remarkable. When Linda is threatened with capture by Mr. Dodge (her new master via his marriage to Emily Flint), the second Mrs. Bruce not only helps Linda escape once more but proposes she take Mrs. Bruce's own baby with her. If Linda is found, she reasons, the slavecatchers would be forced to return the white child to its mother before taking Linda south; Mrs. Bruce could then intervene on her behalf. Brent writes: "It was a comfort to me to have the child with me, for the heart is reluctant to be torn away from every object it loves. But how few mothers would have consented to have one of their own babies become a fugitive, for the sake of a poor, hunted nurse."[54] The sisterhood of that earlier Edenic image can be regained. Mrs. Bruce does recognize Linda as her neighbor. By risking her child, she assumes that neighbor's danger as her own.

But Linda's tale here also is "bittersweet," a word which reappears throughout the text. While Linda is in hiding with Mrs. Bruce's child, Mrs. Bruce writes that she intends to buy her from Mr. Dodge and end her persecution. Linda's response is sharply mixed. Although she is grateful, "The more my mind had become enlightened, the more difficult it was for me to consider myself an article of property; and to pay money to those who had so grievously oppressed me seemed like taking from my sufferings the glory of triumph." Linda writes to thank Mrs. Bruce but also to say "that being sold from one owner to another seemed too much like slavery, that such a great obligation could not be easily cancelled, and that I preferred to go to my brother in California."[55] She will take her stand on principle, uncompromised, passionate. Mary Helen Washington is correct in seeing this statement as Linda Brent's forthright assertion of selfhood, which is comparable to Frederick Douglass's rejection of any master, kind as well as cruel.[56]

Yet, here too, there is a difference; without Linda's knowledge, Mrs. Bruce goes ahead with the negotiations and purchases her friend's freedom. Again, Linda's response is deeply ambivalent. In her description of the bill of sale, the sentences themselves are split, pitting feeling against feeling: "I well know the value of that bit of paper, but much as I love freedom I do not like to look upon it. I am deeply grateful to the generous friend who procured it, but I despise the miscreant who demanded payment for what never rightfully belonged to him or his."[57] Despite her objections to the means, the end has been reached. Linda confesses that "when it was done I felt as if a heavy load had been lifted from my weary shoulders." She accepts the gift and does not judge Mrs. Bruce for dealing with slaveholders, any more than she judged her brother William for going to his mistress instead of his father, or her grandmother for preferring a living slave child to a lost free one. Mrs. Bruce has compromised a principle to gain Linda's freedom, and though Linda's bitterly resents the necessity, she forgives the act. After all, she has struck her own bargains with the devil.

"When I reached home, the arms of my benefactress were thrown round me, and our tears mingled." The imagery echoes the language of Dr. Flint's blasphemous letter at Nancy's death, but here the mutual identification is real. As Mrs. Bruce explains, "You wrote me as if you thought you were going to be transferred from one owner to another. But I did not buy you for your services. I should have done just the same if you were going to sail to California tomorrow. I should, at least, have the satisfaction of knowing that you left me a free woman."[58] Linda cannot help but remember how her father and grandmother had struggled to buy her freedom, and failed: "But God had raised me up a friend among strangers, who had bestowed on me the precious, long-desired boon." Mrs. Bruce, Brent writes, is her friend. "Friend! It is a common word, often lightly used. Like other good and beautiful things, it may be tarnished by careless handling; but when I speak of Mrs. Bruce as my friend, the word is sacred." As her narrative closes Linda Brent describes herself as "bound" to Mrs. Bruce's side, not by slavery and not only by economic circumstances but also by "love, duty, gratitude. . . ."[59]

"Reader, my story ends with freedom, not in the usual way, with marriage." The difference, however, goes even deeper. If her story does not end in the conventional feminine way, neither does it represent freedom in the conventional masculine way. Linda Brent's narrative ends, not with a solitary speaker, but with a woman gratefully acknowledging her bonds to her children and friends, bonds freely chosen. She has recovered her two children, Benjamin and Ellen. Although she still does not have a home of her own, her family is intact and free. The nineteenth-century vision of domesticity has become a kind of operative fiction: a Christian community of true sisterhood and brotherhood, based on mutual interdependence and identification, neighbor love. The power of this text, however, is its demonstration that moral action is not the work of pure, ego-less angels but of loving, self-determined women and men. The community of care cannot be sustained in a fallen, corrupted world merely through the innocence of the dove but requires the wisdom of the serpent to survive and prevail. Principled yet pragmatic, defiant and compassionate, Linda Brent's bittersweet voice is the voice of moral experience. Like Ralph Ellison's invisible man deep below his city's streets, she has emerged from her hiding place with a painful, healing knowledge. Ellison's hero closes by offering us that knowledge: "Who knows but that, on the lower frequencies, I speak for you."[60] Perhaps Linda Brent does too.

NOTES

1. See Jean Fagan Yellin, "Introduction," in Harriet A. Jacobs, *Incidents in the Life of a Slave Girl, Written by Herself*, ed. Jean Fagan Yellin (Cambridge, Mass.: Harvard University Press, 1987), xiii–xxxiv; also, Charles T. Davis and Henry Louis Gates, Jr., eds., "Text and Contexts of Harriet Jacobs' *Incidents in the Life of a Slave Girl: Written by Herself*," in *The Slave's Narrative* (New York: Oxford University Press, 1985), 262–82. For the text itself I have used the Yellin edition of Jacobs's work. In recognition of the fictional aspects of autobiography, I have referred to the author throughout as "Linda Brent." Finally, I would like to thank the anonymous readers of the *NWSA Journal* for their suggestions, as well as Patrocinio Schweickart and Lester A. Fisher for their encouragement and comments. This project was generously supported by a Faculty Summer Stipend from Dean Stuart Palmer and the College of Liberal Arts at the University of New Hampshire.
2. On the ideology of true womanhood see Barbara Welter, "The Cult of True Womanhood," *American Quarterly*, 18 (Summer 1966): 151–74; Nancy Cott, *The Bonds of Womanhood: "Woman's Sphere" in New England, 1780–1835* (New Haven, Conn.: Yale University Press, 1977); Lucy Freibert and Barbara A. White, eds., *Hidden Hands: An Anthology of American Women Writers, 1790–1870* (New Brunswick, N.J.: Rutgers University Press,

1985); and Judith Fetterley, ed., *Provisions: A Reader from 19th-Century American Women* (Bloomington: Indiana University Press, 1985). For a discussion of nineteenth-century Afro-American women's responses to the cult of true womanhood, see Frances Smith Foster, "Adding Color and Contour to Early American Self-Portraitures: Autobiographical Writings of Afro-American Women," in *Conjuring: Black Women, Fiction, and Literary Tradition*, ed. Marjorie Pryse and Hortense J. Spillers (Bloomington: Indiana University Press, 1985), 25–38.

Recent key studies of Jacobs's text include: Mary Helen Washington, "Meditations on History: The Slave Woman's Voice," in *Invented Lives: Narratives of Black Women, 1860–1960*, ed. Mary Helen Washington (Garden City, NY. .: Doubleday Anchor, 1987), 3–15; Hazel Carby, *Reconstructing Womanhood: The Emergence of the Afro-American Woman Novelist* (New York: Oxford University Press, 1987), 40–61; Valerie Smith, *Self-Discovery and Authority in Afro-American Narrative* (Cambridge, Mass.: Harvard University Press, 1987), 28–43; and Yellin, "Introduction," in *Incidents*, xxvii–xi. Also, Thomas Doherty, "Harriet Jacobs' Narrative Strategies: *Incidents in the Life of a Slave Girl*," *Southern Literary Journal* 19 (Fall 1986): 79–91.

3. For a discussion of the genre's conventions and Frederick Douglass's achievement within them see Houston A. Baker, Jr., "Autobiographical Acts and the Voices of the Southern Slave"; and James Olney, "'I Was Born': Slave Narratives, Their Status as Autobiography and as Literature," in *The Slave's Narrative*, 245–55; 148–75. On canon formation see Henry Louis Gates, Jr., "Canon Formation, Literary History, and the Afro-American Tradition: From the Seen to the Told," in *Afro-American Literary Study in the 1990s*, ed. Houston A. Baker, Jr. and Patricia Redmond (Chicago: University of Chicago Press, 1989), 14–50; also Nina Baym, "Melodramas of Beset Manhood: How Theories of American Fiction Exclude Women Authors," *American Quarterly* 33 (Summer 1981): 123–39.

4. The themes of moral innocence and experience are, of course, central to many literatures in many cultures. This problem of the fortunate fall, however, was especially important to the fiction of Jacobs's better-known contemporaries, such as Nathaniel Hawthorne and Herman Melville. Hawthorne, in

particular, provides an interesting parallel because, although a representative of elite culture, he worked within some of the same codes that Jacobs did, namely evangelical Protestantism and Victorian female ideology. See *The Marble Faun* and *The Scarlet Letter* (which painted a sympathetic portrait of another mother who bears an illegitimate child and whose experience forces her to question conventional morality). Significantly, these texts, among the most valued in the Anglo-American canon, are known for their exploration of moral conflict and ambiguity. Like Linda Brent's, their narrative voices are complex.

5. On this history see Jacqueline Jones, *Labor of Love, Labor of Sorrow* (New York: Basic Books, 1985); Eugene D. Genovese, *Roll, Jordan, Roll: The World the Slaves Made* (New York: Vintage, 1972); Herbert C. Gutman, *The Black Family in Slavery and Freedom, 1750–1925* (New York: Random House, 1976).

6. Daniel Scott-Smith, "Family Limitation, Sexual Control, and Domestic Feminism in Victorian America," *Feminist Studies* 1 (Winter/Spring 1973): 40–57; Nancy F. Cott, "Passionlessness: An Interpretation of Victorian Sexual Ideology, 1790–1850," *Signs* 4 (Spring 1978), 219–36.

7. For the evidence behind this judgment see the "Introduction" and annotations to Yellin's edition of *Incidents*, as well as the appended letters by Harriet Jacobs herself. However, the issue has not been completely laid to rest. Yellin recently chaired a roundtable discussion of the issue, "The Ending of a White Novel? The Beginning of a Black Narrative? Authorship, Genre, and *Incidents in the Life of a Slave Girl*," at the American Studies Association Convention in Toronto, Canada (3 November 1989). During the discussion panelist Alice Deck argued that Lydia Maria Child's editorial advice rendered the authorship of *Incidents* problematic, while fellow panelists Frances Smith Foster and Henry Louis Gates, Jr. affirmed Jacobs's ultimate authorship and authority. Here, as elsewhere, Jacobs deals with the constraints of her cultural context; here, as elsewhere, she exercises her power to choose.

For the relationship between *Incidents* and the classic seduction plot, see John Blassingame, "Critical Sources on Texts," in *The Slave Community: Plantation Life in the Antebellum South*, 2d ed. (New York: Oxford University Press, 1979),

367–82; John F. Bayliss, *Black Slave Narratives* (New York: MacMillan, 1970), 108; Frances Smith Foster, *Witnessing Slavery: The Development of the Ante-Bellum Slave Narrative* (Westport, Conn.: Greenwood Press, 1979), 58–59; Doherty, "Harriet Jacobs' Narrative," 83–91; Smith, *Self-Discovery*, 35–43; Carby, *Reconstructing Womanhood*, 45–48.

8. Jacobs, *Incidents*, 201.

9. Jacobs, *Incidents*, 56.

10. Smith, "Introduction," in *Narrative Authority*, 37.

11. Jacobs, *Incidents*, 55.

12. Jacobs, *Incidents*, 55.

13. Jacobs, *Incidents*, 55–56.

14. Jacobs, *Incidents*, 55. Mary Helen Washington discusses the slave woman's need for control over her sexuality and her life in *Invented Lives*, xxiii–xxiv. See also Smith, *Self-Discovery*, 33.

15. Jacobs, *Incidents*, 56–57. A comparison between the grandmother's response and mores among plantation slaves is revealing. According to historians Jacqueline Jones and Eugene Genovese, although the slave community highly valued marital fidelity, it generally tolerated pregnancy before marriage, even when the child's father was not the young woman's eventual husband. Jones, *Labor of Love*, 34–35; Genovese, *Roll, Jordan, Roll*, 458–75, esp. 465.

16. Jacobs, *Incidents*, 57.

17. For a discussion of Ellen's response to her mother's history, see Yellin, "Introduction," in *Incidents*, xiv; and Carby, *Reconstructing Womanhood*, 60–61. For a discussion of the silences within this narrative, see Smith, *Self-Discovery*, 42–43.

18. Ruth Bloch, "American Feminine Ideals in Transition: The Rise of the Moral Mother, 1785–1815," *Feminist Studies* 4 (June 1978): 101–26; Elizabeth Ammons, "Stowe's Dream of the Mother Savior: *Uncle Tom's Cabin* and American Women Writers Before the 1920's," in *New Essays on Uncle Tom's Cabin*, ed. Eric J. Sundquist (New York: Cambridge University Press, 1986). Harriet Jacobs's relationship to Stowe, including Stowe's unneighborly treatment of Jacobs and her daughter, is documented in *Incidents*; see particularly, 232–36.

19. Carby, *Reconstructing Womanhood*, 60.

20. Jacobs, *Incidents*, 62.

21. Jacobs, *Incidents*, 37.

22. Jacobs, *Incidents*, 93, 101.

23. Jacobs, *Incidents*, 86–87, 62.

24. Toni Morrison, *Beloved* (New York: Knopf, 1987).

25. Jacobs, *Incidents*, 78, 79.

26. Jacobs, *Incidents*, 142, 189.

27. Jacobs, *Incidents*, 107, 142.

28. See Washington, "Mediations on History," in *Invented Lives*, 8; Fetterley, "Introduction to *Incidents in the Life of a Slave Girl*," in *Provisions*, 279–85; and Smith, *Self-Discovery*, 27, 33–34.

29. Genovese, *Roll, Jordan, Roll*, 451.

30. Henry Bibb, "Narrative of the Life and Adventures of Henry Bibb, an American Slave," in *Puttin' On Ole Massa: The Significance of Slave Narratives*, ed. Gilbert Osofsky (New York: Harper & Row, 1969).

31. Jacobs, *Incidents*, 91.

32. Jacobs, *Incidents*, 199.

33. Jacobs, *Incidents*, 95.

34. Jacobs, *Incidents*, 92.

35. Jacobs, *Incidents*, 21.

36. Jacobs, *Incidents*, 134.

37. Jacobs, *Incidents*, 158.

38. Jacobs, *Incidents*, 281. According to Yellin, this is one of the few places in which Jacobs fictionalized her history, perhaps to make this moral point.

39. Jacobs, *Incidents*, 72.

40. Jacobs, *Incidents*, 85. Genovese's comments on the role and situation of black mammies are particularly helpful here: "That they loved the white children they raised—hardly astonishing for warm, sensitive, generous women—in no way proves that they loved their own children the less. Rather, their position in the Big House, including their close attention to the white children sometimes at the expense of their own, constituted the firmest protection they could have acquired for themselves and their immediate families." But, as Genovese points out and as *Incidents* demonstrates, this protection was extremely limited, resting as it did solely on personal influence (Genovese, *Roll, Jordan, Roll*, 356–57).

41. Carby, *Reconstructing Womanhood*, 57.

42. Genovese in *Roll, Jordan, Roll*, 360–61, again illuminates the problems which Martha poses to her granddaughter: "More than any other slave, [the mammy] had absorbed the paternalistic ethos and accepted her place in a system of reciprocal obligations defined from above. In so doing she developed pride, resourcefulness, and a high sense of responsibility to white and black people alike, as conditioned by the prevalent systems of values and notions of duties.... Her tragedy lay, not in her abandonment of her own people but in her inability to offer her individual power and beauty to black people on terms they could accept without themselves sliding further into a system of paternalistic dependency."

43. Toni Morrison, *The Bluest Eye* (New York: Washington Square Press, 1970), 87.

44. Toni Morrison, *Beloved*, 70.

45. Alice Walker, *The Color Purple* (New York: Washington Square Press, 1982), 233.

46. Jacobs, *Incidents*, 190, 170.

47. Jacobs, *Incidents*, 29.

48. Jacobs, *Incidents*, 29.

49. Jacobs, *Incidents*, 29.

50. See Minrose C. Gwin, "Green-Eyed Monsters of the Slavocracy: Jealous Mistresses in Two Slave Narratives," in *Conjuring*, ed. Pryse and Spillers, 39–52.

51. Jacobs, *Incidents*, 32.

52. Jacobs, *Incidents*, 7.

53. Jacobs, *Incidents*, 8.

54. Jacobs, *Incidents*, 194.

55. Jacobs, *Incidents*, 199.

56. Washington, "Meditations on History," in *Invented Lives*, 11–12.

57. Jacobs, *Incidents*, 200.

58. Jacobs, *Incidents*, 200.

59. Jacobs, *Incidents*, 201. A related pattern emerges in Sherley Anne Williams, *Dessa Rose* (New York: Berkley, 1986). Though more conflicted than the friendship of Linda Brent and Mrs. Bruce, the relationship of the escaped slave Dessa Rose and the white woman Miss Rufel is also rooted in the bonds of motherhood. Miss Rufel, raised by a beloved black nurse, gives

her breast in turn to Dessa Rose's newborn child. If the white woman here becomes the mammy, in *Beloved* she becomes the midwife. In Denver's caring for the laboring Sethe we also see an unusual white woman able to resist the temptation of racist power. Like the Good Samaritan, she recognizes the other as her neighbor.

60. Ralph Ellison, *The Invisible Man* (New York: Random House, 1947), 439.

THE INTERESTING NARRATIVE OF THE LIFE OF OLAUDAH EQUIANO, OR GUSTAVUS VASSA, THE AFRICAN, WRITTEN BY HIMSELF (OLAUDAH EQUIANO)

"Review of *The Interesting Narrative of the Life of Olaudah Equiano, or Gustavus Vassa, the African, Written by Himself*"
by Mary Wollstonecraft,
in *Analytical Review* (1789)

INTRODUCTION

In an early review of this highly influential slave narrative, Mary Wollstonecraft–author of the seminal feminist text *A Vindication of the Rights of Women* (1792)–describes both the literary qualities and humanity of Equiano's story of enslavement and emancipation.

The life of an African, written by himself, is certainly a curiosity, as it has been a favourite philosophic whim to degrade the numerous nations, on whom the sun-beams more directly dart, below the common level of humanity, and hastily to conclude that nature, by making them inferior to the rest of the human race, designed to stamp them with a mark of slavery. How they were shaded down, from the

---

Wollstonecraft, Mary. "Review of *The Interesting Narrative of the Life of Olaudah Equiano, or Gustavus Vassa, the African, Written by Himself.*" *Analytical Review* no. 4 (May 1789): 28.

fresh colour of northern rustics, to the fable hue seen on the African sands, is not our task to inquire, nor do we intend to draw a parallel between the abilities of a negro and European mechanic; we shall only observe, that if these volumes do not exhibit extraordinary intellectual powers, sufficient to wipe off the stigma, yet the activity and ingenuity, which conspicuously appear in the character of Gustavus, place him on a par with the general mass of men, who fill the subordinate stations in a more civilized society than that which he was thrown into at his birth.

The first volume contains, with a variety of other matter, a short description of the manners of his native country, an account of his family, his being kidnapped with his sister, his journey to the sea coast, and terror when carried on shipboard. Many anecdotes are simply told, relative to the treatment of male and female slaves, on the voyage, and in the West Indies, which make the blood turn its course; and the whole account of his unwearied endeavours to obtain his freedom, is very interesting. The narrative should have closed when he once more became his own master. The latter part of the second volume appears flat; and he is entangled in many, comparatively speaking, insignificant cares, which almost efface the lively impression made by the miseries of the slave. The long account of his religious sentiments and conversion to methodism is rather tiresome.

Throughout, a kind of contradiction is apparent: many childish stories and puerile remarks do not agree with some more solid reflections, which occur in the first pages. In the style also we observed a striking contrast: a few well written periods do not smoothly unite with the general tenor of the language.

An extract from the part descriptive of the national manners, we think will not be unacceptable to our readers.

'We are almost a nation of dancers, musicians, and poets. Thus every great event, such as a triumphant return from battle, or other cause of public rejoicing, is celebrated in public dances, which are accompanied with songs and music suited to the occasion. The assembly is separated into four divisions, which dance either apart or in succession, and each with a character peculiar to itself. The first division contains the married men, who in their dances frequently exhibit feats of arms, and the representation of a battle. To these succeed the married women, who dance in the second division. The young men occupy the third; and the maidens the fourth. Each represents some interesting scene of real life, such as a great achievement, domestic employment, a pathetic story or some rural sport; and as the subject is generally founded on some recent event, it is therefore ever new. This gives our dances a spirit and variety which I have scarcely seen elsewhere.[1] We have many musical instruments, particularly drums of different kinds, a piece of music which resembles a guitar, and another much like a stickado. These last are chiefly used by betrothed virgins, who play on them on all grand festivals.

'As our manners are simple, our luxuries are few. The dress of both sexes is nearly the same. It generally consists of a long piece of calico, or muslin, wrapped loosely round the body, somewhat in the form of a highland plaid. This is usually dyed blue, which is our favourite colour. It is extracted from a berry, and is brighter and richer than any I have seen in Europe. Besides this, our women of distinction wear golden ornaments, which they dispose with some profusion on their arms and legs. When our women are not employed with the men in tillage, their usual occupation is spinning and weaving cotton, which they afterwards dye, and make it into garments. They also manufacture earthen vessels, of which we have many kinds. Among the rest tobacco pipes, made after the same fashion, and used in the same manner, as those in Turkey.'[2]

NOTES

1. 'When I was in Smyrna I have frequently seen the Greeks dance after this manner.'
2. 'The bowl is earthen, curiously figured, to which a long reed is fixed as a tube. This tube is sometimes so long as to be borne by one, and frequently, out of grandeur, by two boys.'

"The Penal Colony"
(Franz Kafka)

"Enslavement and Emancipation in Franz Kafka's 'In the Penal Colony'"
by Lorena Russell, University of
North Carolina at Asheville

Franz Kafka's disturbing, enigmatic short story "In the Penal Colony" was first written in 1914, published as "Der Strafkolonie" in 1918, but not translated into English until 1941. Kafka, who lived from 1883–1924, is recognized as a leading European expressionist, one whose cryptic and elusive stories capture the absurdity of modern life through an abstract and often surrealist style. In particular, Kafka's stories such as "The Judgment," *The Trial*, and "The Metamorphosis" emphasize the dehumanization of the working man as he is trapped in an increasingly indifferent bureaucratic structure, a place so irrational that humane actions have no meaning and injustice prevails. "In the Penal Colony" follows in this tradition, as it engages the theme of enslavement and emancipation in a remote penal colony marked by alienation, irrationality, and injustice.[1]

The setting of the story and nature of the characters, as is so often the case in Kafka, remain scantily sketched and ill defined. Kafka's intentional withholding of "backstory," detailed characterization, and context effectively creates a kind of dreamworld in which individuals seem unmoored from their pasts as well as from others, and their actions and motivations remain largely unexplained.[2] Because the story lacks the details and context that typically guide readers toward understanding, we are forced to derive what meanings we can from the relationships that exist or develop between characters, and whatever clues the texts offer in terms of situational context.

"In the Penal Colony" involves four primary characters, none of whom are actually named: a traveler/explorer[3] who has recently arrived on the island, an officer who presides over the impending execution, the condemned man, and his guard. We learn from the officer that the colony is in a state of transition: The old commandant has died, and the officer, as one of the few remaining loyalists, fears his growing redundancy under the rule of the new commandant. In particular, he clings to his former commandant's method for execution. This extended, torturous process is carried out by an elaborate apparatus, a machine that enfolds the condemned within a glass-tipped harrow that inscribes the violated commandment on the prisoner's body in ever-deepening layers, slowly killing him[4] in an excruciating, twelve-hour process.

It is worth noting that the title of a text that offers the reader so few cues clearly places the story within the context of a penal colony, a place of state-sanctioned confinement, isolation, and virtual enslavement. As Peter Redfield notes in his study of French Guiana, the penal colony has a history of alignment with slavery as well as with colonization: "The penal colony has antecedents on the one hand in practices of slavery and forced labor in galleys, mines and public works, and on the other in traditions of exile for political figures, nobles and other members of fallen elites" (Redfield 54). Countries such as England and France were accustomed to remote administration of outposts as extensions of their empires, and these remote prison posts became a key component of the general movement of colonization and empire. Kafka's "In the Penal Colony," in its very title, thus alerts readers to the story's engagement with state-sanctified oppression and suffering that links abuses within the penal system with broader abuses that were also part of colonization.[5] While the plot of the short story deals with the relationship among a handful of men on a scene of execution, the broader situation has been set into motion by a remote nation. It is in fact largely the disjunction between the state and its remote colony that has led in part to the irrational and inhumane events that unfold in this distant setting, and that make such a mockery of justice.[6] For it is only justice that distinguishes imprisonment from enslavement, and in the penal colony, injustice prevails.

The state does not play an obvious role in the actions of the colony, but the ludicrous nature of the colonial relationship is made apparent through various details in the story. For example, the officers on the island suffer from wearing inappropriate uniforms that are "too heavy for the tropics," but nevertheless persist because "[the uniforms] represent our homeland, and we don't want to lose touch with our homeland" (Kafka 36). Interestingly, the traveler is himself removed from the pressures of national identification, and therefore retains a certain level of objectivity: "He was neither a citizen of the penal colony nor a citizen of the country to which it belonged" (46). His objectivity is at once what makes him a useful focalizer for readers while it also lends him a distance that makes him a mere observer, a passive onlooker in a situation that on many levels demands intervention. No matter how disturbing the scene, "he was traveling with the sole purpose of observing and by no means altering other people's legal institutions" (46). Even though he is witness to torture carried out in a system bereft of any justice, his claim on his outsider status forgives any impulse toward interference. He effectively becomes an excused, passive observer to murder.

Still, the traveler's status as an outsider becomes an important part of how readers can identify with his position. The officer senses the difference that sets the explorer apart from the system he is trying so desperately to defend: "You are conditioned by European points of view, maybe you are fundamentally opposed to the death penalty in general and this kind of execution by a machine in particular . . . would it not be easily possible that you would not consider my procedure correct?" (49). He imagines the objections that the traveler might offer the commandant: "'In our country the defendant is interrogated before the judgment,' or 'In our country the condemned man is informed of his judgment,' or 'In our country not all penalties are death penalties,' or 'In our country we used torture only in the Middle Ages'" (50). All of these imagined claims are ones that the reader of the story is likely to share, therefore establishing another level of alignment between the traveler and the reader. Like the traveler, the reader has arrived fresh upon a perplexing scene and must make full use of interpretation to make sense of events. In some sense the reader shares a state of neutrality as well: "I can no more help you than I can harm you" speaks to the moral indifference of a reader as well as a traveler (51).

The sense of injustice and irrationality in the story is heightened by the multiple absurdities of the story itself. The action begins with the traveler's conversation with the officer at the scene of the impending execution. From the first line, the focus is perversely set upon a decrepit execution apparatus that the officer praises as a model of efficiency and justice. However, as the story unfolds and the actual mechanisms of execution become clear, readers (alongside the traveler) come to recognize the apparatus as a mere torture device, one that effectively dehumanizes as it inflicts pain, drawing out an elaborated death with maximized suffering that outstrips any sense of justice. This literal perversion of justice, and the reader's perception of the perversion, depend largely on our ability to read the irony at the center of the story: that gap between the officer's perception of an execution performed in the name of justice, and the traveler's growing awareness of a place where injustice is meted out through the madness of those in power. Because the story is told so insistently through the reverse lens of irony, readers must work against the grain to unravel these coded meanings.

The presiding officer is chafing over the change in command; the previous commandant was the one who had invented the machine and instituted this perverse and torturous display, and the officer makes it quite clear that (from his perspective) the new commandant is a failure on many levels, not least of which is his failure to appreciate the apparatus. The officer works on the assumption (later denied by the traveler) that he is there as a specialist to observe the execution and make recommendations to the new commandant regarding the apparatus and process. Much of the story, therefore, consists of the officer's attempts to sway the traveler/explorer to appreciate the machine.

This focus on the machine is in itself symptomatic of the general lack of an ethical perspective that marks the outdated and inhumane law of the old regime. The officer's defense and adoration of the machine and its aura of progress creates a misplaced emphasis that displaces the fact of the condemned man and his suffering. The opening line highlights this misplaced focus, as the story begins through the approving eyes of the officer: "It is a peculiar piece of machinery,' said the officer to the traveler and with a look that contained some admiration surveyed the machine that was after all so familiar to him" (36). It is only secondarily that we are invited to consider the human being who will be subjected to the device. An execution is state-sanctioned murder, but here the sense of spectacle promised by the machine somehow displaces the human drama of a determined death at the center of the story. Our attention is being directed not on the suffering man, but on the technology of death.[7]

The lack of context and history also means that the relationships that develop between the characters provide the reader with much of the basis of understanding. As befits the quasi-military nature of the penal colony, this is a series of relationships built on clear lines of power, a strict hierarchy of domination and subordination. The commander pines for his lost commandant, and the prisoner is being executed because of a perceived failure to respect his superiors.

It is in fact the condemned man who offers the most interesting commentary on subordination and the psychology of enslavement. We initially encounter him as someone who has seemingly embraced his subordinate role, one who has adapted to his fate of imprisonment by making himself as lowly and nonthreatening as possible. This man, condemned to death for the offense of sleeping during duty, does not speak the language of the colonizers, and therefore seems blissfully unaware of his pending fate. We might expect a prisoner accused of a capital offense to be a violent and threatening type, but this character is marked by docility and fawning, like a loyal dog.[8] Bound in layers of elaborate chains, "the condemned man looked so doggishly submissive and one would only have to whistle at the start of the execution for him to come" (36). He seemingly embodies docility, though ironically his offence was one of insubordination.[9]

Kafka wrote "In the Penal Colony" at the same time he was writing his novel *The Trial*. Both texts share a central concern with the question of justice. The machine and its harrow-like apparatus literally inscribe the judgment on the body of the man. In the pending case, the machine will write "Honor thy superiors!" on the man's back (39). For the commander, the very physicality of the execution and the fact that the accused will literally "read" the judgment through his body speaks to a kind of exact justice. The traveler, however, expresses concern that the accused does not speak the language and will enter into the torture with no idea why he is being executed. The illogical nature of the story progresses largely in this manner, with the officer presenting arguments lodged in minute details or limited observations, while the traveler counters the officer's rationale with appeals to broader principles.

A lack of meaningful communication pervades the story, and further contributes to the mechanisms of enslavement, injustice, and oppression. The accused (who, again, does not speak the language of the ruling class) had worked as an orderly for a captain and was assigned to keep watch and sleep outside his door. He is furthermore expected to wake every hour "to salute the captain's door" (41). When the orderly is caught dozing by his superior on the stroke of two, the captain strikes the man in the face with a riding crop, and the orderly responds with defiance, saying "Throw the whip away, or I'll eat you alive" (41).[10] The captain then makes a statement to the officer, who "immediately added the judgment" (41). But the officer's judgment is clearly removed from any real sense of justice, based as it is on the guiding principle that "Guilt is always beyond all doubt" (40). He dismisses the traveler's notion that accused men should have an opportunity to defend themselves, arguing on the basis of expediency and simplicity that to let him speak "would have only led to confusion. He would have lied . . ." (41).

The traveler receives this account of "justice" with a level of ambivalence. On the one hand he recognizes that justice has been abused, but then he allows that "this was a penal colony, that special disciplinary measures were necessary here, and that military procedures had to prevail throughout" (41). He further holds out hope for the new commandant and the initiation of a new, more humane rule of law. Again, his outsider position allows for an objectivity that is at once useful and disturbing, and his rationalization offers insight into how easily injustice can be rationalized away.

Lack of meaningful communication is also part of what alienates the prisoner from understanding the full implications of his predicament. As the officer invites the traveler to observe the glass needles, the prisoner attempts to follow: "The condemned man had also accepted the officer's invitation to have a look at the harrow up close. . . . One could see how, with shifting eyes, he was searching for what the two gentlemen had just observed, but since he had not grasped the explanation, he could not succeed" (42).

The accused is not the only one in the dark, however. The officer urges the traveler to read the former commandant's designs, but, despite the officer's promise that "you'll be able to see everything clearly," these are illegible: "He saw only labyrinthine lines intersecting at various points, covering up the paper so thickly that it was an effort to detect the white spaces between them" (43). Despite the officer's protestations that the designs are clear, the traveler cannot decipher the message. While the officer is disappointed, he takes comfort in the fact that at least the complexity of the machine has been "impressed" upon the traveler.[11]

As the officer continues with his description, the horror of the torture becomes painfully clear. The harrow writes on the man's body in a stabbing motion, deepening its inscriptions with every pass:

> During the first six hours the condemned man lives almost as he did before, except that he is in pain. After two hours the felt plug is removed, since the man no longer has the strength to scream.... But how quiet the man becomes around the sixth hour! Understanding dawns on even the dumbest. (44)

It is at this moment of "understanding," the fetishized "sixth hour," that the process reaches an apotheosis for the officer, as he gains satisfaction from watching the condemned "read" the judgment on his body, written in the same undecipherable script that marked the design: "You've seen that it is not easy to decipher the script with your eyes, but our man deciphers it with his wounds" (45).

Much of the work of the machine seems designed around these issues of communication, both written and verbal. The condemned has no opportunity to speak in his defense. The felt plug is designed for stopping the condemned from speaking. The prisoner cannot speak the language and mimics the traveler in ways that he finds most disturbing.[12] In its ability to bypass normal modes of communication, the machine seems to be designed to "impress," and the officer himself is eager to make an "impression" on the traveler. Once the prisoner is stripped of his clothes and strapped into the machine, the officer scrutinizes the traveler, as though to understand by his expression: "From the side the officer looked uninterruptedly at the traveler, as if he were trying to read his face for the impression the execution ... was making on him" (45). There's a whole lot of reading going on in this story, but very few coherent results.

When the machine malfunctions, the officer bemoans his current lack of support, and jury-rigs a substitution for the broken strap. Once again, the traveler reacts by retreating into an attitude of passive observation: "They could say to him: you're a foreigner, keep quiet ...

he was traveling with the sole purpose of observing and by no means altering other people's legal institutions" (46). In one final desperate plea the officer urges the traveler to take action despite his outsider status: "' . . . Is such a lifework'—he pointed to the machine—'to be ruined? Can we let that happen? Even if one is only a foreigner visiting our island for a few days?'" (47). He reminisces about the old days when everyone in the colony attended the executions: "everyone knew: Now justice is being done. In the silence you heard only the condemned man's moans, muted by the felt plug" (48). Here the ironic subversion is driven home in part by the notion that justice could be achieved by stifling communication.[13]

When the officer realizes that the traveler will not intervene on his behalf, the story takes an unexpected turn. In a gesture of resignation, the officer frees the condemned man from the machine, notably speaking the words "You are free" in the prisoner's language. This injunction toward freedom marks a turning point in the text. Clearly the condemned does not understand the rationale behind the turn of events, but he quickly shifts in his role from utter subordination to an almost playful interaction with his former guard. They frolic with the handkerchiefs as the officer, recognizing the hopelessness of his case and the final end of the old regime, replaces the script in the machine with the exhortation "Be just," strips naked, and enters the harrowing machine to accept his self-imposed death sentence. As the machine begins its workings, the gears fall apart, and much to the horror of the traveler, the officer is killed: "This was not the torture that the officer had wanted to achieve, this was plain murder" (57).

One might expect this tale to end in a gesture of liberation: The old machine and its final loyalist have been destroyed, and the unjustly convicted prisoner has been freed. But the nature of the island colony means that the guard and the prisoner are still in a sense enslaved: They are not free to leave. While the traveler successfully engages a boat to take him away, he refuses the prisoner's and the guard's efforts to escape with him. His last gesture is to protect his interest, leaving the others to their enslavement on the island. What sets imprisonment apart from slavery is that the former is presumably enacted under a system of justice. But here on the penal colony, justice is perverted by the very nature of the colonial relationship. The prisoner no longer wears chains, but finds in the end that freedom is little more than an illusion.

NOTES

1. Kafka considered grouping the story along with "The Judgment" and "The Metamorphosis" in a volume called *Punishments*. See Eric L. Santner and David J. Levin, "Kafka Symposium: Introduction," *Modernism/Modernity* 8.2 (2001): 277.
2. Peter Heller discusses the inconclusiveness that is central to Kafka. See Peter Heller, "On Not Understanding Kafka," *The German Quarterly* 47.3 (1974).
3. The German word "Forschungreisender" is variously translated into English as "traveler," "explorer," or "researcher." This nuance of meaning that is present in German—the addition of the concept of scholar or seeker of knowledge—makes the "traveler" subject position correlate even more so with the position of the reader, who enters the text as an outsider and a searcher after knowledge.
4. Women are hardly present in this story, save for a few references to "the ladies," a group devoted to doing the biddings of the new commandant, and whose indulgences are a source of aggravation to the officer. They were responsible for feeding the condemned man sweets and adorned him with handkerchiefs that have since been taken by the officer.
5. Critics focusing on colonial themes include Rolf J. Goebel, "Kafka and Postcolonial Critique: *Der Verschollene*, 'in Der Strafkolonie,' 'Beim Bauer Der Chinesischen Mauer'," *A Companion to the Works of Franz Kafka*, ed. James Rolleston, Studies in German Literature, Linguistics and Culture (Rochester, N.Y.: Camden House, 2002). Margaret Kohn, "Kafka's Critique of Colonialism," *Theory & Event* 8.3 (2005). And Paul Peters, "Witness to the Execution: Kafka and Colonialism," *Monatshefte für Deutschsprachige Literatur und Kultur* 93.4 (2001).
6. For an elaboration of this point, see Danilyn Rutherford, "The Foreignness of Power: Alterity and Subversion in Kafka's 'In the Penal Colony' and Beyond," *Modernism/Modernity* 8.2 (2001).
7. For an elaboration on the social function of execution, see Michel Foucault, *Discipline and Punish: The Birth of the Prison*, 2nd Vintage ed. (New York: Vintage Books, 1995).

8. Kafka's *The Trial* ends with the hapless character Michael K. executed "like a dog," and this allegory of powerlessness recurs throughout his writings. For Kafka, as for the contemporary writer J. M. Coetzee, the lack of power and mistreatment that animals suffer is symptomatic of man's enslavement of other men and represents a similar level of injustice. For a discussion of dogs in Kafka, see Peter Stine, "Franz Kafka and Animals," *Contemporary Literature* 22.1 (1981).

9. The writings of Michel Foucault, particularly his work in *Discipline and Punish*, resonate in multiple ways with "In the Penal Colony." Here I'm referencing his concept of "docile bodies," an elaboration of how individuals and their behaviors are largely marked and determined by the social structures that surround and influence them.

10. It is worth noting here that the implications of cannibalism mark another level of dehumanization of the accused man, as well as providing another link between the story and colonial discourse, where the figure of the native cannibal looms large in the colonial imagination.

11. For a reading of "In the Penal Colony" that highlights the story's theme of writing and language, see Stanley Corngold, *Franz Kafka: The Necessity of Form* (Ithaca: Cornell University Press, 1988).

12. Rolf Goebel discusses the role of mimicry in the text and its relationship to the story's critique of colonial oppression. See Goebel, "Kafka and Postcolonial Critique: *Der Verschollene*, 'in Der Strafkolonie,' 'Beim Bauer Der Chinesischen Mauer'."

13. For an interesting discussion of the relationships of silence to justice, see Danielle Allen, "Sounding Silence," *Modernism/ Modernity* 8.2 (2001).

Works Cited

Allen, Danielle. "Sounding Silence." *Modernism/Modernity* 8.2 (2001): 325–34.

Corngold, Stanley. *Franz Kafka: The Necessity of Form.* Ithaca: Cornell University Press, 1988.

Foucault, Michel. *Discipline and Punish: The Birth of the Prison.* 2nd Vintage ed. New York: Vintage Books, 1995.

Goebel, Rolf J. "Kafka and Postcolonial Critique: *Der Verschollene*, 'in Der Strafkolonie,' 'Beim Bauer Der Chinesischen Mauer'." *A Companion to the Works of Franz Kafka*. Ed. James Rolleston. Studies in German Literature, Linguistics and Culture. Rochester, NY: Camden House, 2002. 187–212.

Heller, Peter. "On Not Understanding Kafka." *The German Quarterly* 47.3 (1974): 373–93.

Kafka, Franz. "In the Penal Colony." Trans. Stanley Corngold. *Kafka's Selected Stories: New Translations, Backgrounds and Contexts, Criticism*. Ed. Stanley Corngold. New York: W.W. Norton, 2007. 35–59.

Kohn, Margaret. "Kafka's Critique of Colonialism." *Theory & Event* 8.3 (2005).

Peters, Paul. "Witness to the Execution: Kafka and Colonialism." *Monatshefte für Deutschsprachige Literatur und Kultur* 93.4 (2001): 401–25.

Redfield, Peter. *Space in the Tropics: From Convicts to Rockets in French Guiana*. Berkeley: University of California Press, 2000.

Rutherford, Danilyn. "The Foreignness of Power: Alterity and Subversion in Kafka's 'In the Penal Colony' and Beyond." *Modernism/Modernity* 8.2 (2001): 303–13.

Santner, Eric L., and David J. Levin. "Kafka Symposium: Introduction." *Modernism/Modernity* 8.2 (2001): 277–79.

Stine, Peter. "Franz Kafka and Animals." *Contemporary Literature* 22.1 (1981): 58–80.

THE SPEECHES OF ABRAHAM LINCOLN

"Lincoln the Literary Genius"
by Jacques Barzun, in
The Saturday Evening Post (1959)

INTRODUCTION

In this piece written for the 150th anniversary of Abraham Lincoln's birth, famed critic Jacques Barzun comments upon "Lincoln the artist, the maker of a style that is unique in English prose and doubly astonishing in the history of American literature." In showing us the literary qualities and aspirations of the author of the Emancipation Proclamation, Barzun outlines the "four main qualities of Lincoln's literary art—precision, vernacular ease, rhythmical virtuosity and elegance," concluding that Lincoln had a profound influence on American literary style: "Lincoln's example, plainly, helped to break the monopoly of the dealers in literary plush. After Lincoln comes Mark Twain, and out of Mark Twain come contemporaries of ours as diverse as Sherwood Anderson, H.L. Mencken and Ernest Hemingway. Lincoln's use of his style for the intimate genre and for the sublime was his alone; but his workaday style is the American style par excellence."

Barzun, Jacques. "Lincoln the Literary Genius." *The Saturday Evening Post*, Vol. 231, No. 33 (14 February 1959): 30, 62–4.

A great man of the past is hard to know, because his legend, which is a sort of friendly caricature, hides him like a disguise. He is one thing to the man in the street and another to those who study him closely—and who seldom agree. And when a man is so great that not one but half a dozen legends are familiar to all who recognize his name, he becomes once more a mystery, almost as if he were an unknown.

This is the situation that Lincoln occupies in the United States on the 150th anniversary of his birth. Everybody knows who he was and what he did. But what was he like? For most people, Lincoln remains the rail splitter, the shrewd country lawyer, the cracker-barrel philosopher and humorist, the statesman who saved the Union, and the compassionate leader who saved many a soldier from death by court-martial, only to meet his own end as a martyr.

Not being a Lincoln scholar, I have no wish to deal with any of these images of Lincoln. I want only to help celebrate his sesquicentennial year by bringing out a Lincoln who I am sure is real though unseen. The Lincoln I know and revere is a historical figure who should stand—I will not say, instead of, but by the side of, all the others. No one need forget the golden legends, yet anyone may find it rewarding to move them aside a little so as to get a glimpse of the unsuspected Lincoln I have so vividly in mind.

I refer to Lincoln the artist, the maker of a style that is unique in English prose and doubly astonishing in the history of American literature, for nothing led up to it. The Lincoln who speaks to me through the written word is a figure no longer to be described wholly or mainly by the old adjectives, shrewd, humorous or saintly, but rather as one combining the traits that biography reports in certain artists among the greatest—passionate, gloomy, seeming-cold, and conscious of superiority.

These elements in Lincoln's make-up have been noticed before, but they take on a new meaning in the light of the new motive I detect in his prose. For his style, the plain, undecorated language in which he addresses posterity, is no mere knack with words. It is the manifestation of a mode of thought, of an outlook which colors every act of the writer's and tells us how he rated life. Only let his choice of words, the rhythm and shape of his utterances, linger in the ear, and you begin to feel as he did and, hence, to discern unplumbed depths in the quiet intent of a conscious artist.

But before taking this path of discovery, it is necessary to dispose of a few too-familiar ideas. The first is that we already know all there is to know about Lincoln's prose. Does not every school child learn that the Gettysburg Address is beautiful, hearing this said so often that he ends by believing it? The belief is general, of course, but come by in this way, it is not worth much. One proof of its little meaning is that most Americans also believe that for fifty years Lincoln's connection with the literary art was to tell racy stories. Then, suddenly, on a train journey to Gettysburg, he wrote a masterpiece. This is not the way great artists go to work—so obviously not, that to speak of Lincoln as an *artist* will probably strike some readers as a paradox or a joke. Even so, the puzzle remains: How did this strange man from Illinois produce not a few happy phrases, but an unmistakable style?

On this point the books by experts do no better than the public. The latest collective attempt to write a literary history of the United States does indeed speak of Lincoln's styles, in the plural; but this reference is really to Lincoln's various tones, ranging from the familiar to the elevated. Like all other books that I have searched through, this authoritative work always talks of the subject or the occasion of Lincoln's words when attempting to explain the power of his best-known pieces. It is as if a painter's genius were explained by the land-scapes he depicted.

Lincoln has indeed had praise as a writer, but nearly all of it has been conventional and absent-minded. The few authors of serious studies have fallen into sentimentality and incoherence. Thus, in the Hay and Nicolay edition of Lincoln's works, a famous editor of the '90's writes: "Of style, in the ordinary use of the word, Lincoln may be said to have had little. There was nothing ambitiously elaborate or self-consciously simple in Lincoln's way of writing. He had not the scholar's range of words. He was not always grammatically accurate. He would doubtless have been very much surprised if anyone had told him that he 'had' a style at all."

Here one feels like asking: Then why discuss "Lincoln as a writer"? The answer is unconvincing: "And yet, because he was determined to be understood, because he was honest, because he had a warm and true heart, because he had read good books eagerly and not coldly, and because there was in him a native good taste, as well as a strain of imagination, he achieved a singularly clear and forcible style, which took color from his own noble character and became a thing individual and distinguished."

So the man who had no style, had a style—clear, forcible, individual and distinguished. This is as odd a piece of reasoning as that offered by the late Senator Beveridge: "The cold fact is that not one faint glimmer appears in his whole life, at least before his Cooper Union speech, which so much as suggests the radiance of the last two years." Perhaps a senator is never a good judge of what a President writes; this one asks us to believe in a miracle. One would think the "serious" critics had simply failed to read their author.

Yet they must have read him, to be so obviously bothered. "How did he do it?" they wonder. They think of the momentous issues of the Civil War, of the grueling four years in Washington, of the man beset by politicians who were too aggressive and by generals who were not enough so, and the solution flashes upon them: "It was the strain that turned homespun into great literature." This is again to confuse a literary occasion with the literary power which rises to it. The famous documents—the two Inaugurals, the Gettysburg Address, the letter to Mrs. Bixby—marvelous as they are, do not solve the riddle. On the contrary their subjects have such a grip on our emotions that we begin to think almost anybody could have moved us. For all these reasons—inadequate criticism, over-familiarity with a few masterpieces, ignorance of Lincoln's early work and the consequent suppression of one whole side of his character—we must go back to the source and begin at the beginning.

Pick up any early volume of Lincoln's and start reading as if you were approaching a new author. Pretend you know none of the anecdotes, nothing of the way the story embedded in these pages comes out. Your aim is to see a life unfold and to descry the character of the man from his own words, written, most of them, not to be published, but to be felt.

Here is Lincoln at twenty-three telling the people of his district by means of a handbill that they should send him to the state legislature: "Upon the subjects of which I have treated, I have spoken as I thought. I may be wrong in regard to any or all of them; but holding it a sound maxim that it is better to be only sometimes right than at all times wrong, so soon as I discover my opinions to be erroneous, I shall be ready to renounce them." And he closes his appeal for votes on an unpolitical note suggestive of melancholy thoughts: "But if the good people in their wisdom shall see fit to keep me in the background, I have been too familiar with disappointments to be very much chagrined."

One does not need to be a literary man to see that Lincoln was a born writer, nor a psychologist to guess that here is a youth of uncommon mold—strangely self-assertive, yet detached, and also laboring under a sense of misfortune.

For his handbill Lincoln may have had to seek help with his spelling, which was always uncertain, but the rhythm of those sentences was never taught by a grammar book. Lincoln, as he himself said, went to school "by littles," which did not in the aggregate amount to a year. Everybody remembers the story of his reading the Bible in the light of the fire and scribbling with charcoal on the back of the shovel. But millions have read the Bible and not become even passable writers. The neglected truth is that not one but several persons who remembered his childhood remarked on the boy's singular determination to express his thoughts in the best way.

His stepmother gave an account of the boy which prefigures the literary artist much more than the rail splitter: "He didn't like physical labor. He read all the books he could lay his hands on. . . . When he came across a passage that struck him, he would write it down on boards if he had no paper and keep it there till he did get paper, then he would rewrite it, look at it, repeat it." Later, Lincoln's law partner, William H. Herndon, recorded the persistence of this obsessive habit with words: "He used to bore me terribly by his methods. . . . Mr. Lincoln would doubly explain things to me that needed no explanation. . . . Mr. Lincoln was a very patient man generally, but . . . just go at Lincoln with abstractions, glittering generalities, indefiniteness, mistiness of idea or expression. Here he flew up and became vexed, and sometimes foolishly so."

In youth Lincoln had tried to be a poet, but found he lacked the gift. What he could do was think with complete clarity in words and imagine the workings of others' minds at the same time. One does not read far in his works before discovering that as a writer he toiled above all to find the true order for his thoughts—order first, and then a lightninglike brevity. Here is how he writes in 1846, a young politician far from the limelight, and of whom no one expected a lapidary style: "If I falsify in this you can convict me. The witnesses live, and can tell." There is a fire in this, and a control of it, which shows the master.

That control of words implied a corresponding control of the emotions. Herndon described several times in his lectures and papers the eccentric temperament of his lifelong partner. This portrait the kindly sentimental people have not been willing to accept. But Herndon's sense of greatness was finer than that of the admirers from afar, who worship rather storybook heroes than the mysterious, difficult, unsatisfactory sort of great man—the only sort that history provides.

What did Herndon say? He said that Lincoln was a man of sudden and violent moods, often plunged in deathly melancholy for hours, then suddenly lively and ready to joke; that Lincoln was self-centered and cold, not given to revealing his plans or opinions, and ruthless in using others' help and influence; that Lincoln was idle for long stretches of time, during which he read newspapers or simply brooded; that Lincoln had a disconcerting power to see into questions, events and persons, never deceived by their incidental features or conventional garb, but extracting the central matter as one cores an apple; that Lincoln was a man of strong passions and mystical longings, which he repressed because his mind showed him their futility, and that this made him cold-blooded and a fatalist.

In addition, as we know from other sources, Lincoln was subject to vague fears and dark superstitions. Strange episodes, though few, marked his relations with women, including his wife-to-be, Mary Todd. He was subject, as some of his verses show, to obsessional gloom about separation, insanity and death. We should bear in mind that Lincoln was orphaned, reared by a stepmother, and early cast adrift to make his own way. His strangely detached attitude toward himself, his premonitions and depressions, his morbid regard for truth and abnormal suppression of aggressive impulses, suggest that he hugged a secret wound which ultimately made out of an apparent common man the unique figure of an artist-saint.

Lincoln moreover believed that his mother was the illegitimate daughter of a Virginia planter and, like others who have known or fancied themselves of irregular descent, he had a powerful, unreasoned faith in his own destiny—a destiny he felt would combine greatness and disaster.

Whatever psychiatry might say to this, criticism recognizes the traits of a type of artist one might call "the dark outcast." Michelangelo and Byron come to mind as examples. In such men the sense of isolation from others is in the emotions alone. The mind remains a clear and fine instrument of common sense—Michelangelo built buildings, and Byron brilliantly organized the Greeks in their revolt against Turkey. In Lincoln there is no incompatibility between the lawyer-statesman, whom we all know, and the artist, whose physiognomy I have been trying to sketch.

Lincoln's detachment was what produced his mastery over men. Had he not, as President, towered in mind and will over his cabinet, they would have crushed or used him without remorse. Chase, Seward, Stanton, the Blairs, McClellan had among them enough egotism and ability to wreck several administrations. Each thought Lincoln would be an easy victim. It was not until he was removed from their midst that any of them conceived of him as an apparition greater than themselves. During his life their dominant feeling was exasperation with him for making them feel baffled. They could not bring him down to their reach. John Hay, who saw the long struggle, confirms Herndon's judgments: "It is absurd to call him a modest man. No great man was ever modest. It was his intellectual arrogance and unconscious assumption of superiority that men like Chase and Sumner could never forgive."

This is a different Lincoln from the clumsy country lawyer who makes no great pretensions, but has a trick or two up his sleeve and wins the day for righteousness because his heart is pure. Lincoln's purity was that of a supremely conscious genius, not of an innocent. And if we ask what kind of genius enables a man to master a new and sophisticated scene as Lincoln did, without the aid of what are called personal advantages, with little experience in affairs of state and no established following, the answer is: military genius or its close kin, artistic genius.

The artist contrives means and marshals forces that the beholder takes for granted and that the bungler never discovers for himself. The artist is always scheming to conquer his material and his audience. When we speak of his craft, we mean quite literally that he is crafty.

Lincoln acquired his power over words in the only two ways known to man—by reading and by writing. His reading was small in range and much of a kind: the Bible, Bunyan, Byron, Burns, Defoe, Shakespeare and a then-current edition of Aesop's Fables. These are books from which a genius would extract the lesson of terseness and strength. The Bible and Shakespeare's poetry would be less influential than Shakespeare's prose, whose rapid twists and turns Lincoln often rivals, though without imagery. The four other British writers are all devotees of the telling phrase, rather than the suggestive. As for Aesop, the similarity of his stories with the anecdotes Lincoln liked to tell—always in the same words—is obvious. But another parallel occurs, that between the shortness of a fable and the mania Lincoln had for condensing any matter into the fewest words:

> John Fitzgerald, eighteen years of age, able-bodied, but without pecuniary means, came directly from Ireland to Springfield, Illinois, and there stopped, and sought employment, with no present intention of returning to Ireland or going elsewhere. After remaining in the city some three weeks, part of the time employed, and part not, he fell sick, and became a public charge. It has been submitted to me, whether the City of Springfield, or the County of Sangamon is, by law, to bear the charge.

As Lincoln himself wrote on another occasion, "This is not a long letter, but it contains the whole story." And the paragraph would prove, if it were necessary, that style is independent of attractive subject matter. The pleasure it gives is that of lucidity and motion, the motion of Lincoln's mind.

In his own day, Lincoln's prose was found flat, dull, lacking in taste. It differed radically in form and tone from the accepted models—Webster's or Channing's for speeches, Bryant's or Greeley's for journalism. Once or twice, Lincoln did imitate their genteel circumlocutions or resonant abstractions. But these were exercises he never repeated. His style, well in hand by his thirtieth year and richly developed by his fiftieth, has the eloquence which comes of the contrast between transparency of medium and density of thought. Consider this episode from a lyceum lecture written when Lincoln was twenty-nine:

> "Turn, then, to that horror-striking scene at St. Louis. A single victim was only sacrificed there. His story is very short; and is, perhaps, the most highly tragic of anything of its length that has ever been witnessed in real life. A mulatto man by the name of McIntosh was seized in the street, dragged to the suburbs of the city, chained to a tree, and actually burned to death; and

all within a single hour from the time he had been a freeman, attending to his own business, and at peace with the world."

Notice the contrasting rhythm of the two sentences: "A single victim was only sacrificed there. His story is very short." The sentences are very short, too, but let anyone try imitating their continuous flow or subdued emotion on the characteristic Lincolnian theme of the swift passage from the business of life to death.

Lincoln's prose works fall into three categories: speeches, letters and proclamations. The speeches range from legal briefs and arguments to political debates. The proclamations begin with his first offer of his services as a public servant and end with his presidential statements of policy or calls to Thanksgiving between 1861 and 1865. The letters naturally cover his life span and a great diversity of subjects. They are, I surmise, the crucible in which Lincoln cast his style. By the time he was in the White House, he could frame, impromptu, hundreds of messages such as this telegram to General McClellan: "I have just read your despatch about sore-tongued and fatigued horses. Will you pardon me for asking what the horses of your army have done since the battle of Antietam that fatigues anything?"

Something of Lincoln's tone obviously comes from the practice of legal thought. It would be surprising if the effort of mind that Lincoln put into his profession had not come out again in his prose. After all, he made his name and rose to the Presidency over a question of constitutional law. Legal thought encourages precision through the imagining and the denial of alternatives. The language of the law foresees doubt, ambiguity, confusion, stupid or fraudulent error, and one by one it excludes them. Most lawyers succeed at least in avoiding misunderstanding, and this obviously is the foundation of any prose that aims at clear expression.

As a lawyer Lincoln knew that the courtroom vocabulary would achieve this purpose if handled with a little care. But it would remain jargon, obscure to the common understanding. As an artist, therefore, he undertook to frame his ideas invariably in one idiom, but that of daily life. He had to use, of course, the technical names of the actions and documents he dealt with. But all the rest was in the vernacular. His first achievement was to translate the minute accuracy of the advocate and the judge into the words of common men.

To say this is to suggest a measure of Lincoln's struggle as an artist. He started with very little confidence in his stock of knowledge, and having to face audiences far more demanding than ours, he toiled to improve his vocabulary, grammar and logic. In the first year of his term in Congress he labored through six books of Euclid in hopes of developing the coherence of thought he felt he needed in order to demonstrate his views. Demonstration was to him the one proper goal of argument; he never seems to have considered it within his power to convince by disturbing the judgment through the emotions. In the few passages where he resorts to platform tricks, he uses only irony or satire, never the rain-barrel booming of the Fourth-of-July orator.

One superior gift he possessed from the start and developed to a supreme degree, the gift of rhythm. Take this fragment, not from a finished speech, but from a jotting for a lecture on the law:

> "There is a vague popular belief that lawyers are necessarily dishonest. I say vague, because, when we consider to what extent confidence and honors are reposed in and conferred upon lawyers by the people, it appears improbable that their impression of dishonesty is very distinct and vivid. Yet the impression is common, almost universal. Let no young man choosing the law for a calling for a moment yield to the popular belief—resolve to be honest at all events; and if in your own judgment you cannot be an honest lawyer, resolve to be honest without being a lawyer."

Observe the case with which the theme is announced: "There is a vague popular belief that lawyers are necessarily dishonest." It is short without crackling like an epigram, the word "necessarily" retarding the rhythm just enough. The thought is picked up with hardly a pause; "I say vague, because, when we consider ..." and so on through the unfolding of reasons, which winds up in a kind of calm: "it appears improbable that their impression of dishonesty is very distinct and vivid." Now a change of pace to refresh interest: "Yet the impression is common, almost universal." And a second change, almost immediately, to usher in the second long sentence, which carries the conclusion: "Let no young man choosing the law ..."

The paragraph moves without a false step, neither hurried nor drowsy; and by its movement, like one who leads another in the dance, it catches up our thought and swings it into willing compliance. The ear notes at the same time that none of the sounds grate or clash: The piece is sayable like a speech in a great play; the music is manly, the alliterations are few and natural. Indeed, the paragraph seems to have come into being spontaneously as the readiest incarnation of Lincoln's thoughts.

From hints here and there, one gathers that Lincoln wrote slowly—meaning, by writing, the physical act of forming letters on paper. This would augment the desirability of being brief. Lincoln wrote before the typewriter and the dictating machine, and wanting to put all his meaning into one or two lucid sentences, he thought before he wrote. The great compression came after he had, lawyerlike, excluded alternatives and hit upon right order and emphasis.

Obviously this style would make use of skips and connections unsuited to speechmaking. The member of the cabinet who received a terse memorandum had it before him to make out at leisure. But an audience requires a looser texture, just as it requires a more measured delivery. This difference between the written and the spoken word lends color to the cliché that if Lincoln had a style, he developed it in his presidential years. Actually, Lincoln, like an artist, adapted his means to the occasion. There was no pathos in him before pathos was due. When he supposed his audience intellectually alert—as was the famous gathering at Cooper Union in 1860—he gave them his concentrated prose. We may take as a sample a part of the passage where he addresses the South:

> "Again, you say we have made the slavery question more prominent than it formerly was. We deny it. We admit that it is more prominent, but we deny that we made it so. It was not we, but you, who discarded the old policy of the fathers. We resisted, and still resist, your innovation; and thence comes the greater prominence of the question. Would you have that question reduced to its former proportions? Go back to that old policy. What has been, will be again, under the same conditions. If you would have the peace of the old times, readopt the precepts and policy of the old times."

This is wonderfully clear and precise and demonstrative, but two hours of equally succinct argument would tax any but the most athletic audience. Lincoln gambled on the New Yorkers' agility of mind, and won. But we should not be surprised that in the debates with Stephen A. Douglas, a year and a half before, we find the manner different. Those wrangles lasted three hours, and the necessity for each speaker to interweave prepared statements of policy with improvised rebuttals of charges and "points" gives these productions a coarser grain. Yet on Lincoln's side, the same artist mind is plainly at work:

> "Senator Douglas is of world-wide renown. All the anxious politicians of his party, or who have been of his party for years past, have been looking upon him as certainly, at no distant day, to be the President of the United States. They have seen in his round, jolly, fruitful face, post offices, land offices, marshalships, and cabinet appointments, chargéships and foreign missions, bursting and sprouting out in wonderful exuberance ready to be laid hold of by their greedy hands."

The man who could lay the ground for a splendid yet catchy metaphor about political plums by describing Douglas's face as round, jolly and *fruitful* is not a man to be thought merely lucky in the handling of words. The debates abound in happy turns, but read less well than Lincoln's more compact productions. Often, Douglas's words are more polished:

> "We have existed and prospered from that day to this thus divided and have increased with a rapidity never before equaled in wealth, the extension of territory, and all the elements of power and greatness, until we have become the first nation on the face of the globe. Why can we not thus continue to prosper?"

It is a mistake to underrate Douglas's skill, which was that of a professional. Lincoln's genius needs no heightening through lowering others. Douglas was smooth and adroit, and his arguments were effective, since Lincoln was defeated. But Douglas, unlike Lincoln, sounds like anybody else.

Lincoln's extraordinary power was to make his spirit felt, a power I attribute to his peculiar relation to himself. He regarded his face and physique with amusement and dismay, his mind and destiny with wonder. Seeming clumsy and diffident, he also showed a calm superiority which he expressed as if one half of a double man were talking about the other.

In conduct this detachment was the source of his saintlike forbearance; in his art it yielded the rare quality of elegance. Nowhere is this link between style and emotional distance clearer than in the farewell Lincoln spoke to his friends in Springfield before leaving for Washington. A single magical word, easy to pass over carelessly, holds the clue:

"My friends: No one, not in my situation, can appreciate my feeling of sadness at this parting. To this place, and the kindness of these people, I owe everything . . ." If we stop to think, we ask: "This place"?—yes. But why "*these* people"? Why not "you people," whom he was addressing from the train platform, or "this place and the kindness of *its* people"? It is not, certainly, the mere parallel of *this* and *these* that commanded the choice. "These" is a stroke of genius which betrays Lincoln's isolation from the action itself—Lincoln talking to himself about the place and the people whom he was leaving, foreboding the possibility of his never returning, and closing the fifteen lines with one of the greatest cadences in English speech: "To His care commending you, as I hope in your prayers you will commend me, I bid you an affectionate farewell."

The four main qualities of Lincoln's literary art—precision, vernacular ease, rhythmical virtuosity and elegance—may at a century's remove seem alien to our tastes. Yet it seems no less odd to question their use and interest to the present when one considers one continuing strain in our literature. Lincoln's example, plainly, helped to break the monopoly of the dealers in literary plush. After Lincoln comes Mark Twain, and out of Mark Twain come contemporaries of ours as diverse as Sherwood Anderson, H.L. Mencken and Ernest Hemingway. Lincoln's use of his style for the intimate genre and for the sublime was his alone; but his workaday style is the American style par excellence.

A Narrative of the Life of Frederick Douglass, a Slave
(Frederick Douglass)

"The Slave"
by Frederic May Holland, in
Frederick Douglass: The Colored Orator (1891)

INTRODUCTION

In this early overview to Frederick Douglass's story, Frederic
Holland May introduces readers to this slave narrative that
records Douglass's emancipation through literacy and exam-
ines the origins and development of his rhetorical style.

"It has been a source of great annoyance to me, never to have a
birthday," says Mr. Douglass, in a private letter. He supposes that he
was born in February, 1817; but no one knows the day of his birth
or his father's name. Such trifles were seldom recorded of slaves.
His mother, Harriet Bailey, was one of the five daughters of Isaac
and Betsy Bailey; and as slaves were not often permitted to own a
surname, this must have been one of the old families of Maryland.
Grandmother Betty was especially honored for her skill in planting
sweet potatoes, as well as in making and handling nets for taking
shad and herring. When we find further that the village where she

---

Holland, Frederic May. "The Slave." *Frederick Douglass: The Colored Orator.*
London: Funk & Wagnalls Company, 1891. 7–31.

resided still bore the aboriginal name, Tuckahoe, we may believe that
it was from her, that her grandson derived those high cheek bones,
and other peculiarities of physiognomy, which often caused him to
be mistaken for an Indian in later life. His first master sometimes
called him "My little Indian boy," and his whole history shows that
he sprang from a race of warriors, who had rather die than be slaves.
His oratorical power should be ascribed to his African descent, or to
his European parentage. He himself attributes his love of letters to
the native genius of his mother, who was the only colored person able
to read in the whole village. This rare accomplishment suggests the
probability that she had once been something more than a field hand.
Her son saw her so seldom, however, and lost her so early, that he may
have overestimated her ability, in consequence partly of gratitude and
partly of a popular theory, about the preponderating influence over
great men of gifted mothers, which long investigation justifies my
calling extravagant. Inheritance of genius has come, in actual fact, at
least as much from the father as from the mother; and in the most
illustrious instances it has come from both sides. I suspect that there is
some foundation for the rumor, that the father in this case was a noted
politician. White he undoubtedly was, for the son was of much lighter
color than his mother, whose "deep black, glossy" features, are said by
him to have resembled those of King Rameses the Great, on page 157
of "Prichard's Natural History of Man."

She called him Frederick Augustus Washington Bailey; but after
his escape he took the name which he has made famous. She had an
older son, Perry, and four daughters; but none of them, I think, was
endowed with his peculiar genius. Perhaps there was a different father.
Her services were too valuable for her to be permitted to waste her
time on her children, and Douglass does not remember having ever
seen her before he was six years old.

His earliest memories are of his grandmother's log cabin in his
native village, Tuckahoe, on the bank of the Choptank River, in Talbot
County, on the eastern shore of Maryland. The floor and chimney
were of clay, and there were no windows, nor any bedsteads, except
rails flung over the cross-beams. Food was coarse, but it was abundant,
and the little boy was never scolded for playing in the dirt, or getting
his clothes wet, or not learning his lessons, or using his knife and fork
awkwardly. In fact, he had no lessons, or knife and fork, and scarcely
any clothing, to be troubled about. Year after year went by, during

which he was as free and happy as the squirrels he saw running up the trees, or the minnows for which he used to fish in the mill-pond. His grandmother was always kind, and the only cloud upon his path was the fear of being taken from her, as his brother and his sisters had been. He dreaded to find himself growing taller, and at last the terrible day came.

One summer morning, before he was seven, she took his hand in hers, and led him, or carried him on her shoulder, over the twelve miles which lay between Tuckahoe and the house of their master, Captain Anthony. This man owned three farms in Tuckahoe, and about thirty slaves; but his time was mainly occupied in managing the estates of Colonel Lloyd, who had a thousand slaves and twenty or thirty different farms. All the overseers were under the control of Captain Anthony, whose plain brick house stood near the stately mansion of Colonel Lloyd, on the latter's home plantation, on the banks of the Wye, which flows into Chesapeake Bay, about thirty-five miles southeast of Baltimore.

At the "great house" the Lloyds lived in such luxury as the little boy had never dreamed of; but the suffering outside was almost inde-scribable. Most of the slaves were driven out into the field at the first sign of dawn, with lashes for those who came last; and they were kept there until it was too dark to work. The mending and cooking were done during the night, and the food was carried out to be eaten in the field, where the babies were nursed, when the mothers could not be spared time to go home. There was no public opinion in Talbot County to hinder the worst of cruelties. Our hero saw his Aunt Esther receive from his master, because he was jealous and she loved another slave, thirty or forty stripes, each of which drew screams and blood. One of his cousins once walked the twelve miles from Tuck-ahoe, to show how a drunken overseer had gashed her shoulders with his cowhide, and struck her such a blow over the head with his stick as left her face covered with blood. Her master only told her to tramp back at once or he would take the rest of her skin off her back himself. Such floggings were frequent, and a slave who tried to escape one by running into the creek, was shot down there by the overseer, on the very plantation where the little Frederick was kept. His wife's cousin, a girl of fifteen, was beaten to death in her sleep by her mistress for being unable to hear the cry of a baby who had kept her up night after night. Murders of slaves were frequent on the Eastern Shore, but there was no punishment and little blame. The worst sufferings of the slaves, however, seem to have come from lack of sleep and food. The men and women were given about a quarter of a pound of pork, or a little fish, daily, a peck of coarse corn-meal per week, and nothing else, except a little salt. The corn-cake was full of bran, and covered so thickly, with ashes that no Northerner could eat it. Bed there was none, only a blanket for each adult. The children had no blanket, nor any clothes, except a pair of shirts of sackcloth for each child every year. Whole flocks of little boys and girls, from five to ten years old, might be seen running naked around the "great house," or huddled together in the sun during the frosty days of March.

The little Frederick had to sleep on cold nights with his head and shoulders in a sack, and his feet had cracks big enough to hold a penholder. His share of the mush, which a dozen children at Captain Anthony's ate like pigs out of a trough on the kitchen floor, was so scanty that he was often pinched with hunger. He used to run to pick up the little bones which were flung out for the cats, and he often fought with the dog for the crumbs which fell from the kitchen table. The very taste of white bread was unknown to him; but he was fascinated by the sight of those snowy biscuits, baked in a quick oven, out of unleavened flour, which he saw carried to the Lloyds' table, and he made up his mind that he would have some to eat every morning when he was a man. This ambition has been so far satisfied that precisely such biscuits have been regularly set before him for his Sunday breakfast at Cedar Hill.

The worst of it was that the cook, Aunt Katy, often whipped him or made him go all day without food, except a wretched breakfast. One night, when he had been treated thus and was too hungry to sleep, he managed to steal a few kernels of Indian corn and roast them in the fire. Just as he was about to eat them, his mother came in and took him in her arms. She had walked twelve miles to see him, and her indignation, at hearing that Aunt Katy threatened to starve the life out of him, was loud and fierce. He ate the large ginger cake she gave him, and felt prouder, as he sat on her knee, than a king on his throne. He soon dropped off to sleep, however; before he awoke, his mother had to go back to her work; and he never saw her again, for he was not allowed to stand beside her dying bed. These visits had been rare, for it could only have been under unusually favorable circumstances that she was able to travel the twenty-four miles in a single night.

These scenes show what was the early life of "Cap'n Ant'ney Fed," as he was called in the jargon of the plantation, where the sign of the possessive case was a luxury unknown to the slaves. He was switched into repeating the Lord's Prayer, but had no other religious training, except the information that "God up in the sky" had made white men to be masters and black people to be slaves, and that He knew what was best for them all. The child could not believe that the slaves were as well off as they ought to be, and he used to sit and wonder how slavery could exist if God was good. His trouble often made him weep, and his perplexity was increased by observing that God had not made, by any means, slaves of all the blacks, or slaveholders of all the whites. Light broke in upon his troubled mind as he found that some of his fellow-slaves had been stolen from homes where they were free, and others were children of fathers and mothers who had been thus brought into bondage. Clearly it was man who was responsible, not God. The little boy's Aunt Jennie suddenly disappeared with her husband, and it was whispered about that they had run away to the free States, and would henceforth be free. Before he was eight years old he made up his mind that he would, some day, do what they did. No wonder, for, as he said in 1855, he became "just as well aware of the unjust, unnatural, and murderous character of slavery when nine years old, as I am now."

Among the few bright spots in Fred's plantation life was the kindness of his master's daughter, Mrs. Thomas Auld, still called "Miss Lucretia" by the slaves. When he had a fight with another slave-boy, and came home roaring with pain, and streaming with blood from a wound which left the sign of the cross upon his forehead, it was she who washed away the blood, put on balsam, and bound up the wound. When he was unusually hungry he used to go and sing under her window, and she would give him a slice of bread and butter. It may have been her intercession which saved his boyish spirit from being crushed into submission to his lot, and gave him the key to the prison door.

In the summer of 1825, soon after he had begun his ninth year, she told him that he was to go to Baltimore, which seemed like heaven to the slaves on the Eastern Shore. The next three days were the happiest he had ever known, and were spent mainly in the creek, where he was trying to wash the dead skin off his feet and knees. "Miss Lucretia" had told him she would give him a pair of trousers if he could get himself clean. He had no home to regret, and he hardly dared to go to sleep, for fear he might be left behind.

Early on a Saturday morning he was able to look for the last time, as he hoped, on the plantation, as the sloop carried him over Chesapeake Bay toward Baltimore. He arrived there on Sunday morning and was kindly received by his new Mistress, Mrs. Hugh Auld, sister-in-law of Lucretia's husband Thomas. "Miss Sopha," as the boy called her, gave him a comfortable bed, good clothes, and palatable food, while he had nothing harder to do than to run errands and take care of her son, little Tommy. The three soon grew very fond of each other, and she even granted a request, made under circumstances described thus, in a speech made at Belfast, in 1846:

> I remember the first time I ever heard the Bible read, and from that time I trace my first desire to learn to read. I was over seven years old; my master had gone out one Sunday night, the children had gone to bed. I had crawled under the center table and had fallen asleep, when my mistress commenced to read the Bible aloud, so loud that she waked me. She waked me to sleep no more. I have found since that the chapter she then read was the first of Job. I remember my sympathy for the good old man, and my anxiety to learn more about him led me to ask my mistress to teach me to read.

She complied gladly, and was soon looking forward to see him reading the Bible. Her joy led her to tell her husband, but he at once forbade any more lessons, telling her that learning would spoil any nigger, and that if this one should ever be taught to read the Bible, there would be no keeping him a slave.

This was said in Fred's hearing, and it proved the best lesson he ever had. He heard that knowledge would prevent his remaining a slave, and at once he made up his mind to get all he could. "Miss Sopha" not only taught him no more, but would snatch away any book or newspaper she might see in his hand, while she took great care never to leave him alone with anything he could read. He turned the street into a school-room, and made his white playmates his teachers. He always carried Webster's spelling-book in his pocket, and also bread enough to pay the hungry little boys he met for giving him lessons. He used now and then to ask these white boys if it was right for him to be a slave, and they always agreed with him that it was not. Finding them interested in the "Columbian Orator," he bought a copy with fifty cents, earned by blacking boots in the street. Here he found a dialogue between a runaway slave, just recaptured, and his master. The negro demonstrated the injustice of slavery with such power that he was emancipated. Think how eagerly this was read by the boy of thirteen! He entered with equal zeal into the denunciations of oppression by great orators, and especially by Sheridan in his demand for Catholic emancipation. The speeches of Chatham and Fox, too, in behalf of America, helped him to understand the rights of man. He was all ears when he heard any one speak of slavery, and the heat which his master and other white men showed against Abolitionists made him very curious to know who they were. Evidently they had something to do with slavery, but what could it be? At last he found out from one of the city newspapers, probably in February, 1833, when there was much agitation, that they had been sending petitions to Congress, asking for the abolition of the slave trade between States, as well as of slavery itself in the District of Columbia. Thenceforth he knew that he was not without friends upon the earth. This idea assumed a practicable form, when an Irishman repaid him, for helping to unload a boat full of stones, by telling him that he need only go North to be as free as anybody.

His confidence that he would finally gain both freedom and knowledge was much increased by an interest in religion, which became very strong before he was fourteen. At this time he used to pick up stray pages of the Bible in the gutter, and wash and dry them, in order to pore over them in secret. His leisure was now mostly spent either in attending prayer-meetings, or in holding private worship with a good old colored man, who prayed almost without ceasing, even when on his dray. The boy taught the old man how to make out the hard words, and, in return was shown something of their meaning. Both felt sure that the Lord would call Frederick in due time to preach the Gospel; and the exhortation "to wait in trust and patience until the good time came," may have done much to keep him from making a premature attempt to escape. His master tried in vain to break up the intimacy by threats of the lash. The young church-member resented bitterly the persecution, as he called it; and when the cholera smote Baltimore, in 1833, he thought that the Lord was punishing the whites for holding his people in bondage.

One reason that Frederick did not run away then, was that he wished first to learn how to write a pass for himself. He had now exchanged his easy life, of waiting on "Miss Sopha" and little Tommy, for regular work in Mr. Auld's ship-yard. He noticed that the carpenters marked each piece of timber with a capital letter, S. L. A. or F.; and he soon found that these were the initials of the words "Starboard," "Larboard," "Aft," and "Forward." While the men were at dinner, he taught himself to make these four letters. Then he challenged the white boys to "beat that," and thus made them show him other letters. Thus he "learned to write on board fences, making some of his early capitals with their heads downwards and looking the wrong way." By and by he managed to copy the italics out of the spelling-book. He even ventured, at great risk of a flogging, to take the old writing-books which Master Tommy had brought home from school, and copy off line after line in the vacant spaces. He secretly carried a flour barrel and a chair into the kitchen loft, where he slept, and there he used to work late into the night, copying from the Bible and the Methodist hymn-book.

While the young slave was preparing himself for freedom, he became, in consequence of the death of "Miss Lucretia" and her father, the property of her husband, Captain Thomas Auld. His new master soon quarreled with his brother in Baltimore, and took his chattel away. This was in March, 1833, when Captain Auld had taken up his residence at St. Michael's, a fishing village on the Bay, about forty miles from Baltimore. He had taken a second wife; and her father, a rich slaveholder named Hamilton, lived a few miles away. The kitchen at St. Michael's was not very bountifully supplied; and the appetite of the growing boy was keen enough to tempt him to theft.

Whatever scruples the young aspirant for the ministry felt were quieted by this ingenious argument. Captain Auld's meat continued to be his, after it was taken out of one of his tubs and put into another; so there really was no stealing. As for the neighbors, they were accomplices in deliberately robbing the laborer of his reward, and he was justified in protecting himself against starvation at their expense. Another way in which he used to supply himself with food was letting loose his master's horse. The animal would always dash off to its former stable, on the Hamilton plantation, five miles off. The groom would have to be sent to bring him back, and he would return with bread enough to make him comfortable for a day or two. He gave additional offence by constantly speaking to Mr. Auld, or of him to Mrs. Auld, by his old title, "Captain," and not saying "Master," as was desired by the wife especially. Of course, this led to frequent whippings.

Mrs. Auld was a devout member of the church, and Thomas became one at a camp-meeting that August; but Frederick's new brother disappointed all his hopes of better treatment than before. He ventured, soon after the conversion, to help teach a little Sunday-school. A dozen old spelling-books and a few Testaments were collected. Twenty children came together the first day, and the young teacher thought he had now found something worth living for. Scarcely had school begun on the second Sunday, however, when in rushed a mob, headed by Master Thomas and two Methodist class-leaders. The scholars were driven away with sticks and stones, and forbidden ever to meet again, for they were black. Frederick was told that he wanted to be like Nat Turner, who led a bloody insurrection in Southampton, Va., 1831, and that he would get as many balls in his body as Nat had, if he did not look out. He had seen slave girls treated with unusual cruelty by a pious mistress in Baltimore, and he was soon to have new proof of how little could be done, even by religion, to lessen the essential wickedness of slavery.

The completion of his industrial education was intrusted by Brother Auld to Brother Covey, a devout neighbor, famous for success in breaking unruly slaves. The morning of the first of January, 1834, found the poor boy trudging along, with his little bundle at the end of his stick, to the new master with whom that year must be spent. Covey, too, was a Methodist, and made his slaves hear a great deal of religious talk on Sunday, as well as a short prayer every morning and a long prayer every night. Frederick was depended upon to lead the singing, but he often failed to do so; for such worship seemed to him a mockery. He was no longer starved, but he was overworked systematically, and often kept in the field until almost midnight. It was never too hot or too cold for out-door work—it could never rain, blow, snow, or hail too hard. The longest days were too short, he says, for his master, and the shortest nights were too long. Covey relied mainly on hard work for breaking slaves. When he chose to set them an example, he would "make everything fly before him." He was an experienced overseer, and had peculiar skill in watching his slaves, when they thought him far away, and creeping out upon them unexpectedly. They spoke of him to each other as "the snake," and felt as if they were always under his cruel eye.

The lash was only a secondary feature of his plan; but it was not left out. Frederick had been with him but three days when he was sent, on one of the coldest mornings of January, with a pair of oxen, to bring in wood from the forest. He had never driven oxen before, and these were scarcely broken in. Covey himself would not have dared to take them into the woods, until he had let them work off some of their wildness in the open field. The young driver was told to go to the woods; and thither he went, without daring to make objections. The oxen ran all the way over the fields, pulling him along at the end of the rope with which he was ordered to keep them from running away. When they got in among the trees, they took fright, and rushed about wildly, so that he expected to be dashed to death. At last they stopped, entangled in sapplings, and with the body of the cart, the wheels, and the tongue lying scattered about. It took hard work to get the pieces together and release the oxen. On their way out of the wood they ran away once more, despite a heavy load, broke the gate into splinters, and nearly crushed the driver between the wheel and the post. It was noon when he reached the house, but he was sent back at once with the cart to the woods. Covey followed, overtook him there, and said he would teach him how to waste time and break gates. He cut from a black gum-tree three young shoots, from four to six feet long, such as are used for ox-goads. Then he commanded the slave to take off his clothes. No heed was given to the order; Covey tore them off himself. The tough goads were worn out, one by one, and such sores were left on the back as kept open, under the coarse shirt, for weeks. This was the first instance of what happened every few days for six months.

Douglass says it was then, if at any one time, more than another, that he was "made to drink the bitterest dregs of slavery.""A few months of this discipline tamed me." ... "I was broken in body, soul and spirit." ... "My natural elasticity was crushed; my intellect languished; the disposition to read departed; the dark night of slavery closed in upon me; and behold a man transformed into a brute!" ... "I had neither sufficient time in which to eat or sleep, except on Sunday." ... "I spent this in a sort of beast-like stupor, between sleeping and waking under some large tree." ... "I was sometimes prompted to take my life, and that of Covey, but was prevented by a combination of hope and fear." ... "The over-work, and the brutal chastisement, combined with that ever-gnawing and soul-devouring thought, 'I am a slave—a slave for life—a slave with no rational ground to hope for freedom,' rendered me a living embodiment of mental and physical wretchedness."

On one of the hottest Friday afternoons in August Covey was thrashing out his wheat in barbaric fashion. Horses were treading it loose from the straw; and Frederick was carrying the mixture of wheat, chaff and dirt to the fan. He was in a hurry, for he was to have time to go fishing, if the work was finished before sunset. About three o'clock he broke down, with no strength left, an extreme dizziness, and a violent headache. The fanning had to stop, for every hand was needed for the work. Covey found him lying by the fence, and, with a savage kick in the side, bade him rise. He tried to, but fell back. Another heavy kick brought him to his feet; but as soon as he stooped to pick up the tub in which he had been carrying food for the fan, he fell to the ground, utterly helpless. Then Brother Covey took up the hickory club with which the wheat had been struck off level with the sides of the measure, and gave him such a wound on the head as made blood run freely, saying, "If you have got the headache, I'll cure you." He was still unable to rise, and was left bleeding by the fence.

His head was soon relieved by the flow of blood; and he resolved to go and complain to Captain Auld. He started up while Covey was looking another way, and gained the woods. There he had to lie down, for his strength failed him. At last the bleeding ceased, and he made his way barefoot, through bogs and briars, to St. Michael's. It took him five hours to make the seven or eight miles; and Auld insisted on his going back again to the good, religious man. He did so the next morning, and before the house he met Covey, with rope and cowhide, ready for him. He had but just time to get through the corn into the woods. There he lay down exhausted, for he had lost much blood and eaten nothing since noon the day before. All day he lay unpursued, for it was hoped that hunger would bring him back. His recent experiences with members of his church made prayer seem useless. There he lay all day in pain and despair.

During the night another slave came by, on his way to spend Sunday with his wife. The good couple fed and sheltered the sufferer, at the risk of being treated in the same way. Sandy, as his benefactor was named, advised him not to attempt an escape, which would then have been very difficult, but to trust to the magic power of a root, whose wearer ran no danger of being whipped by any white man. The incredulous listener was reminded that all his book learning had not protected him. Sunday morning found him with his pocket full of roots in front of Covey's house. He was kindly received, for the good man was about to go to church. While regaining his strength, he resolved upon a course worthy of his white as well as of his Indian blood. He knew that those slaves who could be whipped easiest were whipped oftenest; and he felt that he had listened too blindly to sermons in which non-resistance was enjoined as the peculiar virtue of the colored race. "My hands," he says, "were no longer tied by my religion." He had made up his mind to risk being sold South, or incurring the penalty of the State law, which provided that any slave who resisted his master should be hung, and then have his head cut off and set up, with the four quarters of his body, in prominent places.

Long before daylight the next morning he was called out and sent to feed the horses. As he was going up to the loft in the stable, Covey sneaked in behind and tried to slip a rope around his leg, in order to tie him up for a flogging. He fell heavily, but leaped up at once and sprang at his master's throat. There the strong black fingers kept their grasp until the nails drew blood. The white man tried to strike; but every blow was parried, though none was struck in return. He closed with the slave, but went down again and again upon the floor. "Are you going to resist, you scoundrel?" "Yes, sir," was the steady answer. Covey called his cousin to his assistance; but the white boy was at once doubled up with pain by the black boy's kick. "Are you going to keep this up?" "Yes, indeed, come what may. You have treated me like a brute the last six months, and I shall stand it no longer." Covey dragged him out of the stable to a stick of wood, with which he meant to knock him down. Just as he stooped to pick it up, he was seized by the black hands and flung out his full length into the cow-yard. Another slave now came up, and was commanded to take hold of the rebel. He at first pretended not to understand the order, and finally said, "My master hired me here to work, and not to help you whip Frederick." This man's owner would not let him be flogged unless he deserved it; and the two were left to fight it out. The only slave whom Covey owned was a woman who had been avowedly bought for breeding. She, too, was called upon for aid as she came in to milk the cows; and she, too, refused, though she knew she must suffer for it. For two hours the fight had gone on, and Covey had not been able to draw a single drop of blood, while blood had been drawn from him. He had not been able to whip the slave; but at last he said, "Now, go to your work; I should not have whipped you half so much, if you had not resisted." He never tried it again, although he had plenty of opportunity, and even provocation, during the next six months.

Douglass is right in calling this the turning point in his life as a slave. It made him a man instead of a timid boy, "a freeman, in fact, while I remained a slave in form." He was four years more in bondage, but he was never again whipped. It was several times attempted, but without success. Not the slightest punishment was inflicted for his resisting Covey. The latter probably kept his defeat as much of a secret as possible, lest his reputation as a slave-breaker should be forfeited. Captain Auld may have felt even then what he acknowledged forty years afterwards, on his death-bed, to his visitor, then Marshal Douglass, that he always thought him too smart to be a slave.

At all events he was hired out, for the two years after that with Brother Covey, 1835 and 1836, to a neighbor who seldom whipped his slaves, and always gave them plenty of time to sleep and eat, while the supply of food was never stinted. Mr. Freeland did not profess religion, but he was a much better master than the church-members just mentioned, or two ministers in Talbot County, about whom a good deal is said in "My Bondage and My Freedom." The author had reason to think that the religion of slaveholders often put their consciences to sleep. He did not, however, give up all idea of preaching some day himself, and he used, when every one else slept, to try to prepare for the pulpit by going out to the pigs and talking to them as "Dear Brethren." It was much more proper for him to say so to pigs than to white men, according to the laws of the land, and the opinions most revered throughout the United States. He was only a field-hand, and reading matter was more out of reach than in Baltimore. He did, however, manage to re-open his Sunday-school, and this time it escaped attack, although it numbered more than forty scholars. Many learned to read, either there or during the three evenings a week which were devoted to this work in winter; and the teacher afterward met several of his former pupils as freemen.

This employment made the first year pass pleasantly, but early in 1836, the position of a slave, even in this mild form, began to seem intolerable to the young agitator; and the ideas which he had learned from the "Columbian Orator," in Baltimore, were earnestly set forth to his companions. Two of the slaves who labored beside him were fully aroused by his passionate declamations on the rights of man and

the glories of liberty. Two other young men on the plantation of his
owner's father-in-law, Mr. Hamilton, joined them. All agreed to set at
naught the teachings of the pulpit, and the dangers which threatened
fugitives. The conspirators held frequent meetings, and kept up each
other's zeal by songs with a secret meaning, like

"I am bound for the land of Canaan,
I don't expect to stay much longer here," etc.

According to the plan invented by our hero, they were going to
take a large canoe, belonging to Mr. Hamilton, sail and paddle to the
head of the bay, seventy miles off, and then make their way on foot to
the North. The only free city known to them, even by name, was New
York. The leader had written passes permitting the bearers to spend
the Easter holidays in Baltimore, and they were getting ready to start
on the Saturday evening previous. That morning, just as Frederick
had been called in from the field for breakfast, he saw Mr. Hamilton
gallop up to the house; three other white men followed on horseback;
and after them walked two negroes whose hands were tied. He saw
that he was betrayed and that his best plan was to submit, quietly. One
of Mr. Freeland's slaves followed his example, but the other fought
bravely, though pistols were pointed against his heart. The scuffle
gave the writer of the passes a chance to burn his own unobserved,
and the others were eaten, by his advice, as the slaves were dragged
along the road by the mounted constables. Mr. Freeland's mother had
supplied the slaves whom he owned with food, while she scolded the
"long-legged yellow devil," who had made them think of running
away. They stopped during the tramp of fifteen miles at his master's
store, and there, as the leader directed, they all protested that they had
not the slightest intention of absconding, and asked indignantly what
evidence there was against them. At last they reached Easton, the
county seat, and were locked up in the jail. They could expect nothing
better than to be sold to die in the rice swamps. Mr. Freeland and Mr.
Hamilton had the slaves they owned released, however, after the holidays were over, and took them back. The ring-leader was left behind.
Captain Auld would have let him work out the year with Mr. Freeland,
but Hamilton declared that he would shoot the dangerous fellow if he
appeared again in that neighborhood. He was the only slave there who
could read and write. Large sums were offered by the negro-traders,

but Auld declared that money would not tempt him to sell Frederick South. Finally he was sent to Baltimore to learn a trade, and promised that, if he would behave himself, he should be emancipated at twenty-five. He had resisted his master with success, he had taken the lead in a plot to run away, and his courage did not go without its reward.

Three years previous he had left Baltimore an unruly boy. He came back a strong man, resolved to protect himself against injury, and to use the first good opportunity for setting himself free. During the rest of 1836 he worked as apprentice in a large ship-yard, where he was at the beck and call of seventy-five carpenters. These white men, just before he entered the yard, had been led by fear of lower wages to refuse to let colored carpenters work there any longer; and now they encouraged the white apprentices to pick quarrels with the new nigger. In one of these he would have lost his life if he had not succeeded in parrying a blow from an adze. Another time he flung the man who struck him into the dock. Whenever he was struck he struck back again, and thus he held his own for about eight months. At last, the man who had been ducked came at him with three other apprentices. One was in front, armed with a brick, one on each side, and the fourth behind with a heavy hand-spike. They closed in upon him. He defended himself, but a blow from the hand-spike stunned him and brought him to the ground. Then all four fell upon him with their fists, while the carpenters shouted: "Kill the d—d nigger! He struck a white man!" By and bye he came to himself and rose to his hands and knees. As he did so he got a kick in the left eye which closed it completely. Then they left him, but even then he would have run after them with the hand-spike if the carpenters had not interfered.

This scene deserves attention, on account of his dauntless courage. The worst of it is, that he could get no protection from the law. He had been put once more under the charge of his master's brother, Hugh Auld; but when this gentleman applied for a warrant, the magistrate refused to issue one, unless white witnesses would come forward. Neither the word of the colored man, nor the sight of his wounds, was of the slightest importance. The laws of Maryland were for the protection of whites. All that Mr. Auld could do for the slave was to take him, as soon as his wounds had healed, into the yard where he was foreman. There the apprentice became an expert calker, and was able, before the end of 1837, to earn a dollar and a half a day, the highest wages paid to men of that trade in Baltimore. He was allowed to get a job where he could, and to collect the money; but he had to hand over every cent he received. He saw more plainly than before that slaves were not protected, but plundered.

His literary education had stood still while he was away from Baltimore; but now he met colored people who knew more than he did. Some of them were able to teach him geography and arithmetic. The young freedmen even permitted him to enter a club from which other slaves were excluded, "The East Baltimore Mutual Improvement Society;" and he took a prominent part in its debates. He also, in all probability, spoke often in religious meetings; and among his delighted hearers may be supposed to have been Anna Murray, a free woman of color, who afterward became his wife.

As his condition and prospects improved, his desire for freedom grew still stronger; and he longed to have money enough of his own to be able to escape. In May, 1838, he persuaded Hugh Auld to let him hire his time. He had to buy his tools and clothes, pay his board, and hand over three dollars a week, whether work was good or bad. He succeeded in carrying out the bargain and in laying aside some money. One Saturday evening in August, instead of going to Mr. Auld with the sum due, he went off with a party of friends to camp-meeting, and did not return before Sunday night. The privilege of hiring out was taken away, in punishment; and his indignation led him to spend the next week in idleness. On Saturday night there was a violent quarrel in consequence of his having no money to hand over; but, fortunately for him, they did not get to blows. The next day he made up his mind to go to work early Monday morning, to make Master Hugh as well satisfied as possible with him during that week, and the two following, and then to run away.

[...] Thus far we have seen him become familiar with some of the best, as well as the worst, aspects of slavery. He had been a half-starved boy, running wild on a plantation, a petted house-servant, a field-hand, first under a master who fed him so poorly that he was obliged to steal, then under a professional negro-breaker, who over-worked him systematically, and whipped him cruelly, until he saved himself from more torture by making a resistance which might have brought him to the gallows. The result was his coming under a master who gave him plenty of food and rest, and never struck him. His attempt to escape, in company with other slaves, whom he had induced to join him, sent him back to Baltimore, where he was cruelly treated at first, but was soon able to learn a good trade and to support himself in almost complete liberty. He had worked his way upward by his own strength and courage, going through fight after fight, with his life in his hand. He had taught himself not only to read and write, but to speak effectively. He knew what to say about slavery, and how to say it. The principal thing which he needed to do in order to reach the platform was to break his chain.

ONE DAY IN THE LIFE OF IVAN DENISOVICH
(ALEKSANDR SOLZHENITSYN)

"Art isn't what you do, it's how you do it': Enslavement, Ideology, and Emancipation in Solzhenitsyn's *One Day in the Life of Ivan Denisovich*"
by John Becker, Independent Scholar

One Day in the Life of Ivan Denisovich (1962), the first novel of Aleksandr Solzhenitsyn, is the story of prisoner Shcha-854, Ivan Denisovich Shukhov, who is detained in a Soviet forced labor camp. The novel was one of the first works published in the Soviet Union to provide a detailed description of the cruelties and hardships suffered by those enslaved within the Soviet convict labor system in remote settlements far away from their families, as was Solzhenitsyn, who was imprisoned in Ekibastuzlag in northeastern Kazakhstan. As *One Day* records such atrocities, the novel also marks an unprecedented easing of the Communist Party's strict censorship policies under the leadership of Stalin's successor Nikita Khrushchev. Solzhenitsyn's narrative shows camp life as barbarous, yet Shukhov's optimistic refrains ring throughout the last half of the novel; he takes pride in his work and dreams of being free. Though the narrative ends with Shukhov counting off one day of his enslavement, he believes in emancipation: the hope of reaching exile, the promise of an extra portion of nettle gruel, a sick day—anything that adds to his chances of survival.

One Day marked a radical change in Society literary culture with its departure from the state-enforced doctrines of socialist realism—a set of guidelines codified by Stalin's cultural advisor Andrei Zhdanov to discourage artists from experimentation that either deviated from honest and realistic portrayals of life or lacked the proper revolutionary fervor. Socialist realist art is intended to educate the working class and to foster the international uprising of workers Marx prophesied. State-endorsed theorizers of socialist realism might have been pleased with Shukhov's optimistic refrains throughout the last half of the novel, as well as the pride he takes in his work. Shukhov evinces a remarkably intimate relationship with his bricklaying, despite knowing he will probably not be assigned to finish the work he has begun. Solzhenitsyn's protagonist—dehumanized as he is by the brutal workings of the camp labor machine—takes pride in his work. Further, despite the narrator's reiterations that a *zek's* (prisoner's) worst enemy is another *zek*, Shukhov empathizes with many of his fellow prisoners. While being openly hostile to the legacy of Stalin—which Khrushchev and others were in the process of dismantling at the time of *One Day's* publication—Solzhenitsyn's story denounces the most sacred beliefs of Soviet communism.

Rather than portraying his subject matter objectively, Solzhenitsyn draws upon the Russian *skaz* tradition, a genre of folk literature characterized by a fictitious narrator and vernacular language. Solzhenitsyn relates the events of the day through the limited perspective of a simple-minded peasant while a reporting narrator relays the horrid details of prison life. Both the narrator and the novel's protagonist use prison camp jargon as well as old Russian mannerisms and figures of speech—literary devices that complicate the enlightened, historical perspective championed by socialist realism. Solzhenitsyn complicates matters by switching artfully between his third-person narrator's point of view and Shukhov's. One example of the abrupt way Solzhenitsyn moves from third-person reportage to Shukhov's perception of events occurs when he enters the mess hut for breakfast (italics have been added to mark the shift):

> Two or three workers from every gang shouted and shoved their way through the mob, carrying bowls of skilly and gruel on wooden trays and looking for a space to put them down on. *Must be deaf, the blockhead, take that for bumping the tray and making me spill the stuff! That's it—use your free hand—give him one on the neck. That's the stuff! You there, don't get in the way looking for leftovers.* (15)

Such shifts occur frequently throughout the text. Yet, despite these manipulations, the novel provides a realistic, unsparing portrait of camp life.

As we become acquainted with Shukhov, a war veteran from a small village unjustly accused of espionage, Solzhenitsyn conveys a sense of the psychological enslavement inflicted by such camps. The narrative perspective of Solzhenitsyn's novel helps form its political commentary by providing a seemingly neutral, apolitical voice, which Solzhenitsyn uses to critique Soviet communism—not just the legacy of Stalin's terror. In fact, Solzhenitsyn's invective against the camp system and the kleptocracy running it bears a striking resemblance to Marx's famous critique of the way capitalism alienates workers:

> What, then, constitutes the alienation of labor? [...] (1) The relationship of the worker to the *product of his labor* as an alien object exercising power over him.... . (2) The relation of labor to *the act of production* within the labor process. This relation is the relation of the worker to his own activity as an alien activity not belonging to him; it is activity as suffering.... Here we have *self-estrangement*, as previously we had the estrangement of the thing.... Estranged labor turns thus: (3) *Man's species being*, both nature and his spiritual species property, into a being *alien* to him, into a *means* to his *individual existence*. It estranges from man his own body, as well as external nature and his spiritual essence, his *human* being. (4) An immediate consequence of the fact that man is estranged from the product of his labor, from his life activity, from his species being is the *estrangement of man* from *man*. (834–6)

Stalin's camps are designed to alienate prisoners. The narrator's grotesque depiction of camp life recalls Marx's famous critique, which was used to justify the repressive and totalitarian measures Soviet leaders took to create an egalitarian, classless society. Certainly, Solzhenitsyn's characters are alienated in all the ways enumerated by Marx. The novel's details underscore this incongruity, especially in its depictions of the numerous classes of *zeks* Stalinist communism has produced.

The narrator relates the endless duplication of tasks in the camp bureaucracy and its variegated hierarchy of stooges, foremen, warders, and administrators, showing class division and the alienation of both *zek* and guard alike. Descriptions of this absurd system depict those charged with making sure everyone in the work convoy is counted: Two sentries, a lieutenant, an escort party sergeant, the assistant guard commander, and yet another lieutenant count the numbers of *zeks* as they move past the barbed wire of the camp. The narrator states the rationale for such redundancy, which is fear:

> All this on behalf of the administration. Every man more precious than gold. A single head short behind the wire and your own head would make up for it.... All this on behalf of the convoy. On no account must they make a mistake. Sign for one head too many and your own would make up the number. (37)

"More precious than gold," the *zeks* are not valued for their labor or their intrinsic humanity. Rather, their worth is tied to their numbers: Thoroughly quantified, the *zeks* are a commodity that threatens to enslave the guards, who will become commodities themselves if they fail to keep an accurate tally.

The narrator's description of mealtime and its preparation offers a clear example of the camp's stratified caste system. In a lengthy passage, the number and tasks of each stooge that attends the cook and his "hygienist" are systematically laid out by the narrator. Including the hygienist, who does nothing except "watch" the cook prepare the meal, a total of nine people are given an extra portion of prized oatmeal gruel from the caldron (73–5). Even before this happens, half of the fat allotted to the cook for the day's lunch has already been stolen. Solzhenitsyn concludes this catalogue of corruption with the following summary: "What the boss man doles out is all you can get.... There's thieving on the site, there's thieving in the camp, and there was thieving before the food ever left the store.... It's dog eat dog here" (75). Not only does the narrator characterize the spectacle as lawless and primitive, but as the result of one person's will: "the boss man" Stalin. Here, in Stalin's most controlled environment, which ostensibly rehabilitates counterrevolutionaries, *zek* preys on *zek*, prisoners are worked to death, tribes (work gangs) battle one another for survival, and class upon class of stooges and informants proliferate in a harsh winter landscape.

As critic Georg Lukács first suggested, *One Day's* "grey mono-chrome" atmosphere of bureaucratic mishandling, unabated cruelty, mortal fear, and suspicion—though "extreme"—serves as a "symbol of everyday life under Stalin" (Lukács 13). Solzhenitsyn's references to this bleak period in Soviet history are often made through seem-ingly unimportant details, such as the confiscation of his prized boots. Shukhov compares his loss to Stalin's forced collectivization of farms and "how they rounded everybody's horses up for the *kolkhoz*" (13). Thus, Shukhov's nostalgia for his work boots—which he remembers better than his own estranged wife—refers to an event that resulted in the death and enslavement of millions of perceived resisters (13–4). While the novel chronicles this period, the narrator's description of the three artists that touch up the numbers on each *zek's* uniform also comments upon Solzhenitsyn's present: the artistic enslavement of Soviet culture by the doctrines of socialist realism. Reduced to tracing the figures of the dehumanized number-names by which the bureaucracy can best use and discipline the workers, these artists fulfill the role Stalin's cultural policies had relegated all artists to: literally inscribing the worker in the camp's reality, his relationship to the State, and his place in the "revolution" (30).

Solzhenitsyn elaborates further on the plight of artists in Stalin's Russia when Shukhov delivers Tsezar his bowl of gruel. Tsezar, a film maker who was never allowed to finish his first piece, is busy discussing the second part of Sergei Eisenstein's epic biography of Tsar Ivan IV, *Ivan the Terrible*, a political figure credited (especially by Stalin) as a defender and unifier of the Russian state. A censored version of the film premiered in 1946, but Stalin was displeased with Eisenstein's second installment, which recounts Ivan's purges of the disloyal and conniving Muscovites plotting his assassination—a set of historical events that resonate with Stalin's purges during the 1920s and 1930s. Though both Tsezar and his interlocutor, prisoner Kh-123, seem unaware of Stalin's displeasure with the film or its censorship, they argue over the relationship between technical brilliance, integrity, and artistic value:

> "Objectively, you will have to admit that Eisenstein is a genius. Surely you can't deny that *Ivan the Terrible* is a work of genius? The dance of the masked *oprichniki* [members of the Oprichnina, Ivan's "secret police"]! The scene in the cathedral!"

[. . .] "Bogus," he said angrily. "So much art in it that it ceases to be. . . . And the political motive behind it is utterly loathsome—an attempt to justify a tyrannical individual. An insult to the memory of three generations of the Russian intelligentsia!" (He was eating his gruel without savoring it. It wouldn't do him any good.)

"But would it have gotten past the censor if he'd handled it differently?"

"[. . .] A genius doesn't adjust his treatment of a theme to a tyrant's taste."

[. . .]

"Yes, but art isn't what you do, it's how you do it."

[. . .]

"I don't give a damn how you do it if it doesn't awaken good feelings in me!" (86)

Such a conversation, arising as it does in a novel which is highly critical of Stalin's policies, has a special bearing on the nature of Solzhenitsyn's artistry. Whether Eisenstein, in his portrayal of Ivan the Terrible, was being critical of Stalin's regime in the last years of his life is questionable. Nonetheless, many of its audiences (especially in the West) thought so, and such a claim implicitly depends on the ability of art to subversively communicate what cannot be safely imparted in simple terms. Furthermore, the mere suggestion that this level of artistic trickery is possible tempts Solzhenitsyn's readers to treat his sparse narrative commentary with the attentiveness of "a slow moving and circumspect zek" (82). Readers who remain blind to the "treatment of a theme," Solzhenitsyn implies, do not "savour their gruel," and it "does them no good" (86).

At the beginning of the novel, one of Shukhov's first gulag mentors informs us that a different law governs the camp system. The "law of the taiga," or forest, determines a zek's fate: "Know who croaks first? The guy who licks out bowls, puts his faith in sick bay, or squeals to godfather" (4). This law bears an intimate connection with nature, as suggested by the camp's physical isolation from the rest of civilization, as well as the narrator's repeated assertions that a zek's worst enemy is another zek—an echo of philosopher Thomas Hobbes's "state of nature." But this primitive law of self-interest is wedded to the camp's institutionalized corruption and culture of surveillance: "A stoolie will always get by, whoever else bleeds for him" (4). And, of course, this law of the enslaved demands obedience, as reflected by what the narrator calls "the convict's daily 'prayer'":

> "Your attention prisoners! Keep strictly to your column on the march! No spreading out, no running into the column in front, no moving from rank to rank, keep your eyes straight ahead, keep your hands behind your backs and nowhere else! One step to the right or left will be considered an attempt to escape and the guards will open fire without warning! Leader—quick march!" (39)

If this is a summation of Stalin's new religion, then we can clearly see that it is predicated upon fear: A single misstep, no matter how trivial, may (or may not) receive the maximum punishment—execution or punitive starvation.

The fear of such consequences seems to be as innate as the workings of nature, as dependable as the sun rising each morning. The almost "natural" status of Shukhov's enslavement is suggested in the narrator's initial description of the camp:

> Two big searchlights from watchtowers in opposite corners crossed beams as they swept the compound. Lights were burning around the periphery, and inside the camp, dotted around in such numbers that they made the stars look dim. (9)

As the *zeks* prepare to fall into ranks for their daily journey to the work site, the camp is again described as an antagonist of the stars, an artificial and grotesque caricature of nature:

> The camp lights had chased the stars from the sky, and it was dark as before. . . . When they first set up this "special" camp, the guards still had stacks of army surplus flares, and as soon as the light faded they would fill the air over the camp with white, green, and red fires. It was like a battlefield. Then they stopped throwing things around. Probably cost too much. (18)

From the beginning of Solzhenitsyn's novel, this dystopian "nature"— animated by fear rather than utopian longings—is hopelessly inefficient and fraught with error. Even when Shukhov and his fellow *zeks* leave the camp, nature is subject to the Party's dictates. One of the appointed counters at the camp gates, is a captain "fond of explaining things" who, the narrator tells us, can "work out for you whether the moon would be new or old on whatever day in whichever year you liked" (38):

> "It's sure to be twelve," Shukhov announced. "The sun's over the top already."
> "If it is," the captain retorted, "it's one o'clock, not twelve."
> "How do you make that out?" Shukhov asked in surprise. "The old folk say the sun is highest at dinnertime."
> "Maybe it was in their day!" the captain snapped back. "Since then it's been decreed that the sun is highest at one o'clock."
> "Who decreed that?"
> "The Soviet government."
> The captain took off with the handbarrow, but Shukhov wasn't going to argue anyway. As if the sun would obey their decrees! (68)

Although Shukhov does not believe the captain's claim, the government has refashioned his sense of time: "He'd often noticed that days in the camp rolled by before you knew it. Yet your sentence stood still, the time you had to serve never got any less" (67). Even the length of sentence can be arbitrarily changed. As Shukhov comments to the gang prankster Kildigs, "Don't keep counting. Who knows whether you'll be here twenty-five years or not? Guessing is like pitch-forking water" (69).

The arbitrariness of *zek* life, its fate at the whim of a faceless bureaucracy that attempts to change basic laws of nature, prefaces the narrator's relating of Shukhov's arrest. After escaping his Nazi captors and finding his way back to a Soviet unit, Shukhov and his sole surviving companion are deemed traitors, German spies sent back on "a mission" of some sort (70). Shukhov, we are told, was faced with a very clear decision:

> The choice was simple enough: don't sign and dig your own grave, or sign and live a bit longer.
> He signed. (71)

Shukhov's arrest, shocking in its mockery of justice, prefaces an even more atrocious revelation: the story of Senka Klevshin, a veteran captured by the Nazis, interned at the concentration camp, Buchenwald (into which he smuggled weapons for an armed uprising), and then persecuted for his contact with the enemy upon his return home (71). Thus Solzhenitsyn relates a string of controversial revelations whose very utterance would, in Stalin's time, warrant imprisonment after the captain's ludicrous claim that the government had changed the speed of the sun. History, we might infer, is equally unaffected by the pronouncements of Stalin and his legions of cronies, who remained criminally indifferent to war veterans and peasants alike as they continued to engineer a new society by liquidating entire classes of people and suppressing dissent with purges and executions. Solzhenitsyn's narrator, by bearing witness to the lives and circumstances of those unfortunate enough to be swallowed by history (and Stalin's desire to control its development and presentations of its legacy), emancipates what has been left out: the death and suffering of millions of people in the name of progress.

In *One Day*, Solzhenitsyn suggests the *zek's* emancipation is coming, that no apparatus of oppression can conquer the spirit of man. For Solzhenitsyn, the human psyche is mixed, forever capable of barbarity and civility toward itself and others:

> [... A] human being hesitates and bobs back and forth between good and evil all his life. He slips, falls back, clambers up, repents, things begin to darken again. But just so long as the threshold of evildoing is not crossed, the possibility of returning remains, and he himself is still within reach of hope. (*Gulag, Vol. 1* 175)

Thus, good and evil are part of the human condition: Reasonable and just people engage—when under the pressure of the State or the sway of a narrow, intolerant ideology—in the most inhuman activities: "Shakespeare's evildoers stopped short at a dozen corpses. Because they had no *ideology*.... Thanks to *ideology*, the twentieth century was fated to experience evildoing on a scale calculated in the millions" (*Gulag, Vol. 1* 174). Moreover, Solzhenitsyn insists that the Soviet system cannot survive without the camps, that Soviet communism requires enslavement and forced labor: " ... foreseen as far back as Thomas More, the great-grandfather of socialism, in his *Utopia*[, the] labor of *zeks* was needed for degrading and particularly heavy work, which no one, under socialism, would wish to perform" (*Gulag, Vol. 3* 578).

Ekibastuzlag, the camp where Solzhenitsyn was imprisoned, was the site of a mass hunger strike in 1951. Some of the prisoners from that camp also took part in the Kengir Uprising: a 40-day rebellion involving thousands of armed and well-organized *zeks* with a long list of demands, including the prosecution of camp guards for illegal shootings and the reexamination of their cases. Even before the death of Stalin in 1953, many acts of defiance had begun to occur throughout the camp system, usually involving labor strikes rather than full-blown mutinies (Applebaum 472–3). *One Day* foresees these rebellious acts, which presumably transpire shortly after the novel ends (Shukhov was arrested during the war; he has been in camps for eight years). The narrator tells us that *zeks* are starting to smuggle knives past the guards and assassinating informants—a practice known in the camps as "chopping"—whose only refuge is, ironically, the block of isolation cells used to punish unruly prisoners with slow starvation (*One Day* 72; *Gulag Vol. 3* 233–41). Thus the historical circumstances surrounding Solzhenitsyn's novel help us understand Shukhov's optimism. The guards and warders treat prisoners differently after these portentous acts of violence: "Oh, yes. Slitting a few throats had made a difference. Just three of them—and you wouldn't know it was the same camp" (105). The *zeks*—long dehumanized in an atmosphere of constant mortal anxiety, at the whim of an authoritarian, absurd, and bureaucratic machine—are autonomous human beings capable of brutal acts that engender fear and respect.

Solzhenitsyn's technical virtuosity—his subtle use of an ironically naïve peasant's perspective, his deft maneuvering between third person and interior monologue, his combination of suggestive symbols and realistic reportage, his intermingling of camp slang with old Russian proverbs and figures of speech—hides a subversive subtext that seeks to emancipate art from the enslavement of Marxist-Leninist aesthetic dogma, Stalinist repression, and the ideologies underpinning them. The ambiguity created by Solzhenitsyn's narrative framing and limited perspective cloaks a devastating critique of not only Stalin's camps and the evils they inflicted, but of the very foundations of Marxism and its notions of historical progress and human nature. In *One Day*

Solzhenitsyn seeks to enact change, investing art, and especially literature, with the power to bring about cultural renewal and emancipation.
By recounting a "good day" of Shukhov's imprisonment, Solzhenitsyn
reveals the mechanisms of institutionalized servitude and its inability
to control the spirit of the oppressed. The guards frisk Shukhov as he
approaches the camp gates to ensure that he has no bread to survive
an escape attempt or a weapon to resist his enslavement. The narrator
reports his silent response to this indignity, equating his humanity
with bread to survive the barren *taiga* or a knife to use within the
camp walls. At this moment we see the enslaved Shukhov reflect upon
the soul, his only means of emancipation: " . . . go ahead, he told them
silently, have a feel, nothing here except bare chest with a soul inside
it" (35).

WORKS CITED AND CONSULTED

Applebaum, Anne. *Gulag: A History*. New York: Double Day, 2003.

Baker, Francis. "The 'Democratic' Novels." *Solzhenitsyn: Politics and Form*. New
    York: Barnes and Noble, 1977. 14–44.

Barry, Minako. "The References to Eisenstein in *One Day in the Life of Ivan
    Denisovitch*." *Notes on Contemporary Literature* 20.5 (November 1990):
    9–10.

Dunlop, John B., Richard Haugh, and Alexis Klimoff, eds. *Aleksandr
    Solzhenitsyn: Critical Essays and Documentary Materials*. 2nd ed. New York:
    Collier, 1975.

Galler, Myer and Harlan E. Marquess. "Origin of the Glossary" and
    "Introduction." *Soviet Prison Camp Speech: A Survivor's Glossary*. Madison,
    WI: University of Wisconsin Press, 1972. 11–56.

Hosking, Geoffrey. *Beyond Socialist Realism: Soviet Fiction Since Ivan
    Denisovich*. New York: Holmes and Meier, 1980.

Kern, Gary. "Ivan the Worker." *Modern Fiction Studies* 23.1 (Spring 1977):
    5–30.

Lucid, Luellen. "Solzhenitsyn's Rhetorical Revolution." *Twentieth Century
    Literature* 23.4 (December 1977): 498–517.

Lukács, Georg. *Solzhenitsyn*. 1969. Trans. William David Graf. Cambridge,
    MA: The MIT Press, 1970.

Marx, Karl. "Economic and Philosophical Manuscripts of 1844." 1844. Trans.
    Martin Milligan. *Classics of Moral and Political Philosophy*. Ed. Steven M.
    Cahn. Oxford: Oxford University Press, 2002. 832–9.

Rothberg, Abraham. "One Day, Four Decades." *Aleksandr Solzhenitsyn: The Major Novels*. Ithaca, NY: Cornell University Press, 1971. 19–59.

Rus, Vladimir J. "*One Day in the Life of Ivan Denisovich*: A Point of View Analysis." *Canadian Slavonic Papers* 13.2 & 3 (1971): 165–78.

Solzhenitsyn, Aleksandr. *The Gulag Archipelago, 1918–1956: An Experiment in Literary Investigation*. 3 vols. Trans. Thomas P. Whitney and Harry Willetts. New York: Harper and Row, 1973–1978.

———. *One Day in the Life of Ivan Denisovich*. 1962. Trans. H.T. Willetts. New York: Farrar, Straus, and Giroux, 1991.

Toker, Leona. *Return From the Archipelago: Narratives of Gulag Survivors*. Bloomington, IN: Indiana University Press.

Zhdanov, Andrei. "Soviet Literature—The Richest in Ideas, the Most Advanced Literature." *Soviet Writers' Conference 1934: The Debate on Socialist Realism and Modernism in the Soviet Union*. Ed. H.G. Scott. London: Lawrence and Wishart, 1977. 15–26.

ROBINSON CRUSOE
(DANIEL DEFOE)

"Enslavement and Emancipation in *Robinson Crusoe*"
by Luca Prono, Independent Scholar

Even a cursory look at the main events in Daniel Defoe's *Robinson Crusoe* highlights the thematic relevance of enslavement and emancipation to the novel. Sometimes confined within the narrow boundaries of the adventure novel, but more often judged to be a literary classic, *Robinson Crusoe* focuses on the hazardous life of its title hero, whose impulse to travel makes him reject a reliable career as a merchant to seek adventure. In the course of the novel, Crusoe himself is enslaved when, during his second voyage, his ship is captured by Turkish pirates and Crusoe becomes the captain's slave. Once he escapes, Robinson first sells into slavery a Moor pirate, Xury, whom he has taken captive, and upon arriving in Brazil, he buys a "Negro slave" and starts a plantation. Because of his knowledge of Africa and the slave trade, three businessmen hire Crusoe to accompany them on an expedition to Guinea to buy slaves. Crusoe is to do the trading for them and, in return, he will receive slaves of his own. He accepts the offer and embarks again. He is, however, shipwrecked on a desert island in South America because of a violent storm. Here Crusoe proves extremely skillful in making tools and equipment for his survival. He spends several years alone on the island, until one day he discovers that the place is used by cannibals for their rituals. He saves an intended victim, naming him Friday after the day of his rescue and

he immediately teaches him to call him "Master," thus establishing
what many critics consider to be an archetypal master-slave relationship. Together Crusoe and Friday rescue the captain of an English
ship from a mutinous crew and they are taken back to England, where
Crusoe is told that his Brazilian plantation has prospered since he
left it. The novel ends with Crusoe visiting the island where he was
shipwrecked (now inhabited by English and Spanish mutineers and
sailors) and promising to embark on new adventures.

As this summary makes clear, Crusoe's desire for freedom, adventure, and success is predicated on the enslavement of others. The
novel celebrates Crusoe's individual agency and his ability to manipulate and domesticate the exotic locales and people, or "savages" as he
defines them, he encounters in the course of his adventures. As Crusoe
himself puts it, the environment of the desert island where he is shipwrecked is hostile and he has to do every type of work by hand: "But
notwithstanding this, with patience and labour I went through many
things; and indeed every thing that my circumstances made necessary
to me to do, as will appear by what follows" (Defoe 127). Thanks to
his resourcefulness, Crusoe does prosper on the desert island, eventually harvesting crops and raising sheep. Crusoe also succeeds in civilizing Friday, the savage he saves from a cannibalistic ritual. The novel
thus presents Crusoe's entrepreneurial spirit and becomes a strong
contribution to the argument for the civilizing mission of Europeans
in foreign and faraway lands. As the South African novelist and
Nobel laureate J. M. Coetzee writes in his introduction to the novel:
"*Robinson Crusoe* is unabashed propaganda for the extension of British
mercantile power in the New World and the establishment of new
British colonies" (ix). Defoe's narrative inextricably links the enslavement of savages, the advancement of European colonization, and the
spread of Christianity with the financial and economic progress of its
prototypical capitalist hero.

Although it is the relationship between Crusoe and Friday that
has attracted the majority of interest among critics who deal with the
racial dynamics of enslavement and emancipation in the novel, there
are other episodes worth examining in this context. At the beginning of the novel, Crusoe feels the need to emancipate himself from
the authority of family tradition. While still a child, he suffers under
the constraints put upon him by his family milieu and, consequently,
his "head began to be filled very early with rambling thoughts." He

is completely alienated from the mercantile class of his father and family, though by the end of the novel he comes to embody those very values of economic profit seeking (including the profitability of the slave trade). Going against his family wishes and disobeying his father, Crusoe goes to sea at a young age and, while he is traveling to the shores of Africa, he is immediately captured by Turkish pirates and brought to Sallee, "a port belonging to the Moors." The captain of the pirates decides to keep Crusoe as his slave, "being young and nimble and fit for his business." Crusoe reads "this surprising change of . . . circumstances from a merchant ship to a miserable slave" as a punishment for having refused to comply with his father's wishes. Crusoe is ordered to look after his master's little garden and "do the common drudgery of slaves about his house" (Defoe 41). For two years, Crusoe endures servitude. Though he tries to think of ways to escape, he cannot enact his imaginative schemes because he is completely alone and has no fellow slave with whom to talk or plot.

During a fishing trip where he is sent with two Moors, Crusoe finally enacts his plans for his escape. Although he is still a slave, he immediately thinks he would "like to have a little ship at [his] command." Without his master on board of the ship, Crusoe decides that he is to become his own master again and thus furnishes himself "not for a fishing business, but for a voyage" (Defoe 43). Here Crusoe shows his readiness to seize a profitable occasion to deliver himself at the expense of others. While the three are out fishing, Crusoe throws one of the Moors overboard and takes control of the boat, obtaining from the other Moor, Xury, a pledge of complete faithfulness. Xury is immediately subjugated to Crusoe: "The boy smiled in my face and spoke so innocently that I could not mistrust him; and swore to be faithful to me, and go all over the world with me." The two travel together along the coast of Africa, which the novel describes as being populated by threatening wild animals and equally threatening savages. The narrative reinforces several times the comparisons of Africans to savage beasts, thus implicitly legitimizing European claims to the land and civilizing missions toward its inhabitants. According to Crusoe, the African coast is "the truly Barbarian coast, where whole nations of negroes were sure to surround us with their canoes, and destroy us; where we could ne'er once go on shoar but we should be devoured by savage beasts, or more merciless savages of humane kind" (Defoe 45). On the rare occasions that Crusoe and Xury anchor their boat near the shores they hear "horrible noises, and hideous cryes and howlings." Both Crusoe and Xury once again come to the conclusion that "to have fallen into the hands of any of the savages, had been as bad as to have fallen into the hands of lyons and tygers" (Defoe 47).

Crusoe and Xury are eventually rescued by a large European ship bound the Brazilian coast. The captain of the ship offers to take Crusoe to Brazil in exchange for Xury. Crusoe is unsure at first as he was not willing to sell "the poor boy's liberty, who had assisted [him] so faithfully in procuring [his] own." Yet all Crusoe's scruples vanish when the captain promises to set Xury free in ten years, provided that he converts to Christianity. What comes as even more surprising is Xury's acquiescence: Threatened with yet more servitude, he responds by "saying that he was willing to go to him" (Defoe 54). The narrative once again legitimizes the enslavement of people who are not Europeans, linking the institution of slavery to a civilizing and Christianizing mission. The same feature comes to characterize the master-slave relationship between Crusoe and his man Friday.

As Crusoe arrives in Brazil, he starts his own plantation and he immediately develops a slaveholding mindset. He buys himself "a Negro slave" (Defoe 58) and he starts to market himself as a slave merchant among his fellow planters. What Crusoe particularly insists upon in his conversations is "the manner of trading with the negroes there and how easy it was to purchase upon the coast, for trifles, such as beads, toys, knives, scissars, hatchets, bits of glass, and the like, not only gold dust, Guinea grains, elephants teeth, &c., but negroes, for the service of the Brasils, in great numbers." The passage presents Crusoe as a skillful slave trader and compares "negroes" to objects: The value of a slave's life is measured in "beads, toys, knives, scissars, hatchets, bits of glass, and the like." Crusoe's fellow planters are especially interested in "that part which related to the buying of negroes": The prospect of having slaves at low prices, as the narrator makes clear, excites the planters, as all of their slaves were preciously expensive and "excessive dear." Because of his ability to secure slaves at a low cost, Crusoe is hired to bring slaves to the nearby plantations and, in exchange for his services, he is offered an "equal share of the negroes without providing any part of the stock" (Defoe 59).

Pushed by his "rambling desires" as much as by the economic profitability of the offer, Crusoe embarks on his expedition to the coasts of Guinea in order to secure more slaves. His ship, however, is caught in a violent storm and Crusoe ends up on a desert island near the mouth of the Orinoco River. The central part of the novel is devoted to how Crusoe domesticates the island he has been imprisoned on. The novel thus celebrates his individualism, self-sufficiency, and entrepreneurial skills. Critics like Ian Watt have defined Crusoe as the typical *homo economicus*, whose main source of identity is his ability to gain wealth. As John Richetti points out, however, the novel does not simply promote a heroic vision of Crusoe as "the domesticator of the wilderness," but also records his anxieties, inner turmoil, and "the psychological effects of a longing for human contact and a terror of unknown others" (67). When he finally encounters these "unknown others," Crusoe applies his beliefs in the Europeans' civilizing and Christianizing mission: He judges them with European eyes and his descriptions of their savage and cannibalistic nature justifies the colonial enterprise. As Coetzee observes, the native peoples of the exotic territories that European nations wanted to colonize represented an obvious obstacle to the process. Yet, Defoe pushes aside the ethical impasse colonizers must confront while eliminating this obstacle by representing the natives as less than human: dangerous, godless cannibals. The site where these subhumans perform their rituals is "a dreadful sight": "The place was covered with human bones, the ground dy'd with their blood, great pieces of flesh here and there, half eaten, mangled and scorched." Crusoe further elaborates on his description of the remains of the feast: "three skulls, five hands, and the bones of three or four legs and feet, and abundance of other parts of the bodies" (Defoe 210). Because of these descriptions, the reader cannot help but sympathize with Crusoe even when he kills several "savages." As Coetzee ironically notes, "the treatment Crusoe metes out to them is accordingly savage" (ix).

Once Crusoe has succeeded in domesticating his island, he fantasizes about how to best domesticate people: "I fancied my self able to manage one, nay, two or three savages, if I had them, so as to make them entirely slaves to me, to do whatever I should to direct them and to prevent their being able at any time to do me any hurt." The chance to subjugate a savage presents itself when Crusoe witnesses the rituals preceding a cannibalistic feast and rescues its intended victim. Once again, the natives are represented as threatening savages dancing with "barbarous gestures and figures ... round the fire" (Defoe 205). The savage, whom Crusoe will name Friday after the day of his rescue, but whose name in his own language the reader will never know, immediately shows his gratefulness to Crusoe in the form of complete obedience. Even before Crusoe makes clear that he wants to be called "Master," he reads Friday's gestures as displaying his willingness to serve as his slave: "He kneeled down again, kissed the ground, and laid his head upon the ground, and taking me by the foot, set my foot upon his head; this it seems was in token of swearing to be my slave for ever" (Defoe 207). This first act of voluntary submission is repeated a few pages later, accompanied by "all the signs ... of subjection, servitude, and submission imaginable to let me know how he would serve me as long as he lived" (Defoe 207). After this second display of submission, Crusoe begins to teach Friday English: He learns to call him Master and to say yes and no. The narrator makes clear that Friday stands apart from the savages who want to kill him. He is described as having "all the sweetness and softness of an European" and "a very good countenance, not a fierce and surly aspect." His nose is small, "not flat like the negroes" (Defoe 208–209). After his rescue, Friday and Crusoe become inseparable, so much so that critic Hans Turley has argued that their relationship is homosocial, even homoerotic. Sexual dynamics aside, Turley acknowledges that "their relationship is also one of power: Crusoe is, after all, the colonizer of his island and, indeed, the colonizer of Friday himself" (Turley 6–7). Friday lacks autonomy. As J. M. Coetzee has pointed out, he is treated by Crusoe "with self-congratulatory paternalism" (ix).

Crusoe also teaches Friday religious dogma, instructing "him in the knowledge of the true God" (Defoe 218). Crusoe's teachings transform Friday from a "blinded ignorant pagan" (Defoe 219) to a good Christian, and, in the process, Crusoe himself becomes a better Christian. Crusoe makes an explicit point of this when he admits that, while explaining the tenets of Christianity to Friday, "I really informed and instructed myself in many things that either I did not know, or had not fully considered before" (Defoe 221). Thus, the parts of the novel devoted to the conversion of Friday and the strengthening of Crusoe's religious sentiment imply that a man can better himself as a Christian by enslaving another human being, so long as the slave is made Christian, another potent justification of slavery. As J. M. Coetzee has commented, the novel typifies and propagates "the rationale that western colonialism offered for its activities ... : the spreading of the gospel" (ix).

Thanks to Friday's rescue and the relationship between the two, Crusoe concludes that "this was the pleasantest year of all the life I led in this place, Friday began to talk pretty well, and understand the names of almost every thing I had occasion to call for" (Defoe 215). Yet, whenever Crusoe shows interest in Friday's culture, it is because he wants to profit from Friday's knowledge. After talking at length to Friday, he starts to entertain "some hopes, that one time or other, I might find an opportunity to make my escape from this place; and that this poor savage might be a means to help me to do it" (Defoe 218). It is clear from this passage that Crusoe expects complete lasting devotion from Friday. As Toni Morrison, another Nobel Prize-winning novelist, has put it, "the rescuer wants to hear his name not mimicked, but adored" (xxvi). Morrison also observes that Crusoe's intervention does not merely save Friday, but effectively ostracizes him from his culture: "Friday has left and been rescued from not only the culture that threatened him, . . . but also from the culture that loves him. That too he has left behind forever" (xxvi). Friday is "rescued into an adversarial culture" and feels that the debt he owes to his rescuer can only be paid with "lifetime service" (Morrison xvii). As Friday accompanies Crusoe back to his mother country, to "the world of power and salvation," he is "condemned first to mimic, then to internalize and adore, but never to utter one single sentence understood to be beneficial" to his own culture. In Morrison's reading of the novel's racial dynamics, Friday becomes a symbol of all those subjects who have renounced their own culture in favor of their oppressors'.

Crusoe's relationship with Friday is the evidence that, in the course of the novel, the main character becomes, in John Richetti's words, "more and more an unhesitating tactician, openly manipulating" both the environment and the people he encounters. After he saves Friday's father, whose name (like Friday's) remains unknown to the reader, and a Spanish captain from a cannibalistic feast, Crusoe defines himself half-jokingly as an "absolute lord and lawgiver" (Defoe 241). Thanks to his manipulation of both Europeans and non-Europeans at the end of the novel, Crusoe secures his fortune, all the while subjugating others. With its intertwined themes of enslavement and emancipation, *Robinson Crusoe* is a key text for understanding imperialism and the experience of the colonized. As it can be read as both a representation of what took place in Defoe's time and as the representation of the colonial mind, the novel leaves readers to weigh the merits of

Crusoe's emancipation and its ultimate cost: the creation of imperialist culture and the enslavement of the colonized.

WORKS CITED AND CONSULTED

Coetzee, J. M. "Introduction." *Robinson Crusoe*. New York: Oxford UP, 1999. v-xi.

Defoe, Daniel. *Robinson Crusoe*. London: Penguin Classics, 1985.

Morrison, Toni. "Friday on the Potomac." *Race-ing Justice, En-gendering Power. Essays on Anita Hill, Clarence Thomas and the Construction of Social Reality*. Ed. Toni Morrison. New York: Random House, 1992. vii-xxx.

Richetti, John. *The English Novel in History, 1700–1780*. London: Routledge, 1999.

——, ed. *The Cambridge Companion to Daniel Defoe*. Cambridge: Cambridge UP, 2009.

Spivak, Gayatri Chakravorty. "Theory in the Margin: Coetzee's *Foe* Reading Defoe's *Crusoe/Roxana*." *Consequences of Theory*. Ed. Jonathan Arac and Barbara Johnson. Baltimore: The Johns Hopkins UP, 1991. 154–180.

Turley, Hans. "The Sublimation of Desire to Apocalyptic Passion in Defoe's Crusoe Trilogy." *Imperial Desire: Dissident Sexualities and Colonial Literature*. Ed. Philip Holden and Richard J. Ruppel. Minneapolis: U of Minnesota P, 2004. 3–20.

Watt, Ian. *The Rise of the Novel*. London: Chatto and Windus, 1957.

Wheeler, Roxann. *The Complexion of Race: Categories of Race in Eighteenth-Century British Culture*. Philadelphia: U of Pennsylvania P, 2000.

A Room of One's Own
(Virginia Woolf)

"Images of Enslavement and Emancipation in Virginia Woolf's *A Room of One's Own*"
by Deborah C. Solomon,
Auburn University at Montgomery

Although much attention has been given to the abundant wealth of imagery in Virginia Woolf's novels, little has been said of the equally striking and provocative imagery in her nonfiction works, such as *A Room of One's Own*—the very title of which has since become one of the most recognized symbols of feminist emancipation. In this part-narrative, part-expository essay, women burn "like beacons" (42); flawed novels "lie scattered, like small pock-marked apples in an orchard" (73); a "silvery, kindly gentleman" (7) materializes in a doorway like a "guardian angel barring the way with a flutter of black gown" (7); wine warms the body like a "lamp in the spine" (18); a question "runs into its answer as a sheep runs into its pen" (28); and a city shines like "a fiery fabric flashing with red eyes, a tawny monster roaring with hot breath" (39). Even nonvisual images abound; readers are called upon to imagine the "hum of traffic" (94), the sound of an "organ booming" (24), a student's "little grunts of satisfaction" (28), and the "sharp," "sweet" (10) smell of a delectable partridge dish. It is easy to see why this essay has remained so popular and why Susan Gorsky argues that its "artistry" elevates it "well beyond propaganda" (141). In fact, part of the effectiveness of Woolf's argument, as Tracy Seeley points out, lies in the very charm and detail of her imagery:

"[W]here another rhetorician would argue to conclusion or resort to abstraction, Woolf invents. For example, rather than concluding a point about the relative conditions of Oxbridge and Fernham, she juxtaposes images of money bags with lean cows and muddy markets. Rather than presenting a generalized historical account of what our foremothers had been doing with their time, she offers Mrs. Seton and her 13 children.... Substituting a picture or fiction for logical rhetorical moves constitutes the single most powerful strategy of Woolf's argument. (38)

Woolf's "inventions," however, do far more than simply clarify her argument (as Seeley demonstrates) or add to its overall artistry (as Gorsky implies): By appealing to her readers' senses, Woolf liberates deep emotional responses while at the same time exposing a host of related impressions too cumbersome to discuss in full but too persuasive to ignore. In a later essay (*On Being Ill*) Woolf herself attests to the incalculable power of "a sound, a colour," or a visual image; these elements, she argues, "when collected, [evoke] a state of mind which neither words can express nor the reason explain" (200). Such insight proves especially valuable when dealing with the complicated and controversial issues found in *A Room of One's Own*, through which Woolf imaginatively reinvents feminist polemics, thus bringing new meaning to the terms *enslavement* and *emancipation*. Her playful flights of fancy and memorable images bring an unprecedented poignancy to the familiar rhetoric of female empowerment and lead her readers to a fresh understanding of how deeply the bonds of poverty, ignorance, isolation, and criticism have demoralized female artists, and how radically the simplest freedoms, such as the freedom of privacy, can alter the female literary landscape.

Written in a meandering, almost "stream of consciousness" style, the essay follows the thoughts and adventures Mary Beton (or Mary Seton or Mary Carmichael—the name, as Woolf points out, doesn't matter given Mary's symbolic status), who has accepted the task of lecturing on the topic of "Women and Fiction." As she mulls over the complexities of her assigned topic, Mary leads her audience through the manicured grounds of Oxbridge (a conflation of Oxford and Cambridge), where she is shooed off the grass and barred from the library but then handsomely served a luncheon of sole and partridge.

The same evening, she visits Fernham (a fictional representation of Newnham and Girton, the two women's colleges at Cambridge), where she thoughtfully partakes of a meal as bland and meager as her lunch had been extravagant and delicious. The stark contrast between the two institutions brings her to a rather obvious but nevertheless profound realization: "One cannot think well, love well, sleep well, if one has not dined well" (*A Room* 30). Continuing her exploration of the topic of women's relationship to fiction, Mary visits the imposing British Museum, where her research unfortunately yields nothing but male studies of women; she consults George Trevelyan's *History of England*, which leads her to imagine what would have happened "had Shakespeare had a wonderfully gifted sister" (46); she reviews the successes and shortcomings of past female poets and novelists, such as Lady Winchilsea, Margaret Cavendish, Aphra Behn, George Eliot, Jane Austen, and the Brontë sisters; and finally, after evaluating the prose styles of two of her contemporaries (one a man, the other a woman), she suggests that in order to produce a great work of literature, one that "has the secret of perpetual life" (100), a writer must achieve an "androgynous" (97) state of mind. It is here at the conclusion of her essay that Woolf interrupts Mary's voice to address her audience with renewed intensity and to repeat the theme from which her entire essay has sprung: "A woman must have money and a room of her own if she is to write fiction" (4). Intellectual journeys, as Mary's story indicates, often grow from physical journeys, which in turn depend on steady incomes. In fact, Woolf presents Mary's emancipated state as the ultimate goal for every aspiring female writer: "By hook or by crook," she tells her readers, "I hope that you will possess yourselves of money enough to travel and to idle, to contemplate the future or the past of the world, to dream over books and loiter at street corners and let the line of thought dip deep into the stream" (107). The suggestive power of imagery (as that last quoted sentence illustrates) helps to unify, sustain, and develop Woolf's entire argument.

Yet, like all good writers, Woolf also uses her images to add complexity to her themes. Indeed, many of the images she uses to explore enslavement and emancipation—arguably the two most important themes of her essay—easily evoke double readings. Windows, for example, although frequently considered symbols of visionary freedom, can be interpreted as both liberating and limiting; they expand a room's boundaries and offer an outlook on the world but an outlook that is often narrow, fragmentary, or troubling. Janus-like, they represent thresholds between worlds and meeting places of opposites—light and dark, insides and outsides, ends and beginnings, even life and death (one cannot forget the fact that Woolf once tried to kill herself by jumping from a window). Naturally, then, the window scenes in *A Room of One's Own* reflect many of these paradoxes, sometimes revealing an inspiring sense of visionary freedom, sometimes an oppressive sense of distraction, and sometimes a combination of both. When she thinks of the concentration necessary to compose, for instance, Mary turns from the window and its noisy energy, treating it as something that will impair or muddy her creative powers. She advises her readers to seek "peace": "Not a wheel must grate, not a light glimmer. The curtains must be close drawn" (103). Yet, the same potential for distraction can also produce inspiration; in fact, many of Mary's most intriguing soliloquies are inspired by something she sees from a window. In Chapter 1, while relaxing "among the cushions in the window-seat" of the Oxbridge dining hall, she spots "a cat without a tail ... padding softly across the quadrangle" (11). Her vision, now directed "outside," away from the warmth and complacency of Oxbridge, is both expanded and disturbed: "The sight of that abrupt and truncated animal ... changed by some fluke of the subconscious intelligence the emotional light ... It was as if some one had let fall a shade" (11). On the one hand, the view from the window leads her to "think ... [herself] out of the room," to reevaluate her surroundings and speculate on the changes war has brought to conversation, poetry, and romance, but on the other hand, it shakes her confidence and extinguishes the "rich yellow flame of rational intercourse" that had colored her thoughts with such optimism (11). Thus, although the scene from the window releases her mind from the bastion of Oxbridge tradition (or male tradition), it also leads to her first ideas about what is missing in her society and the ways men and women are suppressed, perhaps even imprisoned, by their culture.

At Fernham, Mary experiences another moment of illumination while gazing from a window, only this time the moment reinforces rather than interrupts her previous train of thought. The talk of the evening has been of the "reprehensible poverty of women" (21), of the startling contrasts between Oxbridge and Fernham, of how wealthy men poured treasure into the foundations of Oxbridge but watched the women of Fernham scrimp and struggle to raise "bare walls out

of bare earth" (23). As they talk, Mary and Miss Seton gaze out the
window at the "domes and towers" of Oxbridge shining "beautiful"
and "very mysterious in the autumn moonlight" (23). Moved by the
grandeur of the scene, Mary's inner vision amplifies and sharpens to
include the "books," the "pictures," the "panelled rooms," the "painted
windows," the "tablets and memorials and inscriptions," the "fountains," the "grass," the "quiet rooms looking across the quiet quadran-
gles," the "deep armchairs," the "pleasant carpets," and most tellingly,
the "urbanity, the geniality, [and] the dignity which are the offspring
of luxury and privacy and space" (23). Expanding Mary's vision in this
way not only makes the bareness and poverty of Fernham seem all
the more confining, but it also sets up an intriguing contrast with her
earlier vision at Oxbridge. Although both window scenes juxtapose
contentment and its accompanying mental freedom with privation
and its accompanying mental constraints, the arrangement of each
scene is reversed. At Oxbridge, Mary stands in a lavishly comfortable
interior, looking out upon a symbol of deficiency, while at Fernham
she stands in cramped, economical apartments looking out upon an
expansive picture of prosperity. Dramatizing the differences between
the two institutions in this way makes Woolf's argument all the more
convincing. How will women have time to think if they are worrying
about making ends meet? How will they find inspiration in the
midst of drudgery and blandness? The inferior physical conditions
of women, Woolf argues, have long impeded their intellectual and
creative emancipation.

Yet, not all of the window scenes in *A Room of One's Own* lead to
images of opposition and contrast. In the last chapter, for instance,
the act of looking out the window produces a moment of visionary
freedom that unifies rather than divides the sexes. Having just
discussed the various obstacles barring the "average woman" from
creating a "prose style completely expressive of her mind" (94) and
having just stressed the need for women writers to find a truthful yet
inoffensive way to laugh at, perhaps even criticize, the opposite sex,
the narrator now seems to want to prevent any possible divisiveness
or rancor in her audience. Looking for some insight, she walks to the
window, through which shines the "light of the October morning"
(94), and she looks down upon the bustling streets of London. Of
course, the image of light streaming through a window in itself presents an intriguing symbol of enlightenment, reminiscent of religious

conversion, but Woolf's next few descriptions do even more to build the sense of an impending visionary experience:

> [T]here was a complete lull and suspension of traffic. Nothing came down the street; nobody passed. A single leaf detached itself from the plane tree at the end of the street, and in that pause and suspension fell. Somehow it was like a signal falling, a signal pointing to a force in things which one had overlooked. It seemed to point to a river, which flowed past, invisibly, round the corner, down the street, and took people and eddied them along, as the dead leaves. (95)

What Mary actually sees is "ordinary enough" (95), as she admits: A young woman and a young man approach from opposite directions and meet directly below her window at the same moment that a taxi stops next to them. The two then get into the taxi and drive off together. Yet Mary's mind, her "imagination" (95), inexplicably moved by the sight, transforms the ordinary into the extraordinary and reads meaning into the meaningless. The synchronization of the encounter and the sense of harmony implied by the unification of opposites (opposite sexes as well as opposite directions) leads her to a rather surprising idea: Perhaps "there are two sexes in the mind corresponding to the two sexes in the body" and perhaps "they also require to be united in order to get complete satisfaction and happiness" (97). As she follows this line of reasoning, she begins to realize that freedom from sex, or a complete unconsciousness of one's gender, is the ultimate form of emancipation and a necessary basis for any lasting work of art. To mark the importance of this revelation she writes the "very first sentence" on her "page headed Women and Fiction" (102): "It is fatal for any one who writes to think of their sex" (103). Once again, the act of looking out a window has become not just a narrative device but a powerful strategy of argument as well, a way for Woolf to present her thesis visually and offer a more complex and convincing view of intellectual freedom.

Another powerfully suggestive image that Woolf uses throughout her essay is that of running water. Fluid and unpredictable, rivers have long been associated with the emancipation of the mind and the expression of genius. To mention just a few examples: Horace compares Pindar's verse to an "impetuous river" (31); Dante, in Canto

I of the *Inferno*, describes Virgil as "a fountain / which spreads abroad ... a river of speech" (5); John Denham, in his most famous lines, addresses the river Thames as his "great example" (11) and his "theme" (11), "deep, yet clear ... gentle, yet not dull, / Strong without rage, without o'er-flowing full" (11); Shelley speaks of "Poesy's unfailing River, / Which through Albion winds forever" (Trevelyan 7); and Wordsworth, in his *Prelude*, compares the mind to a "river" (42) whose source is unknown. No doubt well aware of the rich tradition of river imagery in classical and English literature (having been blessed with "the free run" of her father's "large and quite unexpurgated library" [Hussey xi]), Woolf echoes that tradition often and with great aplomb. She describes the wealth of Oxbridge as an "unending stream of gold and silver" (*A Room* 9) and she depicts an absorbing thought as a "current setting in of its own accord and carrying everything forward to an end of its own" (19). Shakespeare's "poetry," she declares, "flows from him free and unimpeded" (56), while Margaret of Newcastle's "untutored intelligence ... poured itself out, higgledy-piggledy, in torrents of rhyme and prose, poetry and philosophy" (61). Thus, in language as flowing and adaptable as water itself, she appropriates a metaphor grounded in a long, male-dominated literary tradition and uses it to "celebrate" not "male virtues," but female virtues, to "enforce" not "male values," but female values, and to "describe" not the "world of men," but the world of women (100). In doing so, she emancipates such imagery from its age-old associations with men.

Indeed, the very fact that Woolf begins her narrative by imagining a woman "sitting on the banks of a river ... lost in thought" (5) is significant, partly because it is usually male writers who had previously been depicted in this way. The image is suggestive of freedom—freedom to think, to dream, to compose. By allowing Mary the same leisurely position by the river that male poets have so long held, Woolf is able to emphasize not just the importance of spare time in the process of intellectual growth and artistic composition, but also the capacity of the female mind to benefit from such freedom. Like the river, which has "reflected whatever it chose of sky and bridge and burning tree" (5), Mary's mind is free to brood over any subject she desires—an autonomy which naturally breeds inspiration. Meanwhile, the extended mind / river metaphor allows readers to recognize that even the most "exciting" (5) ideas take time to develop:

> Thought—to call it by a prouder name than it deserved—had
> let its line down into the stream. It swayed, minute after minute,
> hither and thither among the reflections and the weeds, letting
> the water lift it and sink it, until—you know the little tug—the
> sudden conglomeration of an idea at the end of one's line: and
> then the cautious hauling of it in, and the careful laying of it
> out? Alas, laid on the grass how small, how insignificant this
> thought of mine looked[.] (5)

Yet, even though Mary has plenty of time to let her mind wander
freely, she still seems constrained by feelings of inferiority and self-
doubt. Just as the flowing waters of the river may seem free but are
in fact bounded and confined by their banks, so Mary's thoughts
seem emancipated but are in fact limited by a long tradition of male
criticism and censure. Thus, Woolf once again complicates what could
have been an unambiguous image of mental freedom with suggestions
of restriction and restraint.

As the narrative progresses, of course, Mary discovers just how
severely and consistently the literary pursuits of women have been
disparaged by men, and once again she effectively uses imagery to
add subtlety and emphasis to her arguments. At the British Museum
she learns that "Professor von X" taught the "mental, moral and
physical inferiority of women" (32) and that there were sages who
viewed women as "shallower in the brain" (30) than men. In her
daily conversation, she witnesses that a woman who dares make an
"uncomplimentary statement" about a man is vilified as an "arrant
feminist" (35), while from the evening paper she discovers that a Mr.
Browning from Cambridge considers "'the best woman . . . intellectually the inferior of the worst man'" (53). Although Mary exposes the
absurdity of such views with a sprightly good humor, the underlying
hesitancy and self-criticism of her tone suggest a lingering concern
over male censure—a concern which Woolf herself could not hide (in
her journals she worried that critics might find A Room of One's Own
"shrill" and "feminine" [Gubar xlvii] or belittle it as "easy reading" and
an example of "feminine logic" [xlvii]).

Ultimately, however, Mary's intellectual journey and Woolf's own
engaging prose style prove that even when bound and constrained by
male discouragement, the thinking woman will find a way to carve
out a creative path of her own if allowed the luxuries of free time and

privacy. Thus, in the last chapter of the essay, when Woolf again uses river imagery to illustrate Mary's imagination, the moment produces not another "insignificant" thought, but a revelation worthy of being recorded (5). Perhaps by comparing the female mind to a river, full of undiminished energy and perpetual change, Woolf sought to encourage in her readers a sense of hope for the female literary tradition. At the very least, Mary's vision of the "tremendous stream," eddying and swirling below her window, symbolizes the endless flexibility and potential of a liberated mind (103).

Woolf provides images of enslavement, however, that are just as memorable and just as provocative as her images of emancipation. Her repeated references to locks, keys, and gates, for instance, vividly illustrate the various intellectual privations woman have faced not just from being locked up or locked in, but from being locked out as well. In Chapter 1, Mary finds herself peremptorily turned away from the Oxbridge library: "Ladies," she discovers to her chagrin "are only admitted to the library if accompanied by a Fellow of the College or furnished with a letter of introduction" (8). As the doors of the "famous library" close in her face, Mary jealously begins to picture all the "treasures safe locked" from her reach (8). It is clear that she can no more access the school's "laboratories" and "observatories" and "splendid equipment of costly and delicate instruments" than she can its rare manuscripts. Woolf further reinforces this sense of physical exclusion in her description of Mary's departure: "Gate after gate seemed to close with gentle finality behind me. Innumerable beadles were fitting innumerable keys into well-oiled locks; the treasure-house was being made secure for another night" (13). By envisioning not one gate or even a set number of gates but an endless succession of enclosures and an "innumerable" array of keys and beadles and locks, Woolf seems to be invoking the entire history of female exclusion and enslavement—the long progression of women like the Duchess of Newcastle who "should have had a microscope put in her hand" or been "taught to look at the stars and reason scientifically" (61). The implications of such physical exclusion fall into place with the persuasiveness of a key turning in a lock; how can limiting the scope of a woman's intellectual stimulation not fail to limit the scope of her literary output? It takes "a firebrand," as Woolf later points out to ignore the discouragement of such repeated "snubs" (74) and "say to oneself ... Lock up your libraries if you like; but there is no gate, no lock, no bolt, that you can set upon the freedom of my mind" (75). Ultimately, of course, the "doors that have been shut upon women" (82), the gates and locks and bolts that have barred them from schools and libraries, have not only limited the scope of their mental emancipation but "impoverished" (83) the literary world "beyond . . . counting" (82).

In Chapter 2, Woolf introduces another intriguing image of enslavement, one that involves not a denial of access, but a suppression of identity. When Mary enters the "vast dome" (26) of the British Museum, she pictures herself as a "harassed thought" (29) in a "huge bald forehead" (26), a decidedly male forehead, where she finds women reduced (and confined) to various categories and subcategories of inferiority. Although Woolf presents the image humorously, the idea of existing simply as a thought in someone else's head can be deeply disturbing, particularly if, as in Mary's case, one's very identity is misunderstood and misrepresented. Mary finds she can do little to rectify the distorted opinions men have produced about women and even less to correct the negative influence such opinions have made on the history and continuing development of female thought and creativity. Ironically, the right to research and read has thus led her, not to a sense of enlightenment, but to a renewed sense of enslavement and vulnerability. Which is worse, Mary wonders: to be "locked out" (24) of the elite male world of education or "locked in" (24) to its uncomplimentary assessment of the female gender?

Of course, Woolf's images of confinement point to paradox as surely as her images of emancipation. Being locked up, for example, can represent freedom or captivity, security or helplessness, depending on whether the act is voluntary or involuntary. For the sixteenth-century woman who "refused to marry the gentleman of her parents' choice" (42), being "locked up" (42) must have seemed nothing less than enslavement, but for Woolf (and perhaps many of her contemporaries), a lock became "the power to think for oneself" (105). Woolf reimagines the same rooms that have confined wives and mothers for so long as a source of freedom for the literary woman seeking solitude and peace. The "dark, cramped" (57) place of oppression becomes in Woolf's vision a place of refuge and inspiration, the "room with a lock on the door" (103) the ultimate symbol of freedom. Perhaps by using the image of the locked room to represent both imprisonment and emancipation, Woolf sought to add complexity to her argument and encourage her readers to think on and question the issue for themselves. Does the ability to choose one's surroundings instinctively change one's perception of those same surroundings? How important is privacy to the creative process or to one's own mental freedom?

Ultimately, Woolf's choice of imagery lends an unforgettable charm and power to her claim that "intellectual freedom depends upon material things" (106). After all, she argues, the "spider's web" (41) of imaginative work is not "spun in mid-air by incorporeal creatures" (41); it is the "work of suffering human beings" (42) and is "attached to grossly material things, like health and money and the houses we live in" (42). What better way to argue for the importance of such material things than with tangible, palpable symbols? Yet, the symbols and images that fill Woolf's essay—the windows, for example, and rivers and locked rooms—do more than simply clarify her points; they become a way of expanding the scope of her argument to explore not just the separate issues of emancipation and enslavement, but all the various connections and correlations between intellectual enslavement and physical confinement, between creative autonomy and financial freedom. Furthermore, the fictional nature of such imagery as well as its tendency to reveal paradox obliges her readers to engage in their own search for truth and draw their own conclusions about the kinds of freedoms and limitations inherent to being a women writer. As Ellen Carol Jones points out, "Woolf gives her readers a second sight, asking them to reconsider art and life, and all they entail, from a different perspective, with a new complexity" (236).

WORKS CITED

Alighieri, Dante, Henry Wadsworth Longfellow, Peter E. Bondanella, and Gustave Doré. *The Inferno*. New York: Barnes & Noble, 2003.

Denham, John. *Coopers-Hill.: A Poem*. London: H. Hills, 1709.

Gorsky, Susan Rubinow. *Virginia Woolf*. Boston: Twayne Publishers, 1978.

Gubar, Susan. Introduction to *A Room of One's Own*. Virginia Woolf. Orlando, Fla: Harcourt, 2005.

Horace. *A Poetical Translation of the Works of Horace; With the Original Text, and Critical Notes*. Trans. and Ed. Philip Francis. London: A. Miller, 1750.

Hussey, Mark. Preface to *A Room of One's Own*. Virginia Woolf. Orlando, FL: Harcourt, 2005.

Seeley, Tracy. "Flights of Fancy: Spatial Digression and Storytelling in *A Room of One's Own*." *Locating Woolf: The Politics of Space and Place*. eds. Anna

Snaith and Michael H. Whitworth. New York: Palgrave Macmillan, 2007. 31–45.

Trevelyan, George Macaulay. *English Songs of Italian Freedom*. London: Longmans, Green and Co, 1911.

Woolf, Virginia. *A Room of One's Own*. Ed. Susan Gubar. Orlando, FL: Harcourt, 2005.

———. "On Being Ill." *Collected Essays. Vol. IV*. New York: Harcourt, 1967.

Wordsworth, William. *The Prelude; or, Growth of a Poet's Mind*. New York: D. Appleton & Co., 1850.

SIDDHARTHA
(HERMANN HESSE)

"The Search for Emancipation in Herman Hesse's *Siddhartha*"
by H. Elizabeth Smith, Bronx Community College, City University of New York

In his novel *Siddhartha* (1922), Herman Hesse recounts Siddhartha's epic quest for self-knowledge and the meaning of life, structuring the chronological narrative upon the life of the historical Buddha. Although Siddhartha's journey follows the trajectory of the historical Buddha's life in significant ways, Siddhartha is not intended to be the Buddha per se; perhaps, more accurately, he is a counterpart to the Buddha. Several key parallels do exist, however, between the historical figure of the Buddha and Hesse's literary character, Siddhartha. First, as a young man, like the Buddha, Siddhartha abandons the wealth and comfort of his prominent Brahmin family in order to seek wisdom because he realizes "that his life is empty, that his soul has been left unsatisfied by his devotion to duty and the strict observance of all religious ordinances" (Malthaner 104). Second, as young men, when the Buddha and Siddhartha become disillusioned with their privileged lives, they choose to spend time among mendicant ascetics; in time, however, both realize that this lifestyle is also incomplete and unsatisfactory. Third, the Buddha leaves behind his ascetic lifestyle and meditates under a bodhi tree until he attains Nirvana, enlightenment, experiencing a vision of all his previous existences and the interconnection of all things;

similarly, it is under a mango tree by the river that Siddhartha, too, experiences his own vision of simultaneity and unity.

While Hesse structures the narrative of Siddhartha's numerous movements from enslavement to emancipation upon many of the well-known events in the historical Buddha's life, Hesse also grounds the narrative in the key Buddhist teachings and principles that Siddhartha experiences. Hesse's sweeping narrative moves from Siddhartha's enslavement to religious dogma to his ultimate emancipation from earthly desires; along the way, Siddhartha encounters various obstacles that he confronts, learns from, and incorporates into his life. Siddhartha's life journey is punctuated by key decisions that send him cycling through a series of lessons that mark his enslavement and subsequent attempts at emancipation: among them, his decision to be an ascetic and his subsequent decision to return to the life of a wealthy Brahman, and then again to continue his search for the meaning of life. These experiences culminate in the lesson he learns from the river, a lesson not possible without the previous lessons: that while knowledge can be conveyed, wisdom must be earned through life experiences. Siddhartha learns this monumental lesson when he has reached mid-life, while meditating under a mango tree by the banks of a river:

> Slowly blossomed, slowly ripened in Siddhartha the realization, the knowledge, what wisdom actually was, what the goal of his long search was. It was nothing but a readiness of the soul, an ability, a secret art, to think every moment, while living his life, the thought of oneness, to be able to feel and inhale the oneness. (Hesse 110)

The fundamental difference between the historical Buddha and Hesse's literary Siddhartha lies in the manner in which each man chooses to spend his time after enlightenment: While the Buddha chooses to go on to teach others, Siddhartha chooses to simply *be* by living an unadorned life by the river. This epiphany of the oneness of life and self-realization ultimately sets Siddhartha free, but it probably would not have been possible without the specific life decisions he made as he grew from a boy prodigy into a young man in search of the meaning of his life. Siddhartha's constant questioning, his pursuit of knowledge, and his earnest effort to cycle through various iterations of enslavement and emancipation ultimately earn him the wisdom he seeks.

Siddhartha's movement toward an understanding of his life drives Hesse's narrative. Each stage of Siddhartha's journey is founded upon a prior lesson learned, combined with Siddhartha's relentless, fierce desire to learn more. Hesse divides the novel in two parts, the first of which describes his background and early life, and the second of which delineates his journey of spiritual awakening. The first part of *Siddhartha* includes four chapters in which he describes Siddhartha's wealthy upbringing, his early questioning, his wanderings with the Samanas (an ascetic sect), and his visit to the Gotama Buddha.

In "The Son of the Braman," Hesse describes Siddhartha's early life as the privileged and much adored son of a prominent and wealthy Brahmin family. The second chapter, "With the Samanas," relates how Siddhartha, as an adolescent, rails against his father's posh and privileged home and decides to join the Samanas, who teach Siddhartha to fast, to think, and to be patient. But this impoverished lifestyle also leaves him utterly empty, both physically and spiritually. As a Samana, Siddhartha abandons his fine garments and privileged lifestyle and turns inward. He wears only a loincloth, eats once a day, and fasts frequently; as a result, his body becomes emaciated and unkempt. Siddhartha withdraws further from the world, which, like his own body, he views with contempt as it is unclean, starved, and hypocritical. Hesse describes how Siddhartha's constant fasting impoverishes his life and wreaks havoc on his mind and body:

> The flesh waned from his thighs and cheeks. Feverish dreams flickered from his enlarged eyes, long nails grew slowly on his parched fingers and a dry, shaggy beard grew on his chin. His glance turned to ice when he encountered women; his mouth twitched with contempt when he walked through a city of nicely dressed people. He saw merchants trading, princes hunting, mourners wailing for their dead, whores offering themselves, physicians trying to help the sick, priests determining the most suitable day for seeding, lovers loving, mothers nursing their children—and all of this was not worthy of one look from his eye, it all lied, it all stank, it all stank of lies, it all pretended to be meaningful and joyful and beautiful, and it all was just concealed putrefaction. The world tasted bitter. Life was torture. (Hesse 13)

In the third chapter, "Gotama," Hesse describes the crucial meeting in which Siddhartha challenges the Gotama Buddha—and breaks away from his good friend Govinda. Finally, the fourth chapter, "Awakening," depicts Siddhartha's realization that he has learned as much as he can and is "heading no longer for home, no longer to his father, no longer back" (Hesse 37) but rather on his path toward his deepest self.

The second part of *Siddhartha* includes the eight sections in which Hesse relates how Siddhartha experiences a spiritual awakening that allows him to embark on a new journey. Part Two of Siddhartha contains eight sections: "Kamala," "With the Childlike People," "Sansara," "By the River," "The Ferryman," "The Son," "Om," and "Govinda." Throughout the second section of the novel, Siddhartha continues his life journey: He returns to society, learns to love a woman, experiences professional success and power, and gambles. When he learns as much as he can from the Samanas, Siddhartha—by now a young man—encounters Kamala, a beautiful courtesan who becomes his lover and instructs him in the sensual arts. Siddhartha collects his teachings and his past experiences as his father's son, as a Samana, and as Govinda's friend and lives the comfortable life of a wealthy Brahmin: He works for a powerful businessman, Kamaswami, and becomes successful; he adorns himself in elegant clothing; he enjoys the sensuality of his relationship with Kamala; he eats well and drinks wine and gambles recklessly; and he sleeps on a soft bed. "At first it is all a game; he feels superior to those who pursue worldly pleasures and riches, but gradually he, too, falls under the spell of possessions" (Tuskin 102–103). Ultimately, though, Siddhartha still remains restless and dissatisfied, apart from the rest of society:

> For a long time, Siddhartha had lived the life of the world of lust, though without being a part of it. His senses, which he had killed off in hot years as a *Samana*, had woken again, he had tasted riches, had tasted lust, had tasted power; nevertheless he had still remained in his heart quite a long time a *Samana*; Kamala, being smart, had realized this quite right. It was still the art of thinking, of waiting, of fasting, which guided his life; still the people of the world, the childlike people, had remained alien to him as he was alien to them. (Hesse 65)

Later, as a result of such a debauched lifestyle, Siddhartha becomes disillusioned once again. Gradually, this sense of dissatisfaction overcomes Siddhartha, and he experiences a series of dreams that induce in him "a deep sadness" (Hesse 71) and ultimately force him to leave society and his great love, Kamala, and return to his quest for self. After Siddhartha leaves, Kamala realizes that she is pregnant with his child, but she does not tell him. This relationship does not—indeed, cannot—last because Siddhartha is a seeker; and so he moves on, leaving Kamala and (unknowingly) his unborn son, journeying once again from enslavement to emancipation and then back to yet another form of enslavement.

In the final chapters of the novel, Siddhartha returns, as a middle-aged man, to visit the ferryman Vasudeva. It is only when Siddhartha meets Vasudeva for the second time that he settles down by the banks of the river and learns to operate the ferry. As Siddhartha acknowledges after his encounter with the divine Buddha, the secret is "not the teachings [of the Buddha], but the inexpressible and not teachable, which he had experienced in the hour of his enlightenment—it was nothing but this very thing which he had now gone to experience, what he now began to experience" (Hesse 42). Siddhartha's return to the river teaches him to listen. There he also experiences within himself a spirit of love and the wholeness of life; he learns to accept human separateness, and achieves Nirvana, which completes his search for self-realization. It is the process of Siddhartha's journey toward his discovery of the wholeness and unity of all things, more than his ultimate realization itself, that creates a rich framework for asking fundamental questions about the nature of human existence: suffering, fasting, meditation, timelessness, asceticism, and the renunciation of society and its mores. The lessons that Siddhartha learns on his life journey ground the narrative in fundamental principles of Buddhism: first, that the path to enlightenment must be grounded in the present; second, that until we reach enlightenment, we are all caught in an ongoing cycle of death and rebirth; and third, that we are ultimately all connected, and it is within these interconnections that wisdom is located. Ultimately, Siddhartha realizes "that the way of salvation cannot be taught, that words and creeds are empty sounds, that each man must find the way by himself, the secret of experience cannot be passed on" (Malthaner 106).

Siddhartha, always eager to seek a new understanding, is constantly disappointed. And yet he learns from each of his experiences, which cumulatively add up to the wisdom he attains by the end of the novel. By midlife, however, Siddhartha is ready to listen to and learn from the river, which, he observes, "is everywhere at once, at the source and at the mouth, at the waterfall, at the ferry, at the rapids, in the sea, in the mountains, everywhere at once, and that there is only the present time for it, not the shadow of the past, not the shadow of the future" (Hesse 92). Siddhartha relates what the river teaches him to his own growth and development, and he articulates an understanding of himself as he exists in the present. He tells his friend Vasudeva:

> I looked at my life, and it was also a river, and the boy Siddhartha was only separated from the man Siddhartha and from the old man Siddhartha by a shadow, not by something real. Also, Siddhartha's previous births were not past, and his death and his return to Brahma was not future. Nothing was, nothing will be; everything is, everything has existence and is present. (Hesse 92)

At midlife, Siddhartha understands life to be at once shifting, transitory and isolated—but also deeply connected to other lives; it is within these connections, rather than within himself, that Siddhartha eventually finds meaning. The river, within which all forms of life are contained and which allows all to flow together into a unified whole, transcending time, opposition, and difference, teaches Siddhartha a final lesson. This final lesson both encompasses and brings closure to the entire narrative; it unifies Siddhartha's journey and brings it to a culminating epiphany that privileges the wisdom of experience and the unity of all things ("Om") over the pursuit of knowledge.

Hesse weaves many of the most significant tenets of Buddhist thought throughout *Siddhartha*. While he structures the narrative chronologically, Hesse grounds Siddhartha's journey in very specific Buddhist teachings. Indeed, the titles of a number of chapters throughout the novel are named after the specific religious principles ("Awakening," "Sansara," "Om," for example) that Hesse illustrates through Siddhartha's experiences. Siddhartha lives a full life as he moves from his father's comfortable home to the life of an ascetic; when fasting and asceticism do not provide satisfaction or answers,

Siddhartha attempts to find fulfillment in wealth, a sensual relationship with a beautiful courtesan, and power, but fails here too. It is only at the river that Siddhartha is able to reconcile life and death, joy and sorrow, and human suffering. It is the river that provides the source of Siddhartha's ultimate enlightenment, but it is Siddhartha's actual quest for knowledge as the son of a wealthy Brahmin and later as a young man that powers his journey. By the time Siddhartha meets the Gotama Buddha, he is able to identify a singular flaw in the Gotama Buddha's teachings: that individuals who have come to an understanding of the nature of life through their own experiences cannot teach this by giving away this knowledge because it is impossible to give away one's own experiences. Instead, they can only describe what they have learned. It is Siddhartha's fierce desire to understand his own nature in relation to the nature of knowledge that forces him to reject his family, his friend Govinda, and religious dogma—that of his childhood and, later, that of the Samanas—in order to experience and arrive at his own wisdom.

Siddhartha's perpetual sense of wanderlust and dissatisfaction help him to rail against the shackles of his "enslavement," whether it is his father's comfortable home, the ascetic sect, his beautiful courtesan, the power and wealth he gains, or his reckless gambling. Siddhartha seeks his own path, always questioning and pushing forward. Toward the end of the novel, his former courtesan, Kamala, and their son visit him at the river; Siddhartha's son scorns him just as Siddhartha repudiated his own father when he was young. Siddhartha chooses not to chase his son back to the city, realizing instead that his son must also seek his own path. The repetition of the father-son dynamic is also a form of enslavement: Just as Siddhartha rejected his father's comfortable home, Siddhartha's son also rejects his father's life of contemplation.

While the river is the seminal source of emancipation in Herman Hesse's *Siddhartha*, it is the quest for that emancipation that is significant, perhaps even more so than the final achievement of enlightenment. The lessons Siddhartha learns are incremental in nature: He could not have achieved each new level of knowledge without having his prior experiences. All the lessons Siddhartha learns are valuable both on their own and in the way that they contribute to his ultimate path towards selfhood. From the religious traditions he experiences as a young boy to the patience and self-discipline he learns as a Samana; his interaction with the Gotama Buddha; and the lessons he learns from Kamala, Govinda, the ferryman, and even his own son, Siddhartha learns one final, overarching lesson: Each person must seek and follow his own paths. Siddhartha leads a full and rich life that encompasses a range of seminal human experiences: a rigorous education, the self-denial of an ascetic life, the sensuality of a sexual relationship with Kamala, his sense of aloneness and despair in the world, and his ultimate realization of the unity of all things. Siddhartha's spiritual "emancipation" is a result of his ongoing desire to escape his mental enslavement. He understands that "there was no teaching a truly searching person, someone who truly wanted to find, could accept. But he who had found, he could approve of any teachings, every path, every goal, there was nothing standing between him and all the other thousand any more who lived in that which is eternal, who breathed what is divine" (Hesse 94).

At the same time, it is his relationships with other people—his father, Govinda, the Gotama Buddha, Kamala, Vasudeva, and his son—that help him along his journey and provide him with points of resistance, with ideals and values to question, to wonder at, and—ultimately—to depart from. Just as Siddhartha leaves his father's home to find his own way and his own answers, so does Siddhartha's son leave him; and in spite of the terrible pain of his loss, Siddhartha lets him go, allowing him to pursue his own path in spite of his paternal desire to protect his son: "With the loss of his son, there is nothing left that binds Siddhartha to this world. He realizes that this had to come, so that he would no longer fight what he considered fate but give himself unreservedly to his destiny; thus Siddhartha has overcome suffering at last and with it has attained the last step of his completion, he has entered into Nirvana" (Malthaner 108–109).

The agony of losing his son to the city causes a shift in Siddhartha's attitude toward the people he ferries across the river: "Differently than before, he now looked upon people, less smart, less proud, but instead warmer, more curious, more involved" (Hesse 109). And so Siddhartha lives and works side by side with Vasudeva, the ferryman, learning from the river and from his friend. Siddhartha initially crosses the river when he is a wandering ascetic. The river teaches him that everything passes away and that life is connected to death in a cycle of reincarnation. Siddhartha crosses it again as a ferryman; this time he learns that the river timelessly contains the world's nurturing energies. Siddhartha's profound friendship with Govinda, his childhood friend, and later his friendship with Vasudeva, the ferryman, is a theme that runs through the novel and is deeply connected to Siddhartha's own search for selfhood.

In Sanskrit the name "Siddhartha" means "he who has achieved his goal" (Hutchison). Hesse's Siddhartha fulfills the promise of his name when he learns the lessons of impermanence the river has to teach: that the cosmic cycle of reincarnations means that all things pass away in an endless flow connecting life and death. And while this culminating realization completes the novel, it would not be possible without the lessons Siddhartha learns on his life's journey. In the final chapter, "Govinda," Siddhartha recounts some of the fundamental insights he has gained to his boyhood friend: "that for each truth the opposite is equally true; that excessive searching—as practiced by Govinda—is self-defeating and that to 'find' is, paradoxically, 'to be free, to be open, to have no goal.' One must simply love and enjoy the world in all its aspects, and Govinda's final vision of Siddhartha's face is in fact an experience of universal metamorphosis, of a streaming river of faces of all time and all emotions, all the manifestations of life which Siddhartha has managed to accept" (Hutchison). And, once again, Siddhartha acknowledges that while knowledge can be communicated, wisdom must be experienced (Tuskin 106). Just as the Gotama Buddha could not transfer his experiences to Siddhartha, at the end of his journey, Siddhartha cannot give the wisdom he has gained to Govinda; Govinda must achieve this through his own experiences.

Hesse concludes his novel with Siddhartha not teaching his disciples—like the Gotama Buddha and, indeed, the historical Buddha upon whom Siddhartha is based—but leading the simple life of a ferryman. He lives on the banks of the great river, interacting and connecting with travelers on their own individual quests through life. Siddhartha does not attempt to pass on his knowledge but, instead, he chooses to simply live the wisdom he has earned. Siddhartha's journey is part spiritual and also part *Bildungsroman* (von Molnar 82): the epic quest of a young boy for self-knowledge and separation from his family to find his own way in the world—a quest his son repeats. Siddhartha's story is a quest without an end, and he earns his wisdom through his various life lessons and experiences. He realizes that to learn these life lessons, one must wear "many a robe" (Hesse 118) and change according to life lessons learned well. He appreciates the many teachers he has encountered in his life: from the teachers he had as a young boy in his father's home to Kamala, Vasudeva, the Gotama Buddha and the ferryman Vasudeva. Ultimately Siddhartha learns that "[k]nowledge can be conveyed, but not wisdom" (Hesse 120); wisdom must be experienced on life's journey.

WORKS CITED

Butler, Colin. "Herman Hesse's *Siddhartha*: Some Critical Objections." *Monatshefte: Fur Deutschen Unterricht, Deutsche Sprache un Literatur* 63 (1971): 117–124.

Byrd, Rudolph P. "'Oxherding Tale' and 'Siddhartha': Philosophy, Fiction, and the Emergence of a Hidden Tradition." *African American Review* 30.4 (Winter 1996): 549.

Grislis, Karen and Hsia, Adrian. "Siddhartha's Journey to Brahma/Tao." *Par Rapport: A Journal of the Humanities* 5–6 (1982–1983): 59–66.

Hesse, Herman. *Siddhartha*. 1951. trans. Gunther Olesch, Anke Dreher, Amy Coulter, Stefan Langer, and Semyon Chaichenets. St. Petersburg, Florida: Red and Black Publishers, 2001.

Malthaner, Johannes. "Herman Hesse: *Siddhartha*." *German Quarterly* 25.2 (1952 March): 103–109.

Narasimhaiah, Sanjay. "Herman Hesse's *Siddhartha*: Between the Rebellion and the Regeneration." *The Literary Criterion* 16.1 (1981): 50–66.

Paslick, Robert H. "Dialectic and Non-Attachment: The Structure of Herman Hesse's *Siddhartha*." *Symposium* 27 (1973): 64–75.

Rao, R. Raj. "God-Consciousness in *The Guide* and *Siddhartha*." *The Literary Endeavour: A Quarterly Journal Devoted to English Studies* 3.3–4 (1982 Jan.–June): 87–91.

Shaw, Leroy R. "Time and Structure of Herman Hesse's *Siddhartha*." *Symposium* 11 (1957): 204–224.

Spector, Robert Donald. "Artist Against Himself: Hesse's *Siddhartha*." *History of Ideas News Letter* 4 (1958): 55–58.

Tuskin, Lewis W. *Understanding Herman Hesse: The Man, His Myth, His Metaphor*. Columbia, South Carolina: University of South Carolina Press, 1998.

Verma, Kamal D. "The Nature and Perception of Reality in Herman Hesse's
   Siddhartha." *South Asian Review* 11–12:8–9 (1988 July): 1–10.
Von Molnar, Geza. "The Ideological Framework of Herman Hesse's
   Siddhartha." *Die Unterrichtspraxis / Teaching German* 4.2 (Autumn 1971):
   82–87.

THE TEMPEST
(WILLIAM SHAKESPEARE)

"' . . . with my nobler reason 'gainst my fury / Do
I take part': Enslavement and Emancipation in
Shakespeare's *The Tempest*"
by Robert C. Evans,
Auburn University at Montgomery

Issues of enslavement and emancipation are clearly important in
Shakespeare's *The Tempest*. While Caliban is the character who is most
obviously enslaved to Prospero, Ariel also exists in a kind of indentured servitude, and both characters eagerly desire their freedom.
Although perhaps less prominently, most of the other characters also
live within various kinds of literal or metaphorical bondage, and the
movement of the play can be seen as a progression toward various
sorts of liberty. Before such liberty is achieved, however, the party
of shipwrecked aristocrats, courtiers, and servants from Milan and
Naples temporarily lose their independence thanks to the superior
power of Prospero, and Ferdinand is literally put to work hauling
wood—the same kind of labor imposed on Caliban. Moreover, even
Prospero finds himself burdened by heavy thoughts and emotions,
including a nasty anger and an unappealing desire for revenge. This
spiritual bondage is, in some ways, at least as significant and damaging
as the physical bondage imposed on others. By the end of the play,
however, most of the characters are able to achieve some sort of
freedom, and Prospero's liberation from his baser instincts is perhaps
the most significant emancipation depicted in the play. After all, if

Prospero had remained enslaved to his anger and bitterness, the other characters might never have achieved their final freedom.

Caliban is, of course, the character who is most obviously enslaved in this play, and recent critics have tended to see him as a victim of Prospero's colonial tyranny. Although the play does present Caliban in somewhat sympathetic terms, it is important to remember that Caliban did not begin his relationship with Prospero in bondage. It is true that in almost his first reference to Caliban, Prospero already calls him "my slave" (1.2.309), and Miranda, Prospero's kind and compassionate adolescent daughter, immediately replies, "'Tis a villain, sir, / I do not love to look on" (2.1.310–11).[1] However it soon comes to light that when Prospero first encountered Caliban, who was already a resident on the island, he treated him very well. Caliban himself admits as much:

Caliban

When thou cam'st first
Thou strok'st me and made much of me; woulds't give me
Water with berries in't, and teach me how
To name the bigger light and how the less
That burn by day and night. And then I loved thee ...
(1.2.333–37)

Prospero's initial kindness to Caliban seems, frankly, extraordinary, especially the reference to affectionate physical stroking. His compassion is particularly striking since various other characters are instantly repulsed by Caliban's ugly appearance and noxious smells. Prospero also presumably knew, at the time he showed such emotional and physical affection to Caliban, that Caliban was the orphaned son of Sycorax, the malignant witch who had confined Ariel to twelve painful years of torment, imprisoned within a tree, where Ariel remained until Prospero released him. What is most striking, then, about Prospero's original treatment of Caliban is how little prejudice the magician actually showed: He was willing to love and literally embrace Caliban despite the latter's foreignness, his ugly (in fact, beastly) physical appearance, and his dubious ancestry. Indeed, Prospero was even willing to allow Caliban to live alongside him and his daughter in their own humble residence. It was only after Caliban tried to rape Miranda (who, at the time of the play, is a very young teenager) that

Prospero's attitudes changed. Speaking to Caliban, Prospero explains that "I have used thee / (Filth as thou art) with humane care and lodged thee / In mine own cell, till thou didst seek to violate / The honour of my child" (1.2.346–49).

Caliban not only fails to deny the charge but openly wishes that he had been able to accomplish the crime ("O ho, O ho! Would't had been done; / Thou didn't prevent me, I had peopled else / This isle with Calibans" [1.2.350–52]). Ironically, although it has been common in recent criticism to depict Prospero as a malignant colonialist, it is Caliban who actually sounds, in these words, like a figure with colonial ambitions. In any case, Caliban no sooner defends his attempted rape of Miranda than Miranda herself speaks up and condemns him, calling him an "abhorred slave, / Which any print of goodness wilt not take, / Being capable of all ill" (1.2.352–54) and telling him that he has been "deservedly confined into this rock, / Who hadst deserved more than a prison" (1.2.362–63). There seems little question, then, about the validity of Prospero's charges: Not only does Caliban himself confess to his intentions, but then Miranda confirms them. Caliban is an attempted rapist of a young girl (almost a child); little wonder, then, that the girl's father has made him a slave.

The wonder, in fact, is that Prospero did not immediately impose far harsher penalties, especially in view of the fact that Prospero, on the island, could in essence make his own law. The death penalty was the standard punishment for rape (when rape *was* punished) in England from 1285 to 1840 (Bamford 5), and child-rape was especially likely to be punished (Ruff 145). Admittedly, the death penalty for rape was almost inevitably not imposed, in part because charges of rape were difficult to prove when the accused denied any guilt (Bamford 5). Shakespeare, however, seems to have gone out of his way to make Caliban's guilty intentions not only undeniable but literally undenied. Of course, Caliban did not succeed in committing his planned violation of Miranda, and attempted rape was not always punished in early modern England.[2] In few cases, however, would the real-life father of the victim of an attempted child-rape have it within his power, as Prospero does, to be simultaneously the jury, judge, and potential executioner of the man accused. Given Prospero's extreme license to deal with the offending Caliban in almost any way he might wish, it is surprising that he merely makes him a slave. Indeed, Miranda's impassioned comment that Caliban has been "deservedly confined into this rock" (1.2.362) inadvertently reminds us of the way Caliban's mother, Sycorax, literally did confine Ariel inside a tree for twelve painful years. Caliban, by contrast, has been "confined into this rock" merely in the sense (apparently) that he must live inside a cave (see Vaughan edition, note to line 362). Gentle-minded Miranda, in fact, suggests that he deserves even harsher punishment than her father has imposed (1.2.363), and it seems significant that the equally gentle-hearted Ariel never once speaks up in defense of his fellow "slave," with whom he might have been expected to make common cause.

If Miranda, of course, had been abusive toward Caliban, there might at least be a conceivable motive to explain the attempted rape. Instead, however, she seems to have been at least as kind toward him—at first—as her father was. She didn't, of course, physically stroke him (as Prospero did), for any such behavior might have been used by latter-day critics to justify his attempted assault on her. Instead, she recounts their early contact simply by saying,

> I pitied thee,
> Took pains to make thee speak, taught thee each hour
> One thing or other. When thou didst not, savage,
> Know thine own meaning, but would gabble like
> A thing most brutish, I endowed thy purposes
> With words that made them known. But thy vile race
> (Though thou didst learn) had that in't which good natures
> Could not abide to be with ... (1.2.354–61)

As when he responded to Prospero's earlier speech, Caliban does not here attempt to dispute or deny Miranda's account; indeed, he affirms it, admitting "you taught me language" but then adding, "and my only profit on't / Is I know how to curse" (1.2.364–65). Whose fault (one might ask) is that? Miranda apparently tried to treat Caliban at first as a friend or even a brother, only to be rewarded with attempted sexual assault. Instead of trying to keep Caliban ignorant, illiterate, and inarticulate (a common stratagem of many slave-masters throughout history), Prospero and Miranda went out of their ways ("took pains") to help him learn how to communicate and to profit from real knowledge. It seems significant, in fact, that Miranda says she endowed "thy" (i.e., Caliban's) "purposes / With words that made them known."

Rather than merely teaching him to understand a few rudimentary commands as one might instruct a pet dog or workhorse, she tried to help him learn how to express his *own* thoughts and intentions, so that he could communicate them to her and her father.[3] Neither she nor Prospero seem to have had any original intention to treat Caliban as a slave; it was only when he abused their trust and good intentions that the potential for a more humane relationship among them all was lost.

Although Caliban might thus in some ways seem simply a kind of prisoner, confessedly guilty of attempting a serious crime, who has therefore been justly sentenced to hard labor, he also, in many real and important respects, does in fact seem undeniably a slave. This is especially true of Prospero's ability not simply to impose his will on Caliban, by force if necessary, but to torment him (as it were) from the inside out: "If thou neglect'st, or dost unwillingly / What I command, / I'll rack thee with old cramps, / Fill all thy bones with aches, make thee roar, / That beasts shall tremble at thy din" (1.2.369–72). Prospero thus reveals that he not only has frightening control over Caliban's body (see also, for example, 2.2.3–16) but that he also seeks to impose such control over his mind ("If thou ... dost unwillingly"). In some ways, of course, the punishments he threatens strongly resemble, in both their causes and effects, the punishments imposed on Ariel by Caliban's mother (1.2.287–89), but in some ways the punishments suffered by Ariel were even worse than anything imposed on Caliban, since Caliban at least has a certain freedom of movement and relative freedom of speech. Still, there is no denying that Caliban is definitely enslaved to Prospero and that his lack of freedom is unfortunate. Caliban, however, bears much of the responsibility for that lack of freedom. Ariel, after all, was imprisoned by Sycorax because Ariel "wast a spirit too delicate / To act her earthy and abhorred commands, / Refusing her grand hests" (1.2.272–74). Ariel, in other words, found himself physically imprisoned because he sought to preserve his moral freedom. He refused to obey Sycorax's "abhorred"—and presumably unethical—"commands." Caliban, in contrast, finds himself sentenced to hard labor precisely because he could not (and apparently still cannot) restrain his own abhorrent impulses. He could not contain his passionate fury in the past, and he still cannot at present.

Much of the recent critical sympathy for Caliban runs the risk of simplifying both Shakespeare's play and Caliban's character. If

Shakespeare had intended to present a purely sympathetic victim of tyrannical slavery, he could easily have done so. Instead, in creating Caliban, he crafted a much more intriguing and ambiguous figure—a figure who has much of the moral complexity (and many of the ethical faults and foibles) of a real person. Efforts to depict Caliban as a simple victim tend to rob him of much of his full humanity, making him less a fully developed moral being, responsible for his own choices and conduct, and more a mere allegorical symbol. Shakespeare, in contrast, makes Caliban as morally complex and ethically flawed as any of the other characters in the play—a fact that becomes especially apparent in Caliban's later encounters with Stephano and Trinculo.

Interestingly enough, when Stephano first discovers Caliban lying on the ground, hiding from the storm, his immediate reaction is far different from the initial reactions of Prospero and Miranda. Instead of showing any real compassion to Caliban, or trying to communicate with him, or trying to teach him to speak, or trying to educate him in any other way, Stephano's instant impulse is to exploit this newly discovered creature for his own personal profit. At first, to be sure, his instinct seems gentler: When he discovers that Caliban can speak his own language, Stephano says, "I will give him some relief, if it be but for that" (2.2.66–67). This, however, is merely the prologue to a far more exploitative plan: "If I can recover him and keep him tame, and get to Naples with him, he's a present for any emperor that ever trod on neat's leather" (2.2.67–69). Stephano does, it is true, offer Caliban some wine from his own bottle when he sees that Caliban is agitated, but once more the apparently generous gesture is self-interested and self-serving: "It [i.e., the wine] will go near to remove his fit. If I can recover him and keep him tame, I will not take too much for him! He shall pay for him that hath him, and that soundly" (2.2.77). If anyone, then, instantly responds to Caliban with the instincts of a slave-owner and slave-seller, it is Stephano, not Prospero.

As if, perhaps, to highlight the contrast between the initial motives of Prospero and Miranda (on the one hand) and Stephano (on the other) in their first dealings with Caliban, Shakespeare deliberately reminds us of the magician and his daughter when he describes how Stephano pours wine down Caliban's throat: "Open your mouth. Here is that which will give language to you, cat. Open your mouth! ... You cannot tell who's your friend" (2.2.81–85). Miranda did indeed genuinely try to befriend Caliban and "give language" to him—not, however, by trying to inebriate him or pacify him with alcohol, but by painfully taking the time to help him learn how to speak. (That talent, as it turns out, now makes him seem all the more economically valuable to Stephano.) Stephano addresses Caliban as if he were the latter's "friend," but of course he is anything but. By plying Caliban with wine, Stephano hopes to make him easier to manipulate and control. He hopes to substitute his own sort of alcoholic "spirits" for the supernatural "spirits" (2.2.3) by which Prospero controls Caliban. Unlike Prospero and Miranda, Stephano begins his relationship with Caliban not by offering him genuine kindness and friendship but by instantly seeking to enslave him.

Ironically, the very same Caliban who rejected the heartfelt friendship of Miranda and who protests against his service to Prospero now falls down on his knees to proclaim his willingness to be the "true subject" of the drunken Stephano (2.2.116; 122). Caliban assumes that Stephano has "dropped from heaven" (2.2.134), and Caliban now promises to "adore" Stephano (2.2.137), kiss his foot (2.1.146, 149), treat Stephano as his "god" (2.1.146), and swear to be Stephano's "subject" (2.2.149). Meanwhile, Trinculo, although described in the cast list as a jester, seems wiser than either Caliban or Stephano; he calls Caliban "a very shallow monster" (2.2.141–42), a "most poor credulous monster" (2.2.143), and "a most perfidious and drunken monster" (2.2.147–48), and he prophesies that "when's god's asleep," Caliban will "rob his bottle" (2.2.148). Stephano, in the meantime, willingly accepts Caliban's self-degrading worship, and although some editors (e.g., the Vaughans) see his statement "Come, kiss" as meaning "take another drink," it seems just as plausible that he is (also) urging Caliban to fulfill the latter's offer to kiss Stephano's feet. Caliban, in short, instantly enslaves himself to Stephano in a far more dramatic and unambiguous way than he was ever instantly enslaved by Prospero. He considers Stephano a "wondrous man" (2.2.161) and promises to serve him even as he rejects the service of the "tyrant," Prospero (2.2.157–60).

Kissing (or at least offering to kiss) Stephano's feet might seem self-degrading enough, but it isn't long before Caliban is offering to worship his "god" by begging to engage in even more self-debasing behavior: "Let me lick thy shoe" (3.2.22). He calls Stephano his "honour" (3.2.22), his "lord" (3.2.29), and his "noble lord" (3.2.36)— and both his conduct and his phrasing make his immediately ensuing claim that he is "subject to a tyrant" (i.e., Prospero) seem more than a little ironic (3.2.40). He promises that if Stephano will overthrow Prospero, Stephano will be "lord" of the island, "and I'll serve thee" (3.2.55). Meanwhile, his specific plan for killing Prospero—"I'll yield thee him asleep, / Where thou mayst knock a nail into his head" (3.2.58–59)—links him symbolically with the scheme for murder concocted earlier by Antonio (2.1.292–94), perhaps the least ethical and least appealing character in the play. Likewise, his desire to have Stephano "batter his [i.e., Prospero's] skull, or paunch him with a stake, / Or cut his wezand with thy knife" (3.2.90) makes Caliban seem far more vicious and inhumane than Prospero has ever been shown to be. Instead of asking merely that Prospero be banished, or imprisoned, or enslaved, or made to suffer the kinds of pains that Caliban himself has suffered, he seeks Prospero's violent and brutal death. And, as if to make his purposes seem even more malign, he essentially offers Miranda as a sexual conquest for Stephano: "Ay, lord, she will become thy bed, I warrant, / And bring thee forth a brave brood" (3.2.104–05). Presumably Stephano would have to compel Miranda to have sex with him, or even rape her (it is hard to imagine that she would freely consent to intercourse with the murderer of her father), and so, in a sense, Caliban seeks to enslave Miranda in retribution for his own mistreatment. When Stephano subsequently promises "on mine honour" to kill Prospero (3.2.114), the irony could hardly be more blatant.

The ensuing passage in which Caliban praises the beauty of music (3.2.135–43) has often been used as evidence of the inherent nobility of his character, and there seems some validity to this argument. For most Renaissance Christians, all rational beings would exhibit in some way or to some degree the beauty and nobility built into them by their creator, and Caliban is no exception. But Caliban no sooner praises music and beauty than he calls once more for Prospero's murder (3.2.146), and part of the point of the juxtaposition—like much of Caliban's phrasing and behavior throughout the play—is to emphasize that although he is physically enslaved, he still has freedom of mind and conscience and morality, and in all those respects he chooses to enslave himself by giving into his basest desires. Instead of merely beseeching his "god" to free him from Prospero, he seeks revenge and murder against Prospero and a kind of enslavement for Miranda. By this point in the play, the behavior of many of the characters has made it clear that the worst kind of enslavement is self-enslavement to corrupt motives and ignoble passions. Caliban would be a far more sympathetic "slave"—a "slave" far more deserving of our respect, hopes, and good wishes—if his own nature was not so vicious and corrupt.

Ariel, for instance, though an indentured servant to Prospero and subject in his own ways to Prospero's "tyranny," never debases himself as Caliban does. He always preserves his self-respect and thus wins our respect as well. He never prostrates himself before Prospero (as Caliban does before Stephano) by calling himself his master's "foot-licker" (4.1.219). Instead, Ariel even subtly reverses the expected process of master educating servant by, at a crucial point, helping to educate his own master. Thus he subtly encourages Prospero to be compassionate toward his enemies, including his treacherous, murderous brother, telling Prospero that "your charm so strongly works 'em / That, if you now beheld them, your affections / Would become tender" (5.1.17–19). To this, Prospero responds, "Dost thou think so, spirit?" And then Ariel replies, in one of the most moving lines of the whole play, "Mine would, sir, were I human." To which Prospero immediately answers,

> And mine shall.
> Hast thou, which art but air, a touch, a feeling
> Of their afflictions, and shall not myself
> (One of their kind, that relish all as sharply,
> Passion as they) be kindlier moved than thou art?
> Though with their high wrongs I am struck to th'quick,
> Yet with my nobler reason 'gainst my fury
> Do I take part. The rarer action is
> In virtue than in vengeance. They being penitent,
> The sole drift of my purpose doth extend
> Not a frown further. (5.1.19–30)

It is a beautiful, memorable passage, and it reveals Prospero's willingness not only to engage in real dialogue and communication with one of his servants, but also to learn and profit from the example of someone he could easily dismiss or ignore. This is the sort of relationship he and Miranda might have had with Caliban if Caliban had been more willing to "take part" with his "nobler reason" rather than enslaving himself to his irrational passions. To argue that Caliban had no choice but to give into his baser instincts is to treat him, ironically, with less than full human dignity and respect; it is to treat him as precisely the kind of animal or savage that he is sometimes considered to be. When Prospero and Miranda approached Caliban with kindness and compassion, it was Caliban who chose to enslave himself, both figuratively and literally, by yielding to his own "fury" (in all the various senses of that term), just as it is Caliban who chooses to remain and even further entrench himself within that kind of enslavement, especially by submitting to Stephano. Only near the very end of the play is there any hint that he may possibly choose freedom from this sort of moral slavery (5.1.295–98). The choice, however, is ultimately his—as indeed it has been, all along.

NOTES

1. All quotations are from the Arden edition, edited by Alden and Virginia Vaughans.
2. On attitudes toward rape and attempted rape in Shakespeare's time, see, for instance, Amussen 218–19; Gossett 168–75, and Walker 55–60.
3. Of course, one could always argue that she should have made an effort to learn *Caliban's* language, but nothing in the play suggests that she would have been naturally reluctant to do so. Besides, his language seems to have been rudimentary, and he makes no single effort to speak it in the play, even to himself, seeming to prefer the language Miranda has taught him.

WORKS CITED OR CONSULTED

Amussen, Susan Dwyer. "'The Part of a Christian Man': The Cultural Politics of Manhood in Early Modern England." In *Political Culture and Cultural Politics in Early Modern England*, ed. Susan D. Amussen and Mark Kishlansky. Manchester: Manchester University Press, 1995. 213–33.

Andrews, John F., ed. *The Tempest*, by William Shakespeare. The Everyman Shakespeare. London: Dent, 1994.

Bamford, Karen. *Sexual Violence on the Jacobean Stage*. New York: St. Martin's, 2000.

Gossett, Suzanne. "'Best Men Are Molded Out of Faults': Marrying the Rapist in Jacobean Drama." In *Renaissance Historicism: Selections from English*

Literary Renaissance, ed. Arthur F. Kinney and Dan S. Collins. Amherst: University of Massachusetts Press, 1987. 168–90.

Grizzard, Frank E., Jr., and D. Boyd Smith, *The Jamestown Colony: A Political, Social, and Cultural History*. Santa Barbara, CA: ABC-CLIO, 2007.

Hulme, Peter and William H. Sherman, eds. *The Tempest*, by William Shakespeare. Norton Critical Edition. New York: Norton, 2004.

Lindley, David, ed. *The Tempest*, by William Shakespeare. The New Cambridge Shakespeare. Cambridge: Cambridge University Press, 2002.

Orgel, Stephen, ed. *The Tempest*, by William Shakespeare. The Oxford Shakespeare. Oxford: Clarendon Press, 1987.

Phelan, James D. and Gerald Graff, eds. *The Tempest*, by William Shakespeare. New York: Macmillan, 2000.

Ruff, Julius R. *Violence in Early Modern Europe, 1500–1800*. Cambridge: Cambridge University Press, 2001.

Shakespeare, William. *The Merchant of Venice*. Ed. John Russell Brown. Arden Shakespeare. 2nd series. 1955. London: Thomson Learning, 2006.

———. *Othello*. Ed. E.A.J. Honigmann. Arden Shakespeare. 3rd series. 1997. London: Thomson Learning, 2006.

Vaughan, Virginia Mason and Alden T. Vaughan, eds. *The Tempest*, by William Shakespeare. The Arden Shakespeare. 3rd series. London: Thomson Learning, 1999.

Walker, Garthine. *Crime, Gender, and Social Order in Early Modern England*. Cambridge: Cambridge University Press, 2003.

A Vindication of the Rights of Women and *Woman in the Nineteenth Century* (Mary Wollstonecraft and Margaret Fuller)

"Margaret Fuller and Mary Wollstonecraft"
by George Eliot, in *Leader* (1855)

INTRODUCTION

In her review of Margaret Fuller's *Woman in the Nineteenth Century*, novelist George Eliot, author of *Middlemarch*, compares Fuller's work with Mary Wollstonecraft's *A Vindication of the Rights of Women*. For Eliot, both women describe the enslaved position women occupy in the modern world and call out for emancipation, leaving the reader with "ardent hopes of what women may become" and a vision of "women as they are."

The dearth of new books just now gives us time to recur to less recent ones which we have hitherto noticed but slightly; and among these we choose the late edition of Margaret Fuller's "Woman in the Nineteenth Century," because we think it has been unduly thrust into the background by less comprehensive and candid productions on the same subject. Notwithstanding certain defects of taste and a sort of vague spiritualism and grandiloquence which belong to all but the very best American writers, the book is a valuable one: it has the

Eliot, George. "Margaret Fuller and Mary Wollstonecraft." *The Leader* 6 (13 October 1855): 988–9.

enthusiasm of a noble and sympathetic nature, with the moderation and breadth and large allowance of a vigorous and cultivated understanding. There is no exaggeration of woman's moral excellence or intellectual capabilities; no injudicious insistence on her fitness for this or that function hitherto engrossed by men; but a calm plea for the removal of unjust laws and artificial restrictions, so that the possibilities of her nature may have room for full development, a wisely stated demand to disencumber her of the—

> Parasitic forms
> That seem to keep her up but drag her down—
> And leave her field to burgeon and to bloom
> From all within her, make herself her own
> To gift or keep, to live and learn and be
> All that not harms distinctive womanhood.

It is interesting to compare this essay of Margaret Fuller's, published in its earliest form in 1843, with a work on the position of woman written between sixty and seventy years ago—we mean Mary Wollstonecraft's "Rights of Woman." The latter work was not continued beyond the first volume; but so far as this carries the subject, the comparison, at least in relation to strong sense and loftiness of moral tone, is not at all disadvantageous to the woman of the last century. There is in some quarters a vague prejudice against the "Rights of Woman" as in some way or other a reprehensible book, but readers who go to it with this impression will be surprised to find it eminently serious, severely moral, and withal rather heavy—the true reason, perhaps, that no edition has been published since 1796, and that it is now rather scarce. There are several points of resemblance, as well as of striking difference, between the two books. A strong understanding is present in both; but Margaret Fuller's mind was like some regions of her own American continent, where you are constantly stepping from the sunny "clearings" into the mysterious twilight of the tangled forest—she often passes in one breath from forcible reasoning to dreamy vagueness; moreover, her unusually varied culture gives her great command of illustration. Mary Wollstonecraft, on the other hand, is nothing if not rational; she has no erudition, and her grave pages are lit up by no ray of fancy. In both writers we discern, under the brave bearing of a strong and truthful nature, the beating of a loving woman's heart, which teaches them not to undervalue the smallest offices of domestic care or kindliness. But Margaret Fuller, with all her passionate sensibility, is more of the literary woman, who would not have been satisfied without intellectual production; Mary Wollstonecraft, we imagine, wrote not at all for writing's sake, but from the pressure of other motives. So far as the difference of the date allows, there is a striking coincidence in their trains of thought; indeed, every important idea in the "Rights of Woman," except the combination of home education with a common day-school for boys and girls, reappears in Margaret Fuller's essay.

One point on which they both write forcibly is the fact that, while men have a horror of such faculty or culture in the other sex as tends to place it on a level with their own, they are really in a state of subjection to ignorant and feeble-minded women. Margaret Fuller says:—

> "Wherever man is sufficiently raised above extreme poverty or brutal stupidity, to care for the comforts of a fireside, or the bloom and ornament of life, woman has always power enough, if she choose to exert it, and is usually disposed to do so, in proportion to her ignorance and childish vanity. Unacquainted with the importance of life and its purposes, trained to a selfish coquetry and love of petty power, she does not look beyond the pleasure of making herself felt at the moment, and governments are shaken and commerce broken up to gratify the pique of a female favourite. The English shopkeeper's wife does not vote, but it is for her interest that the politician canvasses by the coarsest flattery."

Again:—

> "All wives, bad or good, loved or unloved, inevitably influence their husbands from the power their position not merely gives, but necessitates, of colouring evidence and infusing feelings in hours when the—patient, shall I call him?—is off his guard."

Hear now what Mary Wollstonecraft says on the same subject:—

> "Women have been allowed to remain in ignorance and slavish dependence many, very many years, and still we hear

of nothing but their fondness of pleasure and sway, their preference of rakes and soldiers, their childish attachment to toys, and the vanity that makes them value accomplishments more than virtues. History brings forward a fearful catalogue of the crimes which their cunning has produced, when the weak slaves have had sufficient address to overreach their masters. . . . When, therefore, I call women slaves, I mean in a political and civil sense; for indirectly they obtain too much power, and are debased by their exertions to obtain illicit sway. . . . The libertinism, and even the virtues of superior men, will always give women of some description great power over them; and these weak women, under the influence of childish passions and selfish vanity, *will throw a false light over the objects which the very men view with their eyes who ought to enlighten their judgement.* Men of fancy, and those sanguine characters who mostly hold the helm of human affairs in general, relax in the society of women; and surely I need not cite to the most superficial reader of history the numerous examples of vice and oppression which the private intrigues of female favourites have produced; not to dwell on the mischief that naturally arises from the blundering interposition of well-meaning folly. *For in the transactions of business it is much better to have to deal with a knave than a fool, because a knave adheres to some plan, and any plan of reason may be seen through sooner than a sudden flight of folly.* The power which vile and foolish women have had over wise men who possessed sensibility is notorious."

There is a notion commonly entertained among men that an instructed woman, capable of having opinions, is likely to prove an impracticable yoke-fellow, always pulling one way when her husband wants to go the other, oracular in tone, and prone to give curtain lectures on metaphysics. But surely, so far as obstinacy is concerned, your unreasoning animal is the most unmanageable of creatures, where you are not allowed to settle the question by a cudgel, a whip and bridle, or even a string to the leg. For our own parts, we see no consistent or commodious medium between the old plan of corporal discipline and that thorough education of women which will make them rational beings in the highest sense of the word. Wherever weakness is not harshly controlled it must *govern*, as you may see when a strong man holds a little child by the hand, how he is pulled hither and thither, and wearied in his walk by his submission to the whims and feeble movements of his companion. A really cultured woman, like a really cultured man, will be ready to yield in trifles. So far as we see, there is no indissoluble connection between infirmity of logic and infirmity of will, and a woman quite innocent of an opinion in philosophy, is as likely as not to have an indomitable opinion about the kitchen. As to airs of superiority, no woman ever had them in consequence of true culture, but only because her culture was shallow or unreal, only as a result of what Mrs. Malaprop well calls "the ineffectual qualities in a woman"—mere acquisitions carried about, and not knowledge thoroughly assimilated so as to enter into the growth of the character.

To return to Margaret Fuller, some of the best things she says are on the folly of absolute definitions of woman's nature and absolute demarcations of woman's mission. "Nature," she says, "seems to delight in varying the arrangements, as if to show that she will be fettered by no rule; and we must admit the same varieties that she admits." Again: "If nature is never bound down, nor the voice of inspiration stifled, that is enough. We are pleased that women should write and speak, if they feel need of it, from having something to tell; but silence for ages would be no misfortune, if that silence be from divine command, and not from man's tradition." And here is a passage, the beginning of which has been often quoted:—

> "If you ask me what offices they (women) may fill, I reply—any. I do not care what case you put; let them be sea-captains if you will. I do not doubt there are women well fitted for such an office, and, if so, I should be as glad as to welcome the Maid of Saragossa or the Maid of Missolonghi, or the Suliote heroine, or Emily Plater. I think women need, especially at this juncture, a much greater range of occupation than they have, to rouse their latent powers.... In families that I know, some little girls like to saw wood, others to use carpenter's tools. Where these tastes are indulged, cheerfulness and good-humour are promoted. Where they are forbidden, because 'such things are not proper for girls,' they grow sullen and mischievous. Fourier had observed these wants of women, as no one can fail to do who watches the desires of little girls, or knows the ennui that

haunts grown women, except where they make to themselves a serene little world by art of some kind. He, therefore, in proposing a great variety of employments, in manufactures or the care of plants and animals, allows for one-third of women as likely to have a taste for masculine pursuits. one-third of men for feminine. . . . I have no doubt, however, that a large proportion of women would give themselves to the same employments as now, because there are circumstances that must lead them. Mothers will delight to make the nest soft and warm. Nature would take care of that; no need to clip the wings of any bird that wants to soar and sing, or finds in itself the strength of pinion for a migratory flight unusual to its kind. The difference would be that *all* need not be constrained to employments for which *some* are unfit."

Apropos of the same subject, we find Mary Wollstonecraft offering a suggestion which the women of the United States have already begun to carry out. She says:—

"Women, in particular, all want to be ladies. Which is simply to have nothing to do, but listlessly to go they scarcely care where, for they cannot tell what. But what have women to do in society, I may be asked, but to loiter with easy grace? surely you would not condemn them all to suckle fools and chronicle small beer. No. *Women might certainly study the art of healing, and be physicians as well as nurse.* . . . Business of various kinds they might likewise pursue, if they were educated in a more orderly manner. . . . Women would not then marry for a support, as men accept of places under government, and neglect the implied duties."

Men pay a heavy price for their reluctance to encourage self-help and independent resources in women. The precious meridian years of many a man of genius have to be spent in the toil of routine, that an "establishment" may be kept up for a woman who can understand none of his secret yearnings, who is fit for nothing but to sit in her drawing-room like a doll-Madonna in her shrine. No matter. Anything is more endurable than to change our established formulae about women, or to run the risk of looking up to our wives instead of looking down on them. *Sit divus, dummodo non sit vivus* (let him be a god, provided he be not living), said the Roman magnates of Romulus; and so men say of women, let them be idols, useless absorbents of precious things, provided we are not obliged to admit them to be strictly fellow-beings, to be treated, one and all, with justice and sober reverence.

On one side we hear that woman's position can never be improved until women themselves are better; and on the other, that women can never become better until their position is improved—until the laws are made more just, and a wider field opened to feminine activity. But we constantly hear the same difficulty stated about the human race in general. There is a perpetual action and reaction between individuals and institutions; we must try and mend both by little and little—the only way in which human things can be mended. Unfortunately, many over-zealous champions of women assert their actual equality with men—nay, even their moral superiority to men—as a ground for their release from oppressive laws and restrictions. They lose strength immensely by this false position. If it were true, then there would be a case in which slavery and ignorance nourished virtue, and so far we should have an argument for the continuance of bondage. But we want freedom and culture for woman, because subjection and igno-rance have debased her, and with her, Man; for—

> If she be small, slight-natured, miserable,
> How shall men grow?

Both Margaret Fuller and Mary Wollstonecraft have too much sagacity to fall into this sentimental exaggeration. Their ardent hopes of what women may become do not prevent them from seeing and painting women as they are. On the relative moral excellence of men and women Mary Wollstonecraft speaks with the most decision:—

> "Women are supposed to possess more sensibility, and even humanity, than men, and their strong attachments and instantaneous emotions of compassion are given as proofs; but the clinging affection of ignorance has seldom anything noble in it, and may mostly be resolved into selfishness, as well as the affection of children and brutes. I have known many weak women whose sensibility was entirely engrossed by their husbands; and as for their humanity, it was very faint

indeed, or rather it was only a transient emotion of compassion. Humanity does not consist in a 'squeamish ear,' says an eminent orator. 'It belongs to the mind as well as to the nerves.' But this kind of exclusive affection, though it degrades the individual, should not be brought forward as a proof of the inferiority of the sex, because it is the natural consequence of confined views; for even women of superior sense, having their attention turned to little employments and private plans, rarely rise to heroism, unless when spurred on by love! and love, as an heroic passion, like genius, appears but once in an age. I therefore agree with the moralist who asserts 'that women have seldom so much generosity as men'; and that their narrow affections, to which justice and humanity are often sacrificed, render the sex apparently inferior, especially as they are commonly inspired by men; but I contend that the heart would expand as the understanding gained strength, if women were not depressed from their cradles."

We had marked several other passages of Margaret Fuller's, for extract, but as we do not aim at an exhaustive treatment of our subject, and are only touching a few of its points, we have, perhaps, already claimed as much of the reader's attention as he will be willing to give to such desultory material.

VISIONS OF THE DAUGHTERS OF ALBION (WILLIAM BLAKE)

"Blake's Vision of Slavery"
by David Erdman, in *Journal of the Warburg and Courtauld Institutes* (1952)

INTRODUCTION

In his study of William Blake's *Visions of the Daughters of Albion*, David Erdman outlines the ways Blake engaged "concrete historical situations," most notably the institution of slavery. For Erdman, Blake's illuminated manuscripts become "decreasingly inexplicable as we approach them with some knowledge of the facts which his eye saw and the modes of cruelty and prejudice which he wished to make known to the hearts of his contemporaries." In exploring "the three symbolic persons of the poem, their triangular relationship, and their unresolved debate," Erdman argues they are in part "poetic counterparts of the parliamentary and editorial debates of 1789–93 on the bill to abolish the British slave trade–the frustrated lover, for example, being analogous to the wavering abolitionist who cannot bring himself openly to condemn slavery though he deplores the *trade*." By exploring Blake's works and also the sources available to

Erdman, David. "Blake's Vision of Slavery." *Journal of the Warburg and Courtauld Institutes*, 15.3–4 (1952): 242–252.

him, Erdman demonstrates how Blake decries enslavement
and calls for emancipation.

∽⟋⟍∼

"The Eye sees more than the Heart knows," wrote Blake on the title-
page of his *Visions of the Daughters of Albion*, published in Illuminated
Printing in 1793. We no longer think of Blake as the sort of "mystic"
who would have meant that he did not always understand his own
"inexplicable pictures" (thus M. Berger).[1] Nor since the studies of
Mr. Bronowski and Mr. Schorer[2] can we remain content with Mr.
Damon's interpretation—that Blake "could not understand the facts
of this world ... could not believe the cruelty and prejudice which
he saw everywhere."[3] We are coming to recognize that most of the
prophetic books are closely related to concrete historical situations
or clusters of events that "passed before" Blake's face. And we find
his symbolic pictures decreasingly inexplicable as we approach them
with some knowledge of the facts which his eye saw and the modes of
cruelty and prejudice which he wished to make known to the hearts
of his contemporaries.

I

The *Visions of the Daughters of Albion*, though long recognized as in
some sort a companion piece to the obviously historical *America*, of
the same year, has been related to current discussions of "the ethic of
property" but not to any specific background of events. Superficially it
appears to be a lyric debate on free love, with passing allusions to the
rights of man, the rights of woman, and the rights of beasts; to the
injustices of sexual inhibition and prohibition, of the moral tyranny
of "cold floods of abstraction," and of Negro and child slavery. Yet
love and slavery prove to be the two poles of the poem's axis. And the
momentum of its spinning—for it does not progress—is supplied by
the oratory of Oothoon, the "soft soul of America" who is also a female
slave, free in spirit but physically bound; Bromion, the slave-driver
who owns her and has raped her to increase her market value; and
Theotormon, her jealous but inhibited lover who fears to acknowledge
her divine humanity. As a "lament over the possessiveness of love
and the impossible demand for purity,"[4] the poem has been widely
explored in the light of Blake's note-book poems on this theme and

Mary Wollstonecraft's *Vindication of the Rights of Woman*.[5] The other pole, equally important in the dynamics of the work, has scarcely been discovered.[6] Yet we can understand the three symbolic persons of the poem, their triangular relationship, and their unresolved debate if we recognize them as, in part, poetic counterparts of the parliamentary and editorial debates of 1789–93 on the bill to abolish the British slave trade—the frustrated lover, for example, being analogous to the wavering abolitionist who cannot bring himself openly to condemn slavery though he deplores the *trade*.

Blake, in relating his discussion of freedom to the "voice of slaves beneath the sun" (line 31), was directing the light of the French Revolution upon the most vulnerable flaw in the British constitution, and in doing so he was contributing to the most widely agitated reform movement in England at the time. The Society for the Abolition of the Slave Trade was formed in 1787, and Blake's *Little Black Boy* coincided with the early phase of a campaign in which several artists and writers were enlisted. The *Visions* was written at the climax of the first parliamentary phase, which began in 1789 and coincided with the revolution in France and the ensuing revolution in 1791 of slaves in French St. Domingo. It reached its height in 1792–93, and Wordsworth, returning to England early in 1793 after more than a year in France, was struck by the extent of the English movement: "little less in verity Than a whole Nation crying with one voice" against "the Traffickers in Negro blood" (*Prelude*, X). Conservative as well as liberal humanitarians were not unwilling to dissociate British honour and British commerce from "this most rotten branch of human shame." Moreover, the slaves themselves made the trade a risky one, both for slave drivers and for ship owners. And military statesmen complained that merchant seamen died off twice as rapidly in the slave trade as in any other, effecting a loss of manpower for the navy. The abolitionists nevertheless were "baffled." The bill was defeated in Parliament under the pressure of Anti-jacobin attacks by Burke and Lord Abingdon and various slave-agents, of whom Blake's thundering Bromion is a caricature.

In Blake's view the friends of freedom had quailed before the slave traders because the Heart had not kept up with the Eye; and Oothoon, the soft soul of America still in chains, pleads the indivisibility of freedom and love—for the edification of the "enslav'd" Daughters of Albion, an almost silent audience or chorus, who lament upon their mountains and in their valleys and sigh "toward America," and who may be considered the Blakean equivalent of traditional personifications of the trades and industries of Great Britain: in *The Four Zoas* some of them will appear as the textile trades whose "needlework" is sold throughout the earth. In the moral allegory they are, of course, "oppressed womanhood" (as Damon points out).

II

Blake's knowledge of the cruelties of slavery came to him doubtless through many sources, but one source was particularly impressive and, literally, graphic. In 1791 or earlier the liberal publisher Joseph Johnson distributed to Blake and other engravers a sheaf of some eighty sketches of the flora and fauna and conditions of human servitude in the South American colony of Dutch Guiana during some early slave revolts. Blake, on excellent terms with Johnson at the time,[7] received nearly all the pictures illustrating slave conditions. With more than his usual care he engraved at least sixteen plates, and we know he was working on them during the production of *Visions* because he turned in most of his work in batches dated December 1792 and December 1793.[8] The two volumes they illustrate were finally published in 1796 as *A Narrative of a five Years' expedition against the Revolted Negroes of Surinam, in Guiana, on the Wild Coast of South America; from the year 1772 to 1777*, by Captain J. G. Stedman. We may assume that Blake was familiar with the narrative, available in Johnson's shop, at least so far as the portions explanatory of the drawings are concerned. His real interest is shown in the fact that he was the only one of the engravers who subscribed for the published work—if we can assume that he is the subscriber designated "Blake (Mr. Wm.) London."

Blake's engravings, with a force of expression absent from the others, emphasize the dignity of Negro men and women stoical under cruel torture the wise, reproachful look of the 'Negro hung alive by the Ribs to a Gallows,' who lived three days unmurmuring and who upbraided a flogged comrade for crying (Pl. 49a); the bitter concern in the face of the Negro executioner who was compelled to break the bones of a crucified rebel (Pl. 49b); the warm, self-possessed look of his victim, who jested with the crowd and offered to his sentinel "my hand that was chopped off" to eat with his piece of dry bread for how was it "that he, a *white* man, should have no meat to eat along with it?"[9] The image of this courageous rebel during 'The Execution of "Breaking on the Rack'" (Pl. 49b) entered Blake's vision and in the Preludium of *America* he drew Orc in the same posture to represent the spirit of human freedom defiant of tyranny (Pl. 51c).[10]

For the *finis* page Blake engraved according to Stedman's specifications "an emblematical picture" of 'Europe supported by Africa & America'—three comely nude women tenderly embracing each other, the Negro and the European clasping hands in sisterly equality (Pl. 49d). In the text Stedman expresses an "ardent wish" that all peoples "may henceforth and to all eternity be the props of each other" since "we only differ in colour, but are certainly all created by the same Hand."[11] Yet Europe is *supported* by her darker sisters, and they wear slave bracelets while she has a string of pearls—a symbolism rather closer to the historical fact. For one plate Blake had the ironic task of engraving a "contented" slave—with Stedman's initials stamped on his flesh with a silver signet.[12]

In his *Narrative* Stedman demonstrates the dilemma, social and sexual, of the English man of sentiment entangled in the ethical code of property and propriety. A hired soldier in Guiana, Captain Stedman was apologetic about the "Fate" that caused him to be fighting bands of rebel slaves in a Dutch colony: "'Twas *Yours* to fall—but *Mine* to feel the wound," we learn from the frontispiece, engraved by Bartolozzi: 'Stedman with a Rebel Negro prostrate at his feet.' The fortitude of the tortured Negroes and the "commiseration" of their Negro executioners impressed Stedman and led him to conclude that Europeans were "the greater barbarians." Yet he could repeat the myth that these same dignified people were "perfectly savage" in Africa and would only be harmed by "sudden emancipation." His "ears were stunned with the clang of the whip and the dismal yells"; yet he was reassured by the consideration that the tortures were legal punishment and were not occurring in a *British* colony.[13]

To the torture of female slaves Stedman was particularly sensitive, for he was in love with a beautiful fifteen-year-old slave, Joanna, and in a quandary suggestive of that of Blake's Theotormon, who loves Oothoon but cannot free her. Stedman managed "a decent wedding" with Joanna, for which he is shamefaced, and a honeymoon during which they were "free like the roes in the forest." But he was unable to purchase her freedom, and when he thought Joanna was to be sold at auction, he fancied he "saw her tortured, insulted, and bowing under

the weight of her chains, calling aloud, but in vain, for my assistance."
Even on their honeymoon, Stedman was harrowed by his inability to
prevent the sadistic flagellation of a slave on a neighbouring estate.
We have Blake's engraving of this 'Flagellation of a Female Samboe
Slave' (Pl. 49c). Naked and tied "by both arms to a tree," the "beautiful Samboe girl of about eighteen" had just received two hundred
lashes. Stedman's interference only prompted the overseer to order the
punishment repeated. "Thus I had no other remedy but to run to my
boat, and leave the detestable monster, like a beast of prey, to enjoy his
bloody feast." The girl's crime had been her "refusing to submit to the
loathsome embraces of her detestable executioner." The captain's own
Joanna, to prove the equality of her "soul" to "that of an European,"
insisted on enduring the condition of slavery until she could purchase
freedom with her own labour.[14] Blake's Oothoon invites vultures to
prey upon her naked flesh for the same reason. Her lover, Theotormon,
is also unable to interfere or to rescue her:

> Why does my Theotormon sit weeping upon the threshold,
> And Oothoon hovers by his side, perswading him in vain?[15]

The persons and problems of Stedman's *Narrative* reappear,
creatively modified, in the text and illustrations of Blake's *Visions*:
the rape and torture of the virgin slave, her pride in the purity and
equality of her soul, and the frustrated desire of her lover and husband.
Oothoon advertised as pregnant by Bromion is the slave on the
auction block whose pregnancy enhances her price; Oothoon chained
by an ankle is the 'Female Negro Slave, with a Weight chained to
her Ancle'—or the similarly chained victim of the infamous Captain
Kimber, cited in Parliament in 1791.[16] The cold green wave enveloping
the chained Oothoon (Pl. 50b) is symbolic of the drowning of slaves
in passage from Africa; the flame-like shape of the wave is symbolic
of the liberating fires of rebellion. Her friend beside her hears her
call but covers his eyes from seeing what must be done.[17] In another
picture (Pl. 50c) Oothoon is fastened back-to-back to Bromion; yet
the most prominent chains are on *his* leg, and she has not ceased struggling to be free.[18] Impotent beside these two squats Theotormon, the
theology-tormented man,[19] inhibited by a moral code that tells him
his love is impure. A caricature of paralysed will-power, he simultaneously clutches himself, buries his face in his arms, and scratches

the back of his head. Despite his furtive sympathy ("secret tears") he makes no effective response to

> The voice of slaves beneath the sun, and children bought with
>   money,
> That shiver in religious caves beneath the burning fires
> Of lust, that belch incessant from the summits of the earth.[20]

Stedman's anxieties shed light on the moral paralysis of Theo-tormon; yet we must also be aware of the analogous but more impersonal and political quandary of the Abolition Society, whose equivocal announcement in February 1792, that they did not desire "the Emancipation of the Negroes in the British Colonies" but only sought to end "*the trade* for Slaves," conflicted with their own humanitarian professions and involved an acceptance of the basic premises of the slavers: that slaves were legitimate commodities and that the rebellion of slaves was legally indefensible.[21] William Wilberforce, the Society's zealous but conservative spokesman in Parliament, became increasingly preoccupied in 1792 with efforts to clear his humanitarian reputation of the taint of liberalism and to be known as a great friend of the slaves yet an abhorrer of "democratical principles." Also he had obtained a "Royal Proclamation against vice and immorality" and was promoting what became known as the Vice Society, based on the Urizenic proposition that woman's love is Sin and democracy is Blasphemy.[22] Blake's deliberate emphasis on the delights of "happy copulation" and "lovely copulation" could be expected to shock such angelic moralists, as if to say: you cannot free any portion of humanity from chains unless you recognize the close connection between the cat o' nine tails and the moral code.[23]

III

The situation or story of Blake's poem is briefly this. Oothoon, a virgin bride, loves Theotormon and is not afraid to enter the experience of love. She puts a marigold between her breasts and flies over the ocean to take it to her lover; she is willing, that is, to give him the flower of her virginity. But on the way she is seized by Bromion, who rapes her despite her woeful outcries, and advertises her as a pregnant slave (harlot).[24] Her lover—or husband, for he thinks more of the legal than the amorous side of their relationship—responds not by coming to her rescue but by accusing her and Bromion of adultery and secretly bemoaning his fate and hers. And so Oothoon and Bromion remain "bound back to back" in the barren relationship of slavery, while Theotormon, failing as a lover, sits "weeping upon the threshold." The rest of the poem consists of their three-sided soliloquy. Oothoon argues that she is still pure in that she can still bring her lover flowers of joy, moments of gratified desire; but he cannot act because he accepts Bromion's definition of her as a sinner.

Interpretation of the story on this level is sometimes blurred by failure to distinguish Oothoon's offer of herself to Theotormon from her rape by Bromion. The flower-picking is mistaken for a symbol of the rape, and her later argument is mistaken for defence of an "affair" with Bromion. But Oothoon resists Bromion; and in Blake's plot-source, Macpherson's *Oithona*, where the heroine is similarly raped in her lover's absence, the lover returning does what obviously Theotormon ought to do, considers her still faithful and goes to battle at once in her defence, against great odds.[25] Oothoon's argument is not that she likes Bromion or slavery but that she refuses to accept the status of a fallen woman: only if her lover lets Bromion's invective intimidate him will she be "a whore indeed."[26] She is not asking merely for toleration but for love.

The allegorical level, indicated by Oothoon's designation as "the soft soul of America," must not be neglected. Bromion's signet brands not simply a woman but "thy soft American plains," and Bromion is no simple rapist but the slaver whose claim to "thy north & south" is based on his possession in both North and South America of African slaves: "stampt with my signet ... the swarthy children of the sun." When the soul of America goes "seeking flowers to comfort her" she is looking for a further blossoming of the revolutionary spirit (compare the Preludium of *America*) and when she finds a "bright Marygold" in the "dewy bed" of "the vales of Leutha," she is apparently taking note of the insurrections in St. Domingo in the Caribbean, around which the debate in Parliament raged: "Bromion rent her with his thunders."[27] The first risings did not succeed, but the flower or nymph comforts "Oothoon the mild" both with her own "glow" and with the observation that the spirit of liberty is irrepressible: "Another flower shall spring, because the soul of sweet delight Can never pass away." On this level Theotormon, to whom Oothoon wings over the waves in "exulting swift delight" expecting him to rejoice at the good news, acts like those English abolitionists who were embarrassed by the thunders of the Anti-jacobins.

Blake's acquaintance with the abolition debates is evident. The Bromions in Parliament cried that Africans were "inured to the hot climate" of the plantations and therefore needed for "labour under a vertical sun." Under Bromion's words Blake draws a picture, stretching across the page, of a Negro worker smitten into desperate horizon-tality, wilted like the heat-blasted vegetation among which he has been working with a pickaxe, and barely able to hold his face out of the dirt (Pl. 50d).[28] The apologists for slavery argued also that Negroes understood only firmness, were contented and happy and supersti-tious, and were now "habituated to the contemplation of slavery." Bromion utters the same arguments: that "the swarthy children of the sun . . . are obedient, they resist not, they obey the scourge; Their daughters worship terrors and obey the violent."

In Parliament Lord Abingdon accused the "abettors" of abolition of promoting the new philosophy of levelling: "Look at the state of the colony of St. Domingo, and see what liberty and equality, see what the rights of man have done there." They have dried up the rivers of *commerce* and replaced them with "fountains of human blood." More-over, according to Abingdon, the levellers are prophesying that

> all being equal, blacks and whites, French and English [*sic*], wolves and lambs, shall all, "merry companions every one," promiscuously pig together; engendering . . . a new species of man as the product of this new philosophy.[29]

It is this sort of argument that Blake's Oothoon turns right side up again. For, as Abingdon put it, "what does the abolition of the slave trade mean more or less in effect, than liberty and equality?" Wilberforce joined Burke in a committee for the relief of emigrant royalist priests partly, as he admitted, "to do away French citizen-ship"—for the French had misinterpreted his liberalism and named him an honorary French citizen along with Paine and Priestley! Yet this demonstration did not prevent Burke from attacking the Aboli-tion Bill as "a shred of the accursed web of Jacobinism."[30] Blake's Theotormon is tangled in the suspicion that his own desires are part of an accursed web.

IV

The argument of Oothoon is triplex, as she herself is. Stedman's emblematical picture treats Europe, Africa, and America as three separate women: Blake makes them into one. He can do this because Oothoon is not a person but a "soul." Pictured in chains she is the female slave, but she does not have the black skin and tight ringlets of the Africa of the emblem. Only in the picture of the exhausted worker is the Negro slave directly represented. The shape of Oothoon is, allowing for difference in mediums, the American Indian of the emblem, with the same loose black hair, sad mouth, and angular limbs. (See especially the illustration on the title-page, where she runs along the trough of a green wave pursued by the mistaken God of tyranny.)

Yet her skin is not the copper colour of the engraved America either, but theoretically "snowy" white, according to the text.[31] "I am pure," she cries, "because the night is gone that clos'd me in its deadly black." Speaking as America she means that the night of oppressive chivalry is gone with the dawn of freedom. Speaking as Africa she means that the time is gone when people's vision was limited to their five senses and they could see only her dark skin and not her inward purity.

Blake had explained this symbolism in his *Little Black Boy*:

> My mother bore me in the southern wild,
> And I am black, but O! my soul is white;
> White as an angel is the English child,
> But I am black, as if bereav'd of light.

To avoid a chauvinistic interpretation Blake explained that any skin colour is a cloud that cannot obscure the essential brotherhood of man in a fully enlightened society, such as Heaven. "These black bodies and this sunburnt face," said the little black boy, are "but a cloud." If the Negro is to be free of his black cloud, the little English boy must be likewise free from his "white cloud," which is equally opaque. "When I from black and he from white cloud free," I will "be like him, and he will then love me." In the second illustrated page of this Song of Innocence the black boy, it should be observed, appears as light-skinned as the English boy—or as Oothoon.

Oothoon's reason for letting vultures[32] prey upon "her soft snowy limbs" (Pl. 50a) is to let Theotormon, who is an adult version of the English child, *see* that beneath the skin her "pure transparent breast" really reflects the same human "image" as his—that her colour is morally that of "the clear spring, mudded with feet of beasts," which again "grows pure & smiles." As Africa she is urging the London citizen to ignore colour differences. As America she is urging British law-makers to rescue her from the muddy feet of the slaver. As a woman enslaved by Marriage Act morality, she is imploring her lover to rise above accusations of adultery.

Beyond arguing her essential purity, she indicates by several analogies that there is something especially beautiful about dark skin and (she suggests both points at once) about pregnancy. Consider the dark skin of worm-ripened fruit, which is "sweetest"; or the darkness of "the soul prey'd on by woe"; or

> The new wash'd lamb ting'd with the village smoke, & the
>   bright swan
> By the red earth of our immortal river. I bathe my wings,
> And I am white and pure to hover round Theotormon's breast.[33]

It is the soul rather than the body of the slave that is "inured," in being richer in experience. The black boy already loves the English boy and is thus better prepared than he to "bear the heat" of God's presence.

And still we have not done with the complexity of Blake's symbolism, for in one illustration, on the page of the "Argument," Oothoon appears not as an American Indian but as the European woman of the emblem (Pl. 51a). Or rather in this illustration the Stedman influence is supplanted by that of a French neo-classical painter, Vien. Here the focus is on the buying and selling of woman's love, and Blake is reversing Vien's picture (based on a Roman original) of a procuress offering "loves" for sale in a basket: 'La Marchande d'Amours' (Pl. 51b).[34] Oothoon kneels in the same posture as that of the love-merchant; her hair is knotted at the back of her head in a similar fashion. But whereas Vien's procuress holds one of her cupids by his wings like a captive bird, Oothoon keeps her hands to herself and lightly "kisses the joy as it flies," springing not from a basket but from the stem of a marigold.[35]

V

In the most general sense the soaring joys which Oothoon offers to Theotormon are sparks of Promethean fire or winged thoughts calculated to widen his brow (see *A Song of Liberty*). In her effort to prod him to cross the threshold of indecision, Oothoon insists that the revolutionary dawn is at hand and overdue and that the corn is ripe:

> I cry: arise, O Theotormon! for the village dog
> Barks at the breaking day; the nightingale has done lamenting;
> The lark does rustle in the ripe corn, and the Eagle returns
> From nightly prey and lifts his golden beak to the pure east,
> Shaking the dust from his immortal pinions to awake
> The sun that sleeps too long.[36]

Yet this "citizen of London" does not look up but remains confused. He is not at all sure "what is the night or day"; he is nearly deaf to the cries of slaves and blind to visions of a new day: he cannot arise. The springs of rebellion are as obscure to him as those of moral purity. "Tell me what is a thought," he pleads:

> Tell me what is a joy . . . and upon what mountains
> Wave shadows of discontent? and in what houses dwell the
>   wretched,
> Drunken with woe, forgotten, and shut up from cold despair?[37]

His countenance has begun hesitantly to open to Oothoon's winged thoughts:

> Tell me where dwell the thoughts forgotten till thou call them
>   forth?
> . . . .
> Where goest thou, O thought? to what remote land . . . ?

But the remote land is America, the land of freedom, and he is immediately suspicious of the new philosophy:

> Wilt thou bring comforts on thy wings, and dews and honey
>   and balm,
> Or poison from the desart wilds, from the eyes of the envier?

And he grows silent when Bromion shakes the cavern with rhetorical questions, just as some of the Abolitionists were silenced in 1793 by the clamour of Anti-jacobinism.

In the debates a Mr. Baillie, slavery's "agent for Grenada," argued that the very Empire was based on the right to flog:

> I wish to ask such members as have served in his majesty's navy and army, if it is possible to maintain that subordination that is absolutely necessary among bodies of men, without the fear of punishment? ... Have we never heard of seamen being flogged from ship to ship, or of soldiers dying in the very act of punishment, under the lash of the drummer, when tied up to the halberds, and exposed in as shameful and ignominious a manner as can possibly be conceived [i.e. treated as the slaves are treated]? Have we not also heard, even in this country of boasted liberty, of seamen being kidnapped and carried away ... without being allowed the comfort of seeing their wives and families?

Nor was the misery of the slaves extraordinary:

> I declare [continued Baillie] there is more wretchedness and poverty in the parish of St. Giles, in which I live, than there is in the whole of the extensive colonies.[38]

Bromion's rhetorical questions are on the same order:

> Ah! are there other wars beside the wars of sword and fire?
> And are there other sorrows beside the sorrows of poverty?
> And are there other joys beside the joys of riches and ease?
> And is there not one law for both the lion and the ox?
> And is there not eternal fire and eternal chains
> To bind the phantoms of existence from eternal life?

In other words, dare anyone question that subordination must be maintained? Has anyone even in this land of liberty and poverty yet heard of any way to maintain order without fear of punishment? Are not war and slavery the basis of our Empire? Is not sorrow intended for the poor, joy for the rich? Is not fear of Hell necessary to keep the laborious poor from pursuing *life*?

Oothoon replies with a vigorous assertion of "Love! Love! Love! happy, happy Love! free as the mountain wind!" But she remains shackled to Bromion, and Theotormon "sits," and "The Daughters of Albion hear her woes, & echo back her sighs." "The End."

NOTES

1. P. Berger, *William Blake, Poet and Mystic*, New York, 1915, p. 50.
2. J. Bronowski, *Man Without a Mask*, London, 1944; Mark Schorer, *William Blake, the Politics of Vision*, New York, 1946.
3. S. Foster Damon, *William Blake, His Philosophy and Symbols*, Boston and New York, 1924, p. 332.
4. Bernard Blackstone, *English Blake*, Cambridge, 1949, p. 291, in an excellent chapter on "Desire, Love and Marriage."
5. See Damon, Schorer, Blackstone, and, for a detailed exposition, Henry Wasser, "Notes on the *Visions of the Daughters of Albion* by William Blake," *MLQ*, IX, September 1948, pp. 292–7. Wasser develops Middleton Murry's theory that the poem expresses "Blake's knowledge of the love affair between Mary Wollstonecraft and Henry Fuseli." But one is inclined to agree with Schorer that the theory is implausible, "since Mary Wollstonecraft was never involved in such a situation as Oothoon's." Schorer, p. 290.
6. Northrop Frye, *Fearful Symmetry*, Princeton, 1947, p. 241, points to it with his observation that Bromion "is also the possessive economy founded on slavery." And Jack Lindsay, "Ossian," *Modern Quarterly Miscellany*, London, 1947, p. 91, observes that what crucifies Oothoon "is the ethic of property with its consequences of jealousy."
7. See Johnson's letter to Wedgwood, quoted in Geoffrey Keynes, *Blake Studies*, London, 1949, pp. 68–69.
8. Blake signed thirteen plates (one dated December 1, 1794), and three others are unmistakably his. See Geoffrey Keynes, *Bibliography of Blake*, 1921.
9. Stedman, *Narrative*, I, 109.
10. Cf. *America*, p. 1.
11. Stedman, II, 394.
12. *Ibid.*, I, 206; II, pl. 68. Cf. Bromion: "Stampt with my signet are the swarthy children of the sun." V.D.A. 21.

13. Stedman, I, 107, 201 ff., 297–298.

14. *Ibid.*, I, 86 ff., 104, 207, 310–319; II, 82, 377.

15. V.D.A. 44–45.

16. Plate cited was engraved by Bartolozzi. For the Kimber case see Wilberforce in *Parl. Hist.*, April 2, 1792.

17. V.D.A. Pl. 4.

18. Plate printed variously as frontispiece and tailpiece.

19. The names Oothoon, Theotormon, Bromion, and Leutha have been traced to Ossian's Oithona, Tonthormod, Brumo, and Lutha. Damon, p. 329. The oo-oo doubling may come from African words in Stedman: apootoo, too-too, ooroocoocoo (snake). A *toremon* is a shiny black bird whose name means "a tale-bearer, or a spy"; and the rebels "have an invincible hatred against it." Stedman, I, 367. If *Theo* is God, Theotormon is God's spy, Theo-toremon. Unquestionably he torments and is tormented: see D. J. Sloss and J. P. R. Wallis, *William Blake's Prophetic Writings*, Oxford, 1926, I, 34n.

20. V.D.A. 31–33.

21. *London Chronicle*, February 2, 1792.

22. See Wilberforce, *Memoirs*, pp. 60–66; and W. L. Mathieson, *England in Transition* London, 1920, pp. 70–71.

23. In V.D.A. pl. 6, Theotormon is flaying himself with a three-thonged scourge, while Oothoon runs by unaided.

24. The pregnant slave fetches a higher price than the virgin. Stedman, I, 206.

25. On Blake's use of *Oithona* see Lindsay, *loc. cit.*

26. V.D.A. 170. Were Oothoon and Theotormon married before the story begins? Critics differ. Bromion's "Now thou maist marry" suggests they were not; Theotormon's jealousy of "the adulterate pair" suggests they were. What matters is that the affair was not consummated. Theotormon, like Thel, shrinks from "experience."

27. Leutha's Vale is evidently Blake's place name for French St. Domingo, since Leutha is elsewhere the Queen of France, and when the West Indies docks are located in London's Isle of Dogs, Blake takes to calling it the Isle of Leutha's Dogs; *Jerusalem*, Pl. 31. In a verse fragment the fading of "the British Colonies" is compared to the dying of a dream (of French colonialism?) which has left "obscured traces in the Vale of Leutha."

28. V.D.A. pl. 2. Stedman, I, 201–206. *Parl. Hist.* passim.
29. *Parl. Hist.*, April 11, 1793.
30. Mathieson, pp. 70–71.
31. Blake usually employed brown inks in printing the *Visions*, though sometimes he chose pink, purple, or yellow tints.
32. Blake uses eagles and vultures interchangeably.
33. V.D.A. 75–81.
34. Blake must have been acquainted with this work of the 1760's, which has been called "artistically the revolutionary bombshell of the eighteenth century" (Milton W. Brown, *The Painting of the French Revolution*, New York, 1938, p. 74), and his ironic use of it should be classed as an example of "witty quotation." (See Edgar Wind in the *Warburg Institute Journal*, II, 182–185). Vien's work imitates 'The Dealer in Loves,' a painting of the time of Augustus, discovered at Stabiae in 1758. Monaco, *Le Musée Nationale de Naples*, Pl. 25.
35. See Damon, p. 332, on a parallel quatrain of Blake's. "He who binds to himself a joy Does the winged life destroy" will describe Vien's picture. The next lines, "But he who kisses the joy as it flies Lives in eternity's sun rise," describe Blake's.
36. V.D.A. 46–51.
37. In "from cold despair," *from* has the force of *because of*.
38. *Parl. Hist.*, April 2, 1793.

THE POETRY OF PHILLIS WHEATLEY

"Emancipating Phillis Wheatley"
by Deborah James, University of
North Carolina at Asheville

Born around 1753 in an area that currently includes parts of both Senegal and Gambia, Phillis Wheatley came to America as a slave and became the first published African-American poet. Then as now, some of her fame is based on the specifics of her identity. From the moment her story first reached the public in the 1700s, people have argued over what her life and work demonstrate about the humanity of blacks, both the limitations and capabilities of the race. Critics since the last half of the twentieth century have been especially concerned with determining and accounting for her attitude toward Africa, her own enslavement, and the institution and practice of slavery expressed in her writing. By reassessing her writings, we can see how Wheatley comments upon the experience of being enslaved and how her works may be emancipated from historical misconceptions and racial prejudice.

Susannah Wheatley purchased Phillis in Boston when she was around eight years old. Concerned that the other slaves in her household were aging, Mrs. Wheatley had been searching for a young person to serve her. Her twins (especially her daughter) had reached the age of eighteen, an age at which to leave home, increasing Mrs. Wheatley's need for help. According to several accounts, she found Phillis on the auction block, wrapped only in a piece of dirty carpet—a slight, shy child. Her appearance and demeanor caught Mrs. Wheatley's eye and heart. But though Susannah Wheatley may have originally purchased her out of pity, the talents of this child stunned everyone. Within sixteen months, Phillis had mastered English to such an extent that the daughter of the house began to further educate her in the classics—Latin as well as the works of eighteenth-century British classicists such as Alexander Pope. The result was that this slave girl became better educated than many white women of her day.

Another major influence on her life and work was her Christianity. Wheatley was baptized in Old South Church in Boston (Richmond 39), not the first or last African American to be baptized there. Even though she probably worshipped in the segregated space of the balcony referred to as "Nigger Heaven," Christianity became a dominant theme in her poetry. This relationship of Phillis Wheatley to Christianity, especially complicated by her race and status became an issue for scholars of her work. As they probed her life, they looked for signs of her sense of identity as a black person. What were her relationships to other blacks and how might those have shaped her attitudes? Besides the community members with whom she would have shared worship space, Wheatley must have been introduced to her duties within the Wheatley household by those already in service there. She addressed at least one poem to another fellow slave, the artist, Scipio Moorhead, to whom we owe the one likeness of her that has been passed on through history. An additional important link existed between Wheatley and another slave with whom she corresponded, Obour Tanner of Connecticut. Finally, she also married a free man of color, Mr. John Peters. But Wheatley's life was unlike that of most other blacks of her acquaintance.

For one thing, she was celebrated in her day; she wrote about topics important to the educated classes, in a form to which they responded. But this celebration was not without controversy. In 1772, she could not find a publisher in America. Henry Louis Gates Jr. recreates a scene in which eighteen gentlemen leaders were assembled to determine if, indeed, the young slave girl was the author of the poems ascribed to her (*The Trials of Phillis Wheatley*). They provided her with a signed affidavit attesting to their conviction that she was indeed the author of her poems. But even this did not help her find an American publisher. So with their signed support, she traveled to England in 1773 with a volume of poems dedicated to the Countess of Huntingdon, which was published by A. Bell. This was her only published book although she was advertising a second manuscript for subscription at her death. In England, she was treated well and as a curiosity, continuing the debate about both her talent and its uses.

Wheatley wrote about the topics of the day including death and Christianity. Among those topics, perhaps the most significant one was the quest for freedom by the American colonists. Her poems on these topics often took the form of direct address to military leaders or government officials. As part of that work, she wrote a poem "To His Excellency, General Washington" which she sent to him in October 1775. They actually met in March 1776. But there is no corresponding record of poems advocating freedom of the slaves, a fact which continues to trouble readers and scholars. She did attain her own freedom by 1778. Furthermore, though she married John Peters in the same year, there is no record of poems celebrating either event. In fact, as a free woman, her life seems to have become much more difficult materially. Both she and her husband had a hard time finding work sufficient to support them. And in 1784, she died in poverty after the death of at least two of her own infants.

Thus her life has always been used to illustrate opposing views of blacks. From the days of her publication to the time before the Civil War (1860s), abolitionists argued that her work and life demonstrated the human potential of Africans and the wrongness of slavery. Conversely, slavery's proponents argued that her limitations underscored those of blacks, rendering slavery an acceptable practice. Labeling her work as derivative and as a pale imitation of Pope, they concluded that her accomplishments were more like those of an intelligent pet. Indeed Thomas Jefferson's criticism of her work has been frequently quoted: "Religion, indeed, has produced a Phillis Whatley [sic]; but it could not produce a poet." (As quoted in Gates, *The Trials*, 44).

Jefferson's comments seem to have been prompted by the fact that many of the nearly 40 poems in her published collection focus on death, often of someone's child or spouse but without the intense emotion readers may expect in poetry. Many of these poems offer consolation to the bereaved by admonishing them about their Christian duty. Wheatley routinely urges that they dispense with their grief in order to celebrate their beloved's happy passage to heavenly glory. In them, she adopts a distanced, reasoned mode that sometimes makes her seem almost heartless. Critics have also charged that her poetry is formulaic, especially in her use of classical conventions. She often elaborately invokes the Muses and her poems address such topics as "On Virtue;" she retells classical stories (e.g., "Niobe in Distress for Her Children Slain by Apollo, from *Ovid's Metamorphoses*"). The archaic language and eighteenth-century poetic conventions she employs sometimes pose barriers to readers seeking to engage with her work. But these criticisms provide only a partial view of her work.

From the pre-Civil War days to almost the midfifties, most critics had read only a small sampling of her works. Her published work includes nearly 55 poems, only a handful of which were anthologized. However, from the late 1960s onward, the trend has been to publish more complete collections of her poetry and prose, allowing readers to evaluate her skills themselves. With this more complete record, it becomes clearer why she reached popularity in her day. Sometimes her work rises a bit above those conventions to provide glimpses of an evolving poetic talent, as in this description of a hurricane at sea:

> ... Aeolus in his rapid chariot drove
> In gloomy grandeur from the vault above
> Furious he comes. His winged sons obey
> The frantic fire and madden all the sea.
> The billows rave, the wind's fierce tyrant roars,
> And with his thund'ring terrors shakes the shores ...
>> ("To a Lady on her remarkable Preservation
>> in an Hurricane in North Carolina" 80)

The language used here is clear and dramatic. The pacing and rhythm heighten that drama.

Wheatley's works bring readers to empathize with the plight of her people and help dispel the racial misconceptions of her reading public, forcing them to confront the humanity of slaves and the inhumanity of the institution of slavery. For example, in "On the Death of a Young Gentleman," she demonstrates an awareness of her inability to express grief through her poetic art. She asks,

> To ease the anguish of the parents hearts,
> What shall my sympathizing verse impart?
> Where is the balm to heal so deep a wound?
> Where shall a sov'reign remedy be found? (28)

And to parents who have lost their five-year-old she says, "This know, ye parents, nor her loss deplore/ She feels the iron hand of pain no more" ("On the Death of a Young Lady of Five Years of Age" 25). Simple and yet consoling. In "On the Death of J.C. an Infant," she asks the questions friends and family might ask of Death,

> Could'st thou unpitying close those radiant
>   eyes?
> Or fail'd his artless beauties to surprise?
> Could not his innocence thy stroke controul,
> Thy purpose shake, and soften all thy soul? (92)

Her final description of Niobe, in the long poem entitled "Niobe in Distress for her Children . . . ," after she has lost all of her children and is herself grief stricken, turning to stone, reads thus,

> A marble statue now the queen appears
> But from the marble steal the silent tears. (113)

In all of these pieces, Phillis Wheatley articulates the pain of personal loss, speaks the questions of the heart in the face of grief, and calls to readers in simple language to witness that grief expressed. She manages this over and around her effort to maintain her classical poise characterized by calm reason and detachment. She speaks to readers despite the encumbrance of poetic conventions that sometimes seem strained and archaic.

Critical complaint about Wheatley's work has not been limited to her uses of the tools and conventions of poetry, however. Her work has always been judged as much for what readers think it reveals about *who* she is as about *what* the poems actually say. Those arguments intensified towards the end of the twentieth century.

During the rise of the Black Arts Movement, in the late 1960s and early 70s, African-American artists and scholars began to search out and publicize the work of African-American artists previously neglected by the dominant culture, work sometimes unknown to even African-American audiences. When those artists and critics examined Phillis Wheatley's work, however, they often expressed disappointment. Where, they asked, was Wheatley's outrage at her enslaved state, at the injustice and inhumanity of slavery? Where was her pride in her African homeland? Where was her anguish at the separation and terrors she suffered in the Middle Passage? Where was her rage at Christianity and the claims of its white adherents? Not finding these in her poems, critics often dismissed Wheatley as another sellout, unwilling to risk special treatment to acknowledge injustice, or, even worse, oblivious to the sufferings of others of African descent.

But in a poem entitled "To the Right Honourable William, Earl of Dartmouth, His Majesty's Principal Secretary of State for North America," she says:

> "Should you, my lord, while you peruse my
>   Song,
> Wonder from whence my love of Freedom sprung,
> Whence flow these wishes for the common good,
> By feeling hearts alone best understood,
> I, younger in life, by seeming cruel fate
> Was snatched from Afric's fancy'd happy seat;
> What pangs excruciating must molest,
> What sorrows labour in my parents' breast?
> Steel'd was that soul and by no misery mov'd
> That from a father seiz'd his babe belov'd:
> Such, such my case. And can I then but
>   Pray
> Others may never feel tyrannic sway." (74)

Thus she articulates the pain of slavery. She also makes an important connection between the plight of the enslaved African and the quest for freedom the colonists were beginning to undertake.

Still, in the poem most often anthologized, the views she expresses continue to cause the greatest uproar:

"On Being Brought From Africa to America"

'Twas mercy brought me from my Pagan
    Land,
Taught my benighted soul to understand
That there's a God, that there's a Saviour too:
Once I redemption neither sought nor knew.
Some view our sable race with scornful eye,

"Their colour is a diabolic die."
Remember, Christians, Negros, black as Cain,
May be refin'd and join th' angelic train. (18)

In this poem, Wheatley says (1) she has been blessed by being captured and enslaved since this has allowed her to be "saved" as a Christian; (2) that her African home was a "benighted" place from which her enslavement rescued her. Neither of these attitudes seems understandable, appropriate, or forgivable in light of twentieth- and twenty-first century scholarship about the horrors and anguish of the slave trade. Likewise the role that Christianity played in justifying the kidnapping of innocent people and in maintaining slavery seems in modern view to have been cynical, even diabolical. Wheatley's celebration of her Christianity, therefore, especially attributing her spiritual salvation to her enslavement, seems untenable. Based solely on this poem, readers are left to conclude that either she was unaware of the horrors of slavery, or, worse, accepted her master's reasoning as her own. Thus the question remains: In view of such sentiment, how are Wheatley's life and work to be understood?

Consider first the facts as scholars understand them at this point. Wheatley was probably five or six when she was captured, possibly younger since her one recorded memory of her life in Africa suggests that her mother and family were Islamic (Richmond 12). That would have meant a long inland journey as well as a coastal stay of several months awaiting a slave ship. Wheatley seems to have remembered very little of her African past; therefore, what she "knows" of it must have come to her through the people around her—the Wheatleys, their friends and associates, and possibly other servants. Yet at that moment in history, the common view of Africa was that it was a "dark continent" full of idolatry, superstition, and savagery. With the Wheatleys, she received good food, shelter, and protection; she also received education plus time and space in which to write. She lived with them from her sale in Boston at about age eight until she was past thirty. All she knew of life, she learned in their household owing to their own identities as good Christians. Thus her attitudes about Africa and Christianity would have been taken from that experience.

On the other hand, she also wrote for her audience, primarily white, probably other slaveholding men and women. Would she have shared an antislavery poem even with the members of her own house-hold? There is simply too little to go on to make a definitive statement about her personal attitudes and beliefs about her condition. This single poem, then, embodies the complexity of acknowledging, appreciating, and evaluating Phillis Wheatley's work within the American and African-American literary scene.

A translation of this troubling poem articulates what modern readers most hope for when scouring the works of Phillis Wheatley. Walter Grigo, an amateur wordsmith whose avocation is unlocking anagrams, proposes rereading Wheatley's poem as an anagram.

> "Bitter, Go I, Ebon Human Cargo, From Africa"
> Hail Brethren in Christ! Have ye
> Forgotten God's word? Scriptures teach
> Us that bondage is wrong. His own greedy
> Kin sold Joseph into slavery. "Is there
> No balm in Gilead?" God made us all.
> Aren't African men born to be free? So
> Am I. Ye commit so brute crime
> On us. But we can change thy attitude.
> America, manumit our race. I thank the
> Lord. (Gates *The Trials* 88)

"Moreover, [Grigo] continues, the five italicized words [not included above]—Pagan, Saviour, Christians, Negroes, Cain—are an anagram of 'grasp a great vision: no races in chains'" (89). Was Wheatley, admittedly a child prodigy with impressive skills, capable of such an ingenious linguistic disguise? We know that slave songs, Negro spirituals, were also often signals for the Underground Railroad. Could this be another instance in which the creative genius of a slave found a way to express itself in language that left the slave protected? Unfortunately, at this moment, there is not sufficient evidence to support completely such a claim, but it does suggest an intriguing direction for further research. In the meantime, readers are left with the question still burning—who was Phillis Wheatley and what will her real gifts be to future generations? To ask such questions is to begin to emancipate Wheatley's texts from racist assumptions underlying the critical heritage and our very culture.

WORKS CITED AND CONSULTED

Gates, Henry Louis, Jr. *The Trials of Phillis Wheatley: America's First Black Poet and Her Encounters with the Founding Fathers.* New York: Basic *Civitas* Books, 2003.

Jenson, Marilyn. *Phillis Wheatley: Negro Slave.* New York: Lion Books. 1987.

Mason, Julian D. Jr., *The Poems of Phillis Wheatley: Revised and Enlarged Edition.* Chapel Hill, NC: The University of North Carolina Press, 1989.

Richmond, Merle A. *Bid the Vassal Soar: Interpretive Essays on the Life and Poetry of Phillis Wheatley (ca. 1753–1784) and George Moses Horton (ca. 1797–1883).*Washington, D. C.: Howard Press, 1974.

Robinson, William H., ed., *Critical Essays on Phillis Wheatley.* Boston: G.K. Hall, 1982.

———. *Phillis Wheatley: A Bio-Bibliography.* Boston: G.K. Hall, 1981.

———. *Phillis Wheatley in the Black American Beginnings.* Detroit: Broadside Press, 1975.

Wheatley, Phillis. *The Collected Works of Phillis Wheatley.* Ed. John C. Shields. New York: Oxford University Press, 1988.

THE NOVELS OF ELIE WIESEL

"Witness to the Absurd: Elie Wiesel and the French Existentialists"
by Mary Jean Green, in *Renascence* (1977)

INTRODUCTION

Elie Wiesel's *Night* has introduced generations of readers to his own dramatic story of enslavement in and emancipation from Auschwitz and Buchenwald. Claiming that Elie Wiesel's works "are particularly close to those of Camus and, to a lesser extent, Sartre, and he often seems to have set out with the specific intention of providing a theistic response to the questions raised in their work," Mary Jean Green compares Wiesel's literary works with those of these two legendary existential writers. "While adopting Camus' attitude of revolt and certain other ideas central to the thought of the French existentialists," Green declares, "Wiesel differs fundamentally from his atheistic contemporaries by his firm belief in God." For Green, "Wiesel's novels confront the same contemporary problems of human action in the face of the absurd that dominate the works of Camus and Sartre. While he has adopted many of their fundamental perceptions of the human condition, Wiesel brings to these insights his own, scarring personal experience

Green, Mary Jean. "Witness to the Absurd: Elie Wiesel and the French Existentialists." *Renascence* 29.4 (Summer 1977): 170–184.

> of the death camps and his individual form of belief in God.
> His novels provide a forceful theistic alternative to the atheistic
> philosophies developed by Camus and Sartre, a theism which,
> however, approaches similar problems in similar terms."

⌘

Elie Wiesel has gained a certain reputation in America as a "Jewish writer," a survivor of the Holocaust and a teller of Hasidic tales. As the sales of his books in English translation far surpass those of the original French editions, the fact that Wiesel wrote his novels in French is in danger of being quietly forgotten. Yet, although Wiesel first came to France only in his late teens after his liberation from Buchenwald, his contact with French literature and thought had a considerable influence on his novels. In fact, the central concerns of Wiesel's novels reflect those of the French existentialists, principally Camus and Sartre, who dominated the Parisian literary scene to which Wiesel was exposed in the late 1940's.

In making the themes of these French authors part of his own literary creation, Wiesel has woven them together with the memories of his concentration camp experiences and the Hasidic tales of his childhood to produce a new form which does not immediately reveal its existentialist sources.[1] It is important, however, to unravel these strands from the fabric of Wiesel's work, not only in order to determine Wiesel's place within the French literary tradition, but also, more important, to see how he has used the premises of atheistic existentialism in constructing a vigorous contemporary theism. Wiesel's position as a religious existentialist is not unique in literature: his distinguished predecessors include Pascal, Dostoevsky, Kierkegaard and Kafka, as he himself often reminds us in interviews. His own concerns, however, are particularly close to those of Camus and, to a lesser extent, Sartre, and he often seems to have set out with the specific intention of providing a theistic response to the questions raised in their work.

In part because Wiesel's novels rarely use the existentialist vocabulary of Camus and Sartre, the relationship between his work and theirs is not immediately apparent. The idea of the absurd, for example, the point of departure for the French existentialists, seems, on first reading, relatively unimportant in Wiesel's work. Instead, he begins by confronting the Holocaust, an event fraught with personal meaning for him as a Jewish survivor of the camps. Wiesel considers the Holocaust, however, not only as a personal or even a uniquely Jewish experience, but as an event involving all men. In *The Town beyond the Wall* the protagonist Michael returns to his Hungarian home to confront a bystander who had observed with indifference the deportation of the local Jewish community. Wiesel strongly condemns this man's indifference as an abdication of his identity as a human being. As men, Wiesel is saying, we were all involved in this drama of suffering and death and must all share in facing the problems which it poses.

The Holocaust, then, plays the same role in the Wiesel canon as the allegorical plague of Camus' novel, a plague which itself reflected the era of the Occupation and the concentration camp. For Camus—and for Wiesel—these experiences point beyond themselves to reveal the nature of the human condition: man is condemned to suffering and death by an irrational universe. Wiesel would seem to agree with Camus' use of the term "absurd" to describe the confrontation of man, with his demands for logic and meaning, and a universe which denies these demands. In the work of both writers, the absurd is not an abstract concept, but a reality experienced by the plague victims of Oran and the inmates of the camps, who seeing that the death sentence is imposed without reference to guilt or merit, become aware of the limitations of their mortality and the absence of rational order in the universe. While Camus makes clear the allegorical nature of his fictional plague, Wiesel's treatment of the Holocaust may appear to be merely historical. Wiesel states emphatically, however, that the Holocaust is not an event limited in time and space, but rather a manifestation of the enduring nature of human existence. As the Hasidic Rebbe says at the end of *The Gates of the Forest*, "Auschwitz proves that nothing has changed, that the primeval war goes on" (p. 192).[2] Wiesel himself has said of the experience of the camps that it went "to the limits of the human condition."[3] And in a 1967 symposium on the Holocaust, Wiesel described it as both a historical and transhistorical event: "To the sick person, Auschwitz lies in his despair; to the father whose child is dying, Auschwitz has the face of a child."[4]

Through his novels Wiesel has developed a certain number of images which evoke the world as revealed by the Holocaust. The forest is one of these. It expresses the nightmare world of pure contingency which Sartre's protagonist discovers in *La Nausée* and of which Camus speaks in *Le Mythe de Sisyphe*. In *The Gates of the Forest* the forest is the place where the characters are forced to flee from their ordered everyday lives in town and where they must live like hunted animals. Its awesome voice, drowned out by other concerns in normal life, is now audible to them: "this roaring voice which, before creation, before the liberation of the word, already contained form and matter, joy and defeat, and that which separates and reconciles them, from all of which the universe, time, and their own secret life were fashioned" (pp. 122–23). It is the voice which spoke to Job from the thunder, the voice of Chaos: "it's madness, pure madness" (p. 123). Like the experience of the absurd in *La Nausée*, the experience of the forest in *The Town beyond the Wall* strips the world of false meanings and definitions imposed by human habit: "The universe frees itself from the order in which it was imprisoned. Appearance snaps its ties with reality. A chair is no longer a chair, the king no longer king, the fool ceases to be a fool, or to cry" (p. 180). Echoing the words of Dostoevsky often quoted by Camus and Sartre, Wiesel calls it, "the liberty in which anything is permitted" (p. 180).

Camus sums up his understanding of a universe of death and chaos opposed to human strivings in Caligula's statement, "Men die and are not happy." This aspect of the absurd finds its expression in Wiesel's novels in the image of night. This is, in fact, the title of Wiesel's first novel which describes his concentration camp experiences, and it continues throughout his novels to represent those things which deny human values. At the end of *Dawn*, Wiesel's protagonist, after having killed a man, sees his own face reflected back at him in a darkened window pane: his has become the face of night. The progression of Wiesel's personal discovery of meaning in human life is tellingly revealed in the titles of his first three novels: *Night*, *Dawn*, *Day* (in English, *The Accident*).

As the images of night and the forest represent forces of the non-human universe, the prison reflects man's position within it, walled in by the limits which it sets to his freedom. The image of a man in prison, often condemned to death, has been used by writers in the existentialist tradition, at least since Pascal, to describe the human condition, and never more than in the French literature of the 1930's and 40's. Sartre's *Le Mur* and Camus' *L'Etranger* take place in the cells of men condemned to death, and in *La Peste* Camus makes the entire city of Oran into a vast prison. Critics have, in fact, lamented the omnipresent prison cell in the literature of this period, but it is an image almost thrust upon writers of the 30's and 40's by the historical situation and, in addition, one appropriate to their vision of the human condition.

Prisons, similarly, abound in Wiesel's novels, most evidently in the concentration camps described in *Night* and evoked in the other novels. But prison scenes are not limited to the camps. The plot of *Dawn* revolves around two men, a British soldier and a Jewish terrorist, who await execution in a form of cell. In *The Town beyond the Wall*, emprisoning walls are everywhere, a fact noted by the American translator who changed its original French title, *La Ville de la Chance*. Its protagonist Michael is forced to stand with his face to the wall until his legs give out, a torture ironically called The Prayer. Later he is placed in a cell with a religious cellmate who asks him, in a scene reminiscent of the visit of the priest in Camus' *L'Etranger*, whether he has heard the voice of God. "'No,' Michael said, 'It never got through to me. The walls must have been too thick'" (p. 145). There are also the walled garden of Michael's childhood, the walls of his small airless room in Paris, the symbolic wall of the Iron Curtain which Michael and Pedro must traverse to reach their destination. Seen in this way, *The Town beyond the Wall* illustrates the thesis set forth by Gregor's father in *The Gates of the Forest*, "It's man's duty to make a free choice and to push back walls" (p. 34).

Man abandoned in the forest, lost in the night, bound in by prison walls—all of these images reveal Wiesel's vision of the human condition, but none so forcefully questions its justice as the image of the suffering and dying child.[5] Examples of unmerited suffering have traditionally been used to challenge the existence of a just world order, and in literature the child has often embodied the idea of innocence. It is the suffering of innocent children which most troubles Dostoevsky's Ivan Karamazov and which leads him to revolt against God. The theme recurs at the center of Camus' *La Peste*, where the long, agonizing death of a child forms a background for the confrontation of Father Paneloux and Doctor Rieux on the subject of theodicy.

Since Wiesel himself was in a concentration camp when still a child (although just old enough to escape extermination), it is only natural that images of suffering children recur in his work. The little sister Tzipora, who first appears in *Night*, continues to haunt his work, appearing at length in *The Town beyond the Wall* and *A Beggar in Jerusalem.* In the latter novel Katriel's wife mourns a dead child, as does the mother of the would-be suicide of Wiesel's most recent novel, *The Oath.* The most striking and certainly the most horrible treatment of the death of a child occurs in the scene in *Night* where a child, along with two adults, is condemned to death by hanging. The child, being too light to weight the rope, does not die immediately, and the other prisoners are forced to watch his agony. It is this episode which most strongly threatens the protagonist's faith in God: "'Where is God now?' And I heard a voice within me answer him: 'Where is He? Here He is—He is hanging here on this gallows'" (p. 76).

Children also play an important role in *The Town beyond the Wall*, especially little Yankel, an even younger child who has been Michael's companion in the camps. Wiesel follows the hopeless effort of the boy to come to terms with his experience as a *Piepel*, a favored mascot of a camp guard, possessing the power of life and death over the other inmates. This role seems to fascinate Wiesel, perhaps because it so vividly illustrates the irrational nature or the actions taken in the camps. Having too intimate an experience of the absurd, Yankel arranges a suicidal traffic accident. Michael spends a week at his bedside watching his slow death, which calls into question the accepted order of things: "All the men on earth bore a single face: that of my dying friend. Their destinies were measured by his. A child who dies becomes the center of the universe; stars and meadows die with him" (p. 99).

Sharing with the French existentialists a vision of the human condition, Wiesel also shares with them their stress on human freedom. As for Sartre, freedom for Wiesel is the quality which distinguishes humanity: in *The Town beyond the Wall*, Michael says to Pedro, "Freedom is given only to man. God is not free" (p. 101). In the parable of creation told by Gavriel in *The Gates of the Forest*, laughter is seen as the manifestation of human freedom, and in the same novel Gregor's father declares, "It is man's duty to make a free choice ..." (in the original French, more strongly, "se choisir libre").[6]

Sartre views man as a being without previous definition who creates himself by his actions: "man ... is condemned every moment to invent man."[7] Almost echoing these words, Wiesel writes in *The Accident*, "Man must keep moving, searching, weighing, holding out his hand, offering himself, inventing himself" (p.125).

Man is free but how is he to exercise this freedom in the face of the absurd? This question, which preoccupies Camus and Sartre, is at the heart of all of Wiesel's novels, and it seems to reflect a very personal search for meaning. Wiesel's characters are often tempted to give up the struggle by committing suicide. The protagonist of *The Accident* has let himself be run down by a taxi because of his inability to bear the guilt of surviving the Holocaust, a suicide attempt like the child Yankel's. Like all of Wiesel's protagonists, he must find a reason for continuing to live. Camus, too, felt compelled to handle the problem of suicide in his *Mythe de Sisyphe*. Although it may seem a logical human response to the dilemma of the absurd, both Camus and Wiesel strongly reject suicide because it resolves the problem by removing one of the elements in confrontation: to commit suicide is, in effect, to accept the supremacy of an irrational, meaningless world order.

Madness, a suicide of reason, seems to represent a similar temptation for Wiesel's characters. Although madness sometimes has a positive side in his work, revealing an irrationality allied with the divine, in *The Town beyond the Wall* it clearly signifies submission to the chaos of the universe. Old Martha, the madwoman, is a recurrent figure in the novel, offering her favors to the protagonist as a means of escape. At the end of the novel Michael is thrust into endless captivity among fellow prisoners who have already gone mad. The temptation to join them is strong, but he realizes that to accept madness is to admit defeat at the hands of his jailers, to ally himself with the absurd. There is a certain analogy in this situation with that of Camus' Caligula, who reacts to his discovery of the absurd by trying to escape the human condition and himself playing the role of an irrational destiny. For Camus and for Wiesel, man's obligation is to resist the irrational cruelty of the world order rather than to become part of it.

Wiesel's characters are saved from suicide and madness by an attitude of what Camus would call revolt. Whereas the idea of the absurd can itself furnish no basis for positive action, both Camus and Wiesel find such a grounding in the sentiment of revolt aroused in man by consciousness of his condition. The response of many of Wiesel's characters is similar to that of Camus' Sisyphus, eternally condemned to roll his rock up the hill from whose summit it will immediately tumble down. Yet his freedom defies the supremacy of the gods, and his happiness denies the punishment: "There is no fate that cannot be surmounted by scorn. . . . If there is a personal fate, there is no higher destiny, or at least there is but one which he concludes is inevitable and despicable. For the rest, he knows himself to be the master of his days." Thus, Camus concludes, "one must imagine Sisyphus happy."[8] The same feeling of rebellious joy is evoked by the laughter and song of Wiesel's Hasids at the end of *The Gates of the Forest*. The Rebbe explains the peculiar meaning of the Hasid's song to Gregor: "It's his way of proclaiming, 'You don't want me to dance: too bad, I'll dance anyhow. You've taken away every reason for singing, but I shall sing'" (p. 196). Earlier, Gregor's friend Gavriel had told him that God's gift of laughter gave man a weapon of vengeance, and Wiesel's characters typically react to tragedy with a burst of laughter.

The militant Jewishness of Wiesel's protagonists is, in fact, an aspect of their revolt. In the symposium on the Holocaust, Wiesel expressed his own feelings on the subject: "You, God, do not want me to be Jewish; well, Jewish we shall be nevertheless despite your will."[9] For Wiesel, the Jew plays the role of the eternal rebel: throughout their history Jews have felt the irrationality of the human condition and have known the depths of despair. By their very continuing to live and create in the face of this fate, they are revolting against it. Again quoting Camus, Wiesel says of his people,

> I do not like to think of the Jew as suffering. I prefer thinking of him as someone who can defeat suffering—his own and others. For his is a Messianic dimension; he can save the world from a new Auschwitz. As Camus would say: one must create happiness to protest against a universe of unhappiness. But— one *must* create it. And we are creating it. We were creating it. Jews got married, celebrated weddings, had children within the ghetto walls. Their absurd faith in their non-existent future was, nevertheless, an affirmation of the spirit.[10]

For Wiesel, as for Camus, the concept of revolt carries within it a demand for reaching out to other human beings. In the course of his examination of revolt, Camus discovered a new *cogito:* "I rebel,— therefore we exist."[11] That is to say, in his movement of revolt man finds in himself qualities which link him to other men; in his assertion of his own human dignity, he is also necessarily asserting the rights of all men. It is this feeling of responsibility for others which provides a reason for Wiesel's characters to go on living and which gives meaning and direction to their lives. In *The Town beyond the Wall*, Michael's friend Pedro explains, in specifically Camusian terms, "To say 'I suffer, therefore I am' is to become the enemy of man. What you must say is 'I suffer, therefore you are'" (p. 127).

This movement of concern for the other is not mere sentimentalism on Wiesel's part. It results from a philosophical view of man as responsible for all men, a view not far distant from Camus' or even from Sartre's formulations in *L'Existentialisme est un humanisme*: "in making this choice he also chooses all men. In fact, in creating the man that we want to be, there is not a single one of our acts which does not at the same time create an image of man as we think he ought to be."[12] In *The Oath* the narrator's teacher Moshe (another recurring Wiesel character) says: "Every man can and must carry creation on his shoulders; every unit is responsible for the whole."[13] And at the end of *The Gates of the Forest*, the Rebbe explains: "Doesn't helping a human being mean rescuing him from despair? Doesn't it mean subordinating destiny, to your idea of man?" (p. 194). This concept of individual responsibility for all men is an illustration of Wiesel's characteristic blend of existentialist concepts with Jewish belief, in this case, the traditional teaching that the coming of the Messiah is dependent on the faithful behavior of each individual Jew.

This philosophical conclusion is expressed more often through action than in abstract terms. The narrator of *The Accident* abandons his pursuit of death to save his despondent friend Kathleen. Gregor in *The Gates of the Forest* devotes himself to saving his wife Clara from the claims of her dead lover. Michael of *The Town beyond the Wall*, who has withstood torture to protect his friend Pedro, finds a meaning even in hopeless imprisonment by trying to save his demented young cell mate. The old man in *The Oath* breaks his vow of silence to save a young would-be suicide. In fact, a frequently recurring pattern of action in Wiesel's novels involves a somewhat weak and despondent protagonist who, often strengthened by contact with a stronger, more optimistic friend, overcomes his despair in an attempt to save someone yet weaker than himself.

But the relation of man to man in Wiesel's books does not always involve a stronger character reaching out to rescue a weaker. There are also virile friendships, like that of Rieux and Tarrou in *La Peste* which are characterized by long conversations and intimate understanding. These friendships are central to the Wiesel philosophy: they strengthen the protagonist and give him courage to go on. Michael says to Pedro in *The Town beyond the Wall*: "Together, we'll win. When two solitudes unite, there is the world on the one hand, and they on the other—and they are stronger than the world" (p. 134). This type of friendship is often consecrated in Wiesel's work by an exchange of names. In *The Gates of the Forest*, when Gregor meets the stranger Gavriel in the cave, he gives him his name. In *The Town beyond the Wall*, Michael and his friend Pedro feel themselves able to exchange identities, and at the end of the book this exchange is repeated with the madman Michael has begun to cure: "You'll tell me your name and you'll ask me, 'Who are you?' and I'll answer, 'I'm Pedro.' And that will be a proof that man survives, that he passes himself along. Later, in another prison, someone will ask your name and you'll say, 'I'm Michael.' And then you will know the taste of the most genuine of victories" (p. 189). This exchange of names is significant, then, as a device which man may use to overcome his own mortality, again an idea taken from Jewish tradition, which requires that a dead man's name be perpetuated.

If human relationships are the sphere of affirmation against the absurd, then an absence of relationship must contribute to chaos and meaninglessness. In *The Town beyond the Wall*, Wiesel uses the Sartrean concept of the Other, whose glance has the power to reduce a human being to the status of an object. Michael has returned to his former home, now behind the Iron Curtain, in order to confront the man who had passively observed the rounding up and deportation of the Jewish community, including Michael's own family. The man later admits to Michael that, while his wife had cried at the spectacle, he had taken refuge in the idea that the whole episode was only a play in which he himself had no role. Under his gaze, the condemned Jews had become objects, "living sticks of wood" (p. 159). In Wiesel's view, this man is not an exception, but rather, "a symbol of anonymity, the average man" (p. 164). His condemnation of this attitude recalls Sartre's castigation of the bourgeoisie of Bouville in *La Nausée*; Wiesel charges him with leading an inauthentic existence: "You think you're living in peace and security, but in reality you're not living at all. People of your kind scuttle along the margins of existence [perhaps like the insect-like creatures in *La Nausée*]. Far from men, from their struggle, which you no doubt consider stupid and senseless" (p. 172).

Wiesel continues to charge this man with attempting to evade the limits of his existence as a man, reiterating the plea with which Camus ends *L'Homme révolté*: "in order to be a man, to refuse to be a god."[14] At the end of *The Town beyond the Wall*, Michael says to his cellmate: "It's in humanity itself that we find both our question and the strength to keep it within limits. . . . A man is a man only when he is among men. It's harder to remain human than to try to leap beyond humanity" (p. 188).

Wiesel's commitment to action on behalf of his fellow man extends to his own activity as a writer. It seems clear from the fact that all of his novels involve the Holocaust that his novelistic activity is a form of witness. The importance of this witness as a reason for remaining alive is made very forcefully, for example, in *The Oath*, where the Old Man, the sole survivor of the extermination of the village of Kollvillàg, must live on as the keeper of the Chronicle which relates the village history: "And once a messenger, he has no alternative. He must stay alive until he has transmitted his message" (p. 33). The aim of this witness is not only to preserve the past, however, but also to influence the future. Again and again in Wiesel's novels we find the figure of Moché the beadle, who first appears in *Night*. The survivor of the massacre of an entire village, he has returned to the protagonist's town to attempt to warn the population there. But his warnings go unheeded until it is too late. The approach of the Holocaust is also the terrifying message brought to Gregor in *The Gates of the Forest* by Gavriel, whose very name suggests his role as messenger.

Art, for Wiesel, also seems to have a purpose beyond mere communication. The telling of tales, song, dance—all of these activities which are so important in Wiesel's novels are rooted, even more fundamentally, in man's need to create, to "invent himself." In *The Town beyond the Wall*, Wiesel provides a sort of parable on the origin of art:

> if a man has something to say, he says it most perfectly by taking unto him a woman and creating a new man. And then God remembers that he too has something to say; and he entrusts the message to the Angel of Death. . . . The dialogue— or the duel, if you like—between man and his God doesn't end in nothingness. Man may not have the last word, but he has the last cry. That moment marks the birth of art (p. 103).

The dance of the Hasids, the song of the Jews marching off to execution—these are assertions of human qualities in the face of all that denies them, thus an important expression of man's revolt. The activity of witness is itself a way of transcending the physical death of loved ones and the near-annihilation of a tradition of Jewish teachings. As Wiesel says in a review of another novel about a now-extinct Jewish community, "Every literary creation aims to correct injustice."[15] The image which epitomizes this view of art as man's revolt occurs in *Night* when the protagonist's friend Juliek extricates himself and his beloved violin from beneath a pile of dead and dying in order to play a final fragment from Beethoven. "He was playing his life. The whole of his life was gliding on the strings—his lost hopes, his charred past, his extinguished future" (p. 107). What is expressed by Juliek's art is simply man's creative power in the face of death, and his message is not really intended for a human audience barely able to hear him. He plays for himself and, beyond that, for God.

The responsibility for others fundamental to the ethics of Wiesel and the French existentialists makes the issue of violence a particularly complicated one. Discussed by Simone de Beauvoir, Sartre's disciple, in *Pour une morale de l'ambiguité*, it becomes a central issue for Camus in *L'homme révolté*. There Camus admits that in the modern world the taking of life is sometimes a necessary step in the struggle to defend human values, but he questions whether it is a permissible act. He concludes that murder is a denial of the very human solidarity affirmed by the movement of revolt: thus, necessary but impossible. The solution to this dilemma, for Camus, lies in the example of the Russian terrorists portrayed in *Les Iustes*, who killed only to accept death themselves, in order to restore balance to the world.

Wiesel confronts the same problem in his second novel, *Dawn*, and both his statement of the problem and his resolution of it are embodied in a concrete situation. Elisha, the protagonist, has become part of a Palestinian Jewish terrorist organization shortly after his liberation from the Nazi camps. He is convinced that the establishment of a Jewish state represents the only future left to his people, and this belief gives him the strength to engage in raids on British army outposts despite his aversion to violence. One night, however, he is chosen to perform an even more difficult task, the killing of a British hostage whom the terrorists have taken to prevent the execution of one of their own men. The moral case for the murder of the hostage is made as strong as possible. World opinion condemns the execution of the captured terrorist and the British have only to bow to it in order to save their own man. They refuse to give in, however, in large part because they believe the Jews are too moral to go through with the threatened killing. To be merciful to the hostage, then, is to encourage the British to execute more captured Jews and to weaken the cause of a Jewish Palestine, desperately awaited by the boatloads of concentration camp survivors daily being turned back by the British authorities.

Convinced of the necessity of this killing, Elisha nevertheless feels the judgment of his dead parents, teachers and fellow students—and even of the little boy whom he once was. Their silent figures are there to participate in his act: like Sartrean man, in choosing for himself, Elisha must choose for others. As the repository of their teachings and the only living witness to their existence, his actions reflect on the meaning of their lives as well. Elisha poses to himself the objection to murder so forcefully expressed by Camus: in committing murder, man attempts to move beyond human limitations, to become God. Like Camus' moral terrorists, Elisha goes through with the killing, but in doing so he understands that he has changed his role from that of victim to executioner and has identified himself with the Nazi torturers that haunt his memory. Although the protagonist continues to live at the end of the hook, he bears a heavy burden of guilt.

The case against murder is made with similar reasoning by both Camus and Wiesel, and the Wiesel novel, which is clearly more accepting of violence, seems almost to have been written directly in response to *L'Homme révolté*. Wiesel's character does, after all, choose to carry out the execution in full knowledge of what he is doing, and he feels no need to do away with himself afterward. While Camus' abstract discussion of murder and its ideological justifications in *L'Homme révolté* does not seem to relate to any particular cause for which he himself would be ready to kill, Wiesel puts his discussion in the context of Israel, in whose existence he strongly believes. He has publicly defended Israel's actions against such moralists as François Mauriac, who had condemned the Jewish state as "avid for conquest and domination" (*Dawn* is dedicated to Mauriac). To this charge Wiesel replied with a line from the classical French dramatist Corneille: "What do you want them to do?" The implied rhetorical answer is, "Die?"[16]

Thus, despite his aversion to violence, Wiesel seems willing to accept it as the price of continuing human life—without Camus' demand that the murderer forfeit his own life as well. His conclusion is thus similar to that of Sartre in *Le diable et le bon dieu*. The strong male characters in Wiesel's novels do not hesitate to participate in war-like activities: Gad leads the terrorists in *Dawn*, Leib leads the partisans in *The Gates of the Forest*, and the narrator's friends, Gad and Katriel, die fighting in *A Beggar in Jerusalem*. In this last novel, dealing with the 1967 Israeli-Arab war, Wiesel again confronts the moral implications of violence. The victorious Israeli soldiers whom Wiesel describes, both in the body of the novel and in the introduction, are astonished and disconcerted by their victory and even more so by their new-found role as conquerors of innocent Arab children: "victory is gradually losing, not its significance, not its necessity, but its taste of joy" (p. 24). Wiesel thus views the taking of human life as a necessary consequence of moral action, to be accepted not with joyful righteousness but with humility and compassion.

While adopting Camus' attitude of revolt and certain other ideas central to the thought of the French existentialists, Wiesel differs fundamentally from his atheistic contemporaries by his firm belief in God. It is certainly for this reason that he has manifested such hostility to Sartrean philosophy, to the point of refusing to admit the striking parallels between the ideas of the Sartre-de Beauvoir circle and his own. His criticism of the Parisian post-war intellectual atmosphere in *The Town beyond the Wall* clearly has Sartre as its target:

> Despair—they said—stands guard at every exit, hell is the neighbor who snores all night, the absurd has usurped the throne abdicated by God, therefore you have to *do* something!
> ... God is dead, and only the false messiahs, the false prophets, knew it. And no one shouts louder, no one makes himself more clearly understood than a false prophet announcing the arrival of a false messiah. (p. 73)

This expression of hostility to Sartre's atheism is easily understood. While Wiesel has been willing to enter into dialogue with those atheists who have wrestled with the question of God,[17] he seems to recognize that Sartre has never really taken the existence of God seriously.[18]

If Wiesel is less hostile to Camus, it may be because in contrast to Sartre, Camus is in constant sympathetic dialogue with theism, and the problem of belief in God runs throughout his work. For Camus,

God is an intriguing but abstract philosophical concept, one which could resolve a number of problems besetting human existence. In *L'Etranger* the priest offers God as a guarantor of human immortality; in *La Peste* He is proposed as the explanation and justification of human suffering and death; and in *La Chute* as the giver of grace, the restorer of innocence. But Camus steadfastly refuses to accept any of these tempting solutions, which would require belief in an entity inaccessible to human experience. In *L'Homme révolté* he specifically criticizes the existentialist philosophers of the past who, like Kierkegaard, have made a "leap of faith" beyond the limits of human knowledge. Belief in God is, in Camus' opinion, not only unjustified by human experience but even more important, incompatible with an attitude of revolt against an unjust universe for which God would have to be held responsible. "From the moment that man submits God to moral judgment," Camus states, "he kills Him in his own heart."[19]

The problem of evil, which becomes the central issue in *La Peste*, is also of primary importance to Wiesel. As he recounts in *Night*, his personal experience in the Nazi death camps came close to destroying his own faith: "Never shall I forget those flames which consumed my faith forever.... Never shall I forget those moments which murdered my God and my soul and turned my dreams to dust" (p. 44). His novels are filled with accusations against the divine justice, "that transcendent inhuman Justice in which suffering has no weight in the balance" (*The Town beyond the Wall*, p. 59). In *The Gates of the Forest* Gregor tells of a rabbinical court in a concentration camp which tried God for murder and found Him guilty. The Rebbe replies by admitting: "He is guilty. He has become the ally of evil, of death, of murder" (pp. 196–7). Yet, although Wiesel's attitude toward God was profoundly altered by his confrontation with radical evil, he is incapable of denying God's presence. Like his protagonist Michael in *The Town beyond the Wall*, Wiesel's revolt can never go beyond the confines of theism: "I go up against Him, I shake my fist, I froth with rage, but it's still a way of telling Him He's there ..." (p. 123). Wiesel himself has echoed these words: "I have my problems with God, believe me. I have my anger and I have my quarrels and I have my nightmares."[20] But Wiesel's God always retains the unshakeable reality of another person, and his characters, like their author, do not hesitate to dialogue with Him as equals.

The strange Hasidic story which ends *The Town beyond the Wall* illustrates the interdependent relationship between man and God in

Wiesel's work. Legend relates that man and God decided to change places, and that man, now possessing omnipotence, refused to change back. "Years passed, centuries, perhaps eternities. And suddenly the drama quickened. The past for one, and the present for the other, were too heavy to be borne. As the liberation of the one was bound to the liberation of the other, they renewed the ancient dialogue whose echoes come to us in the night, charged with hatred, with remorse, and most of all, with infinite yearning" (p. 190).

This concept of a God open to human criticism is radically different from that of Camus, who sees even the slightest attack on the divine perfection as a fatal flaw in the entire structure of belief. It must be Wiesel's Jewish background, with its stress on the covenantal relationship between God and man, which gives him the basis for his particular response. Even more specifically, the Hasidic stories which colored Wiesel's childhood are filled with examples of such accusatory dialogues with God. In *Souls on Fire*, his non-fiction study of various Hasidic masters, Wiesel speaks at length of the rebellious attitude of such men as Levi-Yitzhak of Berditchev, who did not hesitate to accuse God of injustice. Wiesel explains that such accusations were not considered blasphemous because, "Jewish tradition allows man to say anything to God, provided it be on behalf of man."[21]

Because of their freedom to enter into dialogue with their God, Wiesel's protagonists are able to escape the dilemma of the problem of evil in both its classical form, as expressed, for example, by Hume, and its modern version, made particularly acute by the vivid memory of the Holocaust. One contemporary formulation of the problem of evil was proposed to Wiesel by Richard Rubenstein, a modern Jewish philosopher who has himself adopted a Camusian atheism:

> I have had to decide whether to affirm the existence of a God who inflicts Auschwitz on his guilty people or to insist that nothing the Jews did made them more deserving of Auschwitz than any other people, that Auschwitz was in no sense a punishment, and that a God who could or would inflict such punishment does not exist. In other words, I have elected to accept what Camus has rightly called the courage of the absurd, the courage to live in a meaningless, purposeless Cosmos rather than believe in a God who inflicts Auschwitz on his people.[22]

This situation is similar to that which confronts Camus' characters in *La Peste*. While Father Paneloux collapses under the strain of maintaining his faith in a God who tortures innocent children, the protagonists choose to reject God in order to affirm the innocence of man. Wiesel, in contrast to both Camus and Rubenstein, simply refuses to accept this formulation of the problem. As we have seen, he insists again and again on the innocence of the victims of the Holocaust and does not hesitate to point an accusing finger at God. Yet, for him, such an accusation does not constitute grounds for the denial of God's existence. Without attempting to put forth a detailed explanation of God's seeming injustice, Wiesel's protagonists elect to live with the constant tension of believing in a God whose actions they do not always condone.

Wiesel has never explained in rational terms why they make this choice. He rather leaves us with a question, like the Rebbe in *The Gates of the Forest*, who answers Gregor's anguished question, "After what has happened to us, how can you believe in God?" with the further question, "How can you not believe in God after what has happened?" (p. 192). By implication, the existence of even an incomprehensible God who, nonetheless, provides an overarching framework of meaning is preferable to the acceptance of a state of Hobbesian warfare as the ultimate reality. Wiesel finds the atheistic alternative more destructive to man than the problems and para- doxes of theism. He points out that atheistic humanists were the first to lose their will to survive in the concentration camps and that the survivors of Auschwitz, those who have lived the problem of evil in the most personal way, are not among those who propose a God-is-dead theology.[23] Belief in God is thus, for Wiesel, the very foundation for man's continuing revolt.

In *La Peste* Camus charges that if a man really accepted the exis- tence of God, he would cease to fight against human suffering on earth. He reasons that if God is held responsible for this suffering, He could be expected to provide both its justification and its remedy. As has been pointed out earlier, Wiesel refuses to see such ethical inac- tion as a necessary consequence of belief in God, and his characters work unceasingly on behalf of their fellow men. They are not content to await passively the arrival of a promised Messiah; rather, they elect to bring about his coming through their own action. At the end of *The Gates of the Forest* Gregor says:

Whether or not the Messiah comes doesn't matter; we'll manage without him. . . . We shall be honest and humble and strong, and then he will come, he will come every day, thousands of times every day. He will have no face, because he will have a thousand faces. The Messiah isn't one man, Clara, he's all men. As long as there are men there will be a Messiah. (p. 223)

Wiesel's novels confront the same contemporary problems of human action in the face of the absurd that dominate the works of Camus and Sartre. While he has adopted many of their fundamental perceptions of the human condition, Wiesel brings to these insights his own, scarring personal experience of Auschwitz and Buchenwald and his individual form of belief in God. His novels provide a forceful theistic alternative to the atheistic philosophies developed by Camus and Sartre, a theism which, however, approaches similar problems in similar terms. Wiesel thus must be seen as something more than an "ethnic" novelist whose limited message is directed toward a limited group. Rather, he must be placed in the company of those writers who, like Camus and Sartre, use the novel as a means of exploring the fundamental philosophical and religious questions of the modern era.

Notes

1. Although the topic has not been studied in depth, certain parallels with existentialist thinkers have been suggested by Maurice Friedman in "Elie Wiesel: the Modern Job," *Commonweal* LXXXV (October 14, 1966), 18–52, and Robert Alter in his chapter on Wiesel in *After the Tradition* (New York: E.P. Dutton & Co., 1969), pp. 151–160.
2. All citations in my text from *The Town beyond the Wall, The Gates of the Forest, Night, The Accident,* and *A Beggar in Jerusalem* refer to the English translations by Avon Books. These editions are more easily obtainable than those in the original French, a fact which reflects the complicated nature of Wiesel's literary identity.
3. *New York Times*, February 10, 1970, p. 48.
4. "Jewish Values in the Post-Holocaust Future: A Symposium," *Judaism*, XVI (Summer 1967), 291.

5. This image is discussed in particular by Thomas A. Idinopulos in "The Mystery of Suffering in the Art of Dostoevsky, Camus, Wiesel and Grunewald," *Journal of the American Academy of Religion*, XLIII (March, 1975), 51–61.

6. *Les Portes de la Forêt* (Paris: Editions du Seuil, 1964), p. 32.

7. *Existentialism*, trans. Bernard Frechtman (New York: Philosophical Library, 1947), p. 91.

8. *The Rebel*, trans. Anthony Bower (New York: Vintage Books, 1956), p. 91.

9. "Jewish values in the post-holocaust future," p. 291.

10. Ibid., 293.

11. *The Rebel*, p. 22.

12. *Existentialism*, p. 20. Wiesel's view of the possibility of human relationships, however, is much more optimistic than Sartre's. Directly contradicting Satre's well-known statement in *Huis clos*, Wiesel's protagonist in *The Accident* declares, "Hell isn't others; it's ourselves" (p. 24).

13. *The Oath*, trans. Marion Wiesel (New York: Random House, 1973), pp. 190–191. Further references in my text refer to this edition.

14. *The Rebel*, p. 306.

15. *New York Times Book Reviews*, September 1, 1974, p. 5.

16. *New York Times*, February 10, 1970, p. 48.

17. See, for example, his dialogue with Richard Rubenstein in *The German Church Struggle and the Holocaust*, ed. Franklin H. Littell and Hubert G. Locke (Detroit: Wayne State University Press, 1974), pp. 256–277.

18. As Sartre states in *Les Mots*, any religious élan he may have had in his youth was stifled by the too-ready availability of bourgeois Christianity: "Faute de prendre racine en mon Coeur, il a végété en moi quelque temps, puis il est mort" (*Les Mots*, Paris: Gallimard, 1964, p. 83).

19. *The Rebel*, p. 62.

20. *The German Church Struggle*, p. 271.

21. *Souls on Fire*, trans. Marion Wiesel (New York: Vintage Books, 1972), p. 111.

22. *The German Church Struggle*, p. 262.

23. Ibid., pp. 271–273.

Acknowledgments

Barzun, Jacques. "Lincoln the Literary Genius." *The Saturday Evening Post*, Vol. 231, No. 33 (14 February 1959): 30, 62–4.

Callahan, Allen Dwight. "Exodus." *The Talking Book: African Americans and the Bible*. New Haven: Yale UP, 2006. 83–137. © 2006 by Allen Dwight Callahan.

Cowan, Louise. "*Beloved* and the Transforming Power of the Word." *Classic Texts and the Nature of Authority*. Eds. Donald and Louise Cowan. Dallas: Dallas Institute, 1993. 291–303. © 1993 by The Dallas Institute Publications. Reprinted by permission.

Eliot, George. "Margaret Fuller and Mary Wollstonecraft." *The Leader* 6 (13 October 1855): 988–9.

Erdman, David. "Blake's Vision of Slavery." *Journal of the Warburg and Courtauld Institutes*, 15.3–4 (1952): 242–252. © The Warburg Institute.

Green, Mary Jean. "Witness to the Absurd: Elie Wiesel and the French Existentialists." *Renascence* 29.4 (Summer 1977): 170–184. © *Renascence*. Reprinted by permission.

Holland, Frederic May. "The Slave." *Frederick Douglass: The Colored Orator*. London: Funk & Wagnalls Company, 1891. 7–31.

Schmitz, Neil. "The Paradox of Liberation in *Huckleberry Finn*." *Texas Studies in Literature and Language* Vol. 13, No. 1 (Spring 1971): 125–36. © University of Texas at Austin. Reprinted by permission.

Sherman, Sarah Way. "Moral Experience in Harriet Jacobs's *Incidents in the Life of a Slave Girl*." *NWSA Journal*, Vol. 2, No. 2 (Spring 1990): 167–85. © Sarah Way Sherman. Reprinted by permission.

Tyler, Moses Coit. "Thomas Jefferson and the Great Declaration." *The Literary History of the American Revolution, 1763–1783*, Vol. 1. New York: G.P. Putnam Sons, 1897. 494–521.

Wollstonecraft, Mary. "Review of *The Interesting Narrative of the Life of Olaudah Equiano, or Gustavus Vassa, the African, Written by Himself.*" *Analytical Review* no. 4 (May 1789): 28.

Index